THE DECLINE
OF THE GODDESS

Recent Titles in
Contributions to the Study of World Literature

Promptings of Desire: Creativity and the Religious Impulse in the Works of D. H.
Lawrence
Paul Poplawski

The Second Best Bed: Shakespeare's Will in a New Light
Joyce E. Rogers

Literary Selves: Autobiography and Contemporary American Nonfiction
James N. Stull

Storied Cities: Literary Imagining of Florence, Venice and Rome
Michael L. Ross

Women Writers in Russian Literature
Toby W. Clyman and Diana Greene, editors

Writing the Good Fight: Political Commitment in the International Literature of the
Spanish Civil War
Peter Monteath

Money: Lure, Lore, and Literature
John Louis DiGaetani, editor

Smollett's Women: A Study in an Eighteenth-Century Masculine Sensibility
Robert D. Spector

English Country Life in the Barsetshire Novels of Angela Thirkell
Laura Roberts Collins

Bakhtin, Stalin, and Modern Russian Fiction: Carnival, Dialogism, and History
M. Keith Booker and Dubravka Juraga

Aspects and Issues in the History of Children's Literature
Maria Nikolajeva, editor

Reluctant Expatriate: The Life of Harold Frederic
Robert M. Myers

THE DECLINE
OF THE GODDESS

*Nature, Culture, and Women
in Thomas Hardy's Fiction*

Shirley A. Stave

Contributions to the Study of World Literature,
Number 63

GREENWOOD PRESS
Westport, Connecticut • London

Library of Congress Cataloging-in-Publication Data

Stave, Shirley A.
    The decline of the goddess : nature, culture, and women in Thomas
Hardy's fiction / Shirley A. Stave.
        p.   cm.—(Contributions to the study of world literature,
0738–9345 ; no. 63)
    Includes bibliographical references and index.
    ISBN 0-313-29566-2 (alk. paper)
    1. Hardy, Thomas, 1840–1928—Knowledge—Mythology.   2. Hardy,
Thomas, 1840–1928—Characters—Women.   3. Hardy, Thomas, 1840–1928—
Fictional works.   4. Mythology in literature.   5. Goddesses in
literature.   6. Culture in literature.   7. Nature in literature.
8. Women in literature.   9. Myth in literature.   I. Title.
II. Series.
PR4757.M83S73   1995
823'.8—dc20   94–46928

British Library Cataloguing in Publication Data is available.

Library of Congress Catalog Card Number: 94–46928
ISBN: 0-313-29566-2
ISSN: 0738–9345

First published in 1995

Greenwood Press, 88 Post Road West, Westport, CT 06881
An imprint of Greenwood Publishing Group, Inc.

Printed in the United States of America

The paper used in this book complies with the
Permanent Paper Standard issued by the National
Information Standards Organization (Z39.48–1984).

10 9 8 7 6 5 4 3 2 1

to Madeleine, with gratitude for her light

Contents

Acknowledgments

In the several years over which I have worked on this project, so many different people have been so extremely generous in their support, advice, and assistance that it would be impossible to name them all. However, without one man's continuing encouragement and very practical advice, this work would never have come to fruition. My greatest thanks go to Daniel Schwarz, whom I met as a result of his National Endowment for the Humanities Summer Seminar and whom I have long since come to regard as a friend. I can never repay him for his perseverance in dealing with me and for his attention to all stages of work on this manuscript.

I also wish to thank several of my former professors at the University of Minnesota, specifically William Madden, Chester Anderson, and Gordon Hirsch, who instilled in me an obsession with the Victorian novel and whose enthusiasm for my early work encouraged me to pursue this project even through its most frustrating moments. Equal thanks go to the members of my feminist reading group from those Minnesota days—Brenda Daly, Maureen Reddy, Pat Johnson, and Laura Brady, in particular. These extraordinary women, who remain dear friends, have been a continuing source of strength and inspiration.

To my editor at Greenwood Press, Peter Coveney, I give deep thanks for his attention to my manuscript and excellent advice. Others to who I owe gratitude for assistance in organizing, writing, and editing this work include Jo Glorie, Timothy Sweet, and Dennis Allen.

As perhaps one of the most computer-illiterate members of my profession, I also recognize that this work would not have been possible without one extraordinary man, my "technical assistant," David Crafts, who has been patient with my phone calls at all hours of the day and who has never snickered at the ridiculousness of my questions. He has also been responsible for formatting and printing out working drafts of the manuscript. David Weber, of the University of Wisconsin Center—Waukesha Computer Center, has also been tremendously helpful in this area.

I would also like to acknowledge HarperCollins Publishers Limited for their permission to use Jean Brooks' work, *Thomas Hardy: The Poetic Structure*.

Finally, I would like to thank those people who have come to be my family away from home—my dearest friends Catharine Tipton, Chad Rackowitz, Ina Jane Wundram, and Carolyn Crafts—as well as Michael Grubbs, with whom I share my home and my life. Without their love, their humor, their affection, without our evenings of sharing conversation, laughter, food, and wine, my life would be unspeakably empty and my work would not be the joy that I continue to find it to be.

Chronology of Thomas Hardy's Novels

Desperate Remedies (1871)

Under the Greenwood Tree (1872)

A Pair of Blue Eyes (1873)

Far From the Madding Crowd (1874)

The Hand of Ethelberta (1876)

The Return of the Native (1878)

The Trumpet-Major (1880)

A Laodicean (1881)

Two on a Tower (1882)

The Mayor of Casterbridge (1886)

The Woodlanders (1887)

Tess of the D'Urbervilles (1891)

Jude the Obscure (1895)

The Well-Beloved (1897)

THE DECLINE
OF THE GODDESS

1

In the Beginning: Archetypal Patterns in the Less Well Known Novels

It has become commonplace to approach the novels of Thomas Hardy with the underlying assumption of a tension between agrarian and industrial ways of life. Recently, theoretical distrust of dualism has shifted the emphasis in Hardy criticism away from an overt exploration of this topic; however, it remains impossible to treat the Wessex novels without some discussion of a rapidly fading rural way of life encroached upon by "modern" society. Thus, it may be valuable to reconsider the earlier critical focus, bringing a religio-spiritual concern to the surface-level duality of agrarianism vs. industrialism. In doing so, the readily apparent tension between two ways of life in collision during Victorian England manifests a deeper tension, one that resonates mythically and thereby transcends the boundaries of time and geography. From an archetypal perspective, the struggle between two irreconcilable world views that Hardy repeatedly presents becomes one of the ancient stories, one particularly significant for its implications for gender and social class.

Reading Hardy from the theoretical perspective of myth criticism is also nothing new; Hardy's obvious use of myth throughout his novels invites such an examination. However, leaving behind the allusive use of myth in Hardy, which has been treated thoroughly in Marlene Springer's *Hardy's Use of Allusion*, one can see within the Wessex novels a systemic use of myth that does more than associate certain characters with Greco-Roman or Celtic deities, more than occasionally echo a hero's journey or a sacrificial act. Taken as a whole, the Wessex novels can be read as a repeated exploration of one of the oldest myths of culture, that of a Sky God interacting with an Earth Goddess. However, Hardy's typical association of the Sky God figure with the Christian triune God, particularly in his messianic aspect, makes it possible to narrow the scope of Hardy's use of myth and find the archetype informing Hardy's work within the Bible itself. The Old Testament records an ongoing struggle between Yahweh, the god of the children of Israel and precursor to the Christian god, and Ashtaroth, the agricultural goddess who lost her power as a result of being displaced by those wandering tribes. Hardy fuses that myth with the New Testament's messianic narrative, often depicting the antagonist of the Great

Goddess as a Christ-figure, thereby setting up a bipolar opposition between Christian and Pagan thought. The struggle between these two deities, and specifically between what each represents, bears within it implications for the world at large, reflecting not only the agrarian/industrial tension already mentioned but also a tension of gender that contains within it an exploration of the parameters of patriarchy and an impassioned longing for a world not governed by its logic and its economy.

An exploration of dualities inevitably invites the possibility of oversimplification, especially in the light of theory suggesting that all dualities deconstruct each other. Understanding that such deconstruction can be applied here as well, one can nevertheless explore the terms of the dualism that Hardy, always structuring his texts through the perspective of his finely honed sense of architecture, chose to inscribe in his works. Simply to deconstruct Hardy's agrarian, Pagan world, to reveal it as identical to the culture that is its seeming antithesis, will expose Hardy's nostalgic longing for an edenic world as untenable, his terms as self-contradictory, his bipolar opposition as nonfunctional. But to make such a claim adds little to what has long been known, namely, that it becomes impossible to create in language a representation of an unfallen state. However, to analyze Hardy's treatment of both halves of the equation permits some understanding of one very extraordinary Victorian man's understanding of sexual politics, the implications of gender, the destructiveness of classism, and the role of Christianity in creating and maintaining a system that he saw as immoral and ultimately destructive of not only human spirit but also of the earth itself.

So what exactly are the terms of Hardy's dualism? The original, unfallen world, the world previously aligned with the agrarian side of the equation, is natural, Pagan, nonpatriarchal, and mythic, while the world that threatens it is cultural, Christian, patriarchal, and historical. In making this claim, I have used a series of words, all of which are overdetermined, and hence require some discussion of my sense of them here. While "natural" may initially be the most problematic of the terms, my understanding of that term is predicated upon an understanding of Paganism, which is where I would like to begin. Hardy's exploration of a Pagan-Christian opposition has often been considered a logical outgrowth of the intellectual climate of his time. Matthew Arnold's well-known discussion of Hellenism and Hebraism were of course familiar to Hardy, whose literary notebooks reveal a fascination with Arnold's work. Hardy quotes lengthy sections of Arnold's writing, and, as Lennart Bjork, the editor of the literary notebooks, points out, the dates of the entries indicate that Hardy read a great deal about Greek society shortly before he began *The Return of the Native*, the first of Hardy's novels in which "Hellenism" might be seen to figure significantly (xxviii). Furthermore, the Victorian age in general was intrigued by Greek and Roman mythology, as is obvious from not only the literature of the time but also the painting, for example, the works of the Pre-Raphaelite school. However, I recognize a profound distinction between Hellenism and Paganism, one that is vital to understanding Hardy's agenda in constructing Wessex and its folk. Hellenism, in the sense it is usually understood, figures in Hardy's work on occasion; Paganism informs it. Hellenism is High Culture,

Western thought in its seminal state. It is an intellectual approach to life and art and therefore remains academic. Paganism, in the sense that I use the word, is the antithesis of Hellenism, which it predates just as it predates Hebraism. Paganism is humankind's primal response to the world around it and grows out of an intimate relationship with nature's processes. It has no deities per se; the earth is metaphorized as the Great Goddess, who is essentially all that exists. Paganism is not academic and it is not learned; it is the innate knowledge of the folk who work the land and tend animals, who themselves are determined by the cycle of the seasons. The Wessex folk are by and large Pagan in their response to life; they live what one might call their faith and enact their rituals, which have to do with seasonal changes and human rites of passage. While many Victorian writers flirted with the idea of Hellenism, Hardy is unique in his celebration of the Pagan.

Paganism is inseparable from nature; therefore to claim the Wessex folk are Pagan is simultaneously to say that they are aligned with nature. Perhaps the most significant "tenet"—although the word carries with it a theological, academic sense that makes it inappropriate for a discussion of Paganism—of Pagan thought is the understanding that the human is indistinguishable from the natural. In Pagan thought, no separation exists between self and nature. What Hardy attempts to represent in his Wessex folk is a people existing, for the most part, in an undifferentiated state with the world. While the folk exhibit little "religious" sense, they have a profound sense of the sacredness of the natural world. Ritual becomes a way of affirming their connection with the natural. Hence they jump over balefires, dance around maypoles, and carry peeled willow wands as they walk in procession, acts that mark seasonal changes as well as passages in their own lives. However, since Hardy portrays a Pagan world existing in tension with the Christian system, it is worthwhile to pay particular attention to his construction of Christianity as well as to his depiction of his rustics' interaction with it. While his governing archetype demands that the antagonist of the goddess figure be aligned with the Judeo-Christian tradition in some way, Hardy goes even further by exhibiting narrative disapproval of virtually every ecclesiastical figure he creates, from the lowliest village parson to the loftiest bishop. He emphasizes such a positioning of the clergy by creating a folk, who, as Springer points out, while they have a thorough knowledge of the Bible, also exhibit "a practical habitual attitude towards the Church, occasionally going to services, but certainly with no sense of piety" (83). In the rare cases where one of the rustic characters treats Christianity seriously and devoutly, he is depicted as a comic character, usually as somewhat mentally deficient. Pathetic little Christian Cantle in *Far From the Madding Crowd* immediately comes to mind.

To emphasize the significance of nature in his works, Hardy routinely invests nature with agency; it functions virtually as a character in many of the works, either enabling or thwarting human endeavors, usually in fairly predictable ways. Hardy uses it as a form of narrative voice; those characters and actions of whom he approves, nature blesses, while those he would condemn suffer as a result of nature's intervention. However, Hardy's use of nature transcends what is known as the pathetic fallacy because of the spirituality that he locates within the natural. As Springer points out, "The forces which govern the land regulate his characters, and the two are inextricably united. Cliffs, storms, heaths become instruments of fate that influence both extrinsic and intrinsic action, their timing or their presence either aiding or thwarting human desires" (12). She goes on to speak of Hardy's "skill in transmuting the natural world into an animate force" (31). However, from a Pagan perspective, nature is animate, containing within it all that exists. Hardy's development of it then becomes vital to his creating a sense of living Paganism.

The Pagan unity with nature that characterizes the Wessex folk allows for an alternative construction of gender from that of the historical world Hardy experienced. For these rural folk, who daily observe the workings of nature in the animal life around them, the significance of both female and male experience to the unity of the whole is understood. No useful term exists for such a world view. It is not matriarchal, at least if what is understood as matriarchy is governance by women, but it empowers women and does not assume the same parameters of feminine experience that Victorian society took for granted. What characterizes the mythic world is resistance to hierarchy on the basis of gender and, to some degree, of class. The most capable members of the group assume the position of spokespersons and leaders, as Gabriel Oak does after he repeatedly proves his effectiveness with the flocks and the fields, and as Bathsheba does when she manages her farm efficiently. The world view that is grounded in the myth of the Great Goddess may perhaps be considered gynocentric, since it attributes authority and agency to the female. However, the problem with any term that is set in contrast to patriarchy lies in what is perceived as making up the grounds of the opposition. The simplistic sense that any alternatives to patriarchy must involve women having power over men distorts the issue; the polar issue is power over versus power with. Hardy's Pagan Wessex is not predicated upon an inversion of power; it is not simply upside-down patriarchy, with men positioned as powerless and victimized. Rather, it perceives men and women as equally capable and equally vital to the continuation of the whole. But the implications of such a difference of perception on the structure of daily life are significant. For example, Rosemarie Morgan points out how Hardy's male-dominated households, such as the Swancourts, the Clares, and the Melburys, are very hierarchical, while the female-dominated ones, such as Bathsheba's, Paula's, and Ethelberta's, are not. Furthermore, since a Pagan world view develops from an intimate connectedness with the natural world that understands the human community as innately natural as well, it allows for the evolution of a code of behavior and ethics predicated upon its understanding of the workings of all of nature. Sexuality especially is configured in terms radically different from those articulated by Victorian society. In the natural world, sexuality is responsible for the continuation of life; it is what enables new birth and rebirth, and therefore it becomes a cause for celebration and affirmation rather than a source of shame and guilt.

While Hardy's Wessex remains a fictional construct, while no solid historical evidence suggests a Pagan folk ever lived in an undifferentiated state with nature, free from a sense of sin and guilt, history does reveal that the Victorian obsession with and repression of the sexual was a function of the social and economic factors of the time, all of which Hardy addresses in his novels. Before the rise of industrialization resulted in masses of rural people abandoning the land and what had been an overwhelmingly agriculturally based society, agrarian society had developed a construction of gender and consequently a code of ethics based upon the roles men and women were required to fill if the community were to survive.[1] The nature of agricultural work, which demands intense and immediate participation by the entire community during critical periods such as planting and harvesting, but which also involves lengthy periods of time in which field and crop work demand maintenance rather than actual daily labor, resulted in patterns of gendered behavior far different from those often considered "traditional." As Hardy's novels (as well as other literary and historical sources) repeatedly demonstrate, rural, agrarian society was far freer from restraints of gender than Victorian society was. Women and men participated equally in milking, lambing, shearing, and harvesting, as *Far From the Madding Crowd* and *Tess of the D'Urbervilles* reveal. During the long winter months, when the animals required some tending, but fields lay fallow, men as well as women worked within the house; hence men like Gabriel Oak and Giles Winterbourne are able housekeepers. "Women's work" and "men's work" were labels that solidified in industrialized society, with its burgeoning middle class, who had more leisure time than ever before, and with a high unemployment rate caused by increased mechanization. A signifier of wealth and status among the middle class became a wife who was not required to work, even within the home, other than to oversee the servants. As more and more women were financially supported, the myth of women's helplessness, fragility, and ineptness grew. At the same time, the mores of the middle class spread to the working classes. Working class women, who made up a significant portion of the work force, were required to work for lower wages than their male counterparts, who were perceived as the "breadwinners" of families, a fiction that has extended even to today. Furthermore, as society became less tied to agriculture, as patterns of migration resulted in a very mobile and transient population, sexual ethics changed as well. In rural areas and small towns, no scandal arose when courting couples became sexually involved; rather, such activity was taken for granted. The community assumed the couple would marry when a pregnancy occurred. The identity of the baby's father was no mystery to anyone; the entire community was aware of who "walked with" whom, and no shame attached to what was seen as an inevitable result of nature. Given that agricultural work demanded many hands, it was vital that a marrying couple be capable of procreating if they were to survive. Hence, a pregnancy was seen as a cause for celebration. Furthermore, when massive numbers of people spent their lives working with animals, sexuality was no mystery but rather was understood as a natural act comparable to eating, sleeping, and breathing. The act of sex did not have to be taught. Children, who routinely slept in the same room, if not the same bed, as their parents, inevitably encountered human sexual activity at an early age, and their knowledge of cattle, horses, dogs, and cats resulted in an understanding of pregnancy, gestation, and birth. Furthermore, as Morgan points out, because of the endless labor required of their parents, children in large rural families experienced tremendous amounts of freedom, particularly compared to their city-dwelling, middle class counterparts. No strong authoritarian figures existed in such rural families, which were not "exposed to, or conditioned by, the sexual ethic of the rising Victorian petit-bourgeoisie" (133). However, once the migration to the cities began, children grew up in sexual ignorance. With no animals to learn from and no discourse of sexuality available to parents, sexual confusion led to sexual embarrassment, with sexual repression the inevitable result. In addition, as women were no longer valued for their abilities as farm workers and as bearers of young, as they became status symbols, virginity became the indication of their exchange value. In cities, with the loss of a tightly knit community, the earlier acceptance of a couple's courting until a pregnancy occurred vanished; eager to prove themselves equal to the middle class in what came to be called respectability, the working class came to regard such behavior as immoral and indicative of vice. As such hegemony continued, working class men began to abandon women they had impregnated, women who were subsequently scorned by their families and "respectable society." Tess's story is one fictional representation of a frequently recurring situation and reveals such a clash of values. When Joan sends Tess off to "claim kin," she is perfectly well aware that her daughter and Alec might become sexually involved, but assuming, falsely, that the norms of her community hold in the world at large, she believes that if Tess becomes pregnant, Alec will of course marry her. Joan's rural, Pagan understanding of the world in collision with a differing world view is one example of Hardy's recurring motif, the destruction of Pagan consciousness by a system at odds with it, a destruction that is particularly played out in the lives of women.

The world view that Hardy sets in antithesis to the Pagan one can be defined as patriarchal, Christian, and cultural. It defines itself in opposition to nature, consequently developing laws that attempt to alter or control natural impulses. Privileging male thought and male being, it predicates itself upon the domination of the female. It values academic education over practical know-how, and it celebrates progress, which results in a perception of time as linear rather than cyclical. George Wotton discusses what he sees as a tension between the individual and the communal in Hardy's work (71), which is consistent with the underlying dichotomies I perceive. He also brings education to bear on the duality, claiming, "[T]he result of the educational process is always the same; the acquired ability to 'spaik real language' signifies an alienation from the communal world and also a suppression and domination" (72). The world that Hardy sets in opposition to the Pagan, communal world is, essentially, the world as we experience it. Western culture is both androcentric and patriarchal. In the realm of the symbolic, culture is understood to be male-focused and male-directed. The symbolic translates to the literal system of governance which consistently protects the prerogatives of the male. Even when, as in Victorian England, the power on the throne in female, the system itself does not change, for it works to sustain itself by co-opting women to accept its premises as holy and inviolable. Evidence of the patriarchal, historical world of Victorian England exists consistently throughout Hardy's canon; it becomes the world he opposes, the world view his texts challenge. It becomes manifest in characters such as Clym Yeobright, returning from Paris with the intent of educating the folk of Egdon Heath, and Angel Clare, who in his seeming rejection of Victorian mores has embraced an idealism unshaken by his day-to-day experiences at Talbothay's Dairy. It is also manifest in Hardy's rakes—Sergeant Troy, Damon Wildeve, Alec D'Urberville, among others—men who assume superiority over and possession of women as their birthright and thus trifle with women's lives and love cavalierly. In positing the historical world that threatens and in some cases destroys the mythic world developed in opposition to it, Hardy makes it a familiar world. His portrait reveals a world that emphasizes reason over intuition and mind over the body. It claims its authority from the Judeo-Christian God the Father and therefore becomes inseparable from Christianity, even when seeming schisms occur, as for example, in *Tess of the D'Urbervilles*, when Angel and Alec at various times embrace Christianity overtly as opposed to acting out their enculturation by it. Hardy locates the Pagan consciousness within mythic time, presenting it as a prelapsarian world existing before the onset of time, contrasted with the patriarchal consciousness which is defined by historical time and space. Both systems are contained within the grid that constitutes Wessex, which itself exists simultaneously as myth and as history.

In examining Hardy's novel from an assumption of a bipolar opposition that includes the male/female dyad, I encounter another problem that relates to my feminist agenda. Elizabeth Meese raises a crucial point, "We must consider, for example, whether deconstructive strategy, in presenting the 'female' as one term in a theoretical binary opposition, conceals women's socioeconomic situation and renders the female within feminism, or feminism itself, politically neutral" (78). In treating Hardy's women characters as goddess figures, I reduce them to symbol and to some degree deny the political, social, and economic realities of their lives. However, characters in literary texts are always already doubly articulated. On the one hand, the characters do represent an author's understanding of gender, class, race, ethnicity, and so on. A text can be read as a sociological document that provides important information about actual conditions at a given time. On the other hand, however, characters in texts are also always representational, symbolic, allegorical. They do not live nor have they ever lived. Hardy's goddess figures result from his consciousness of women and his sense of nature; they are informed by his desire, his hostility, his own enculturation, and his actual relationships with women. To expect a Victorian male writer to create women characters from a completely nonsexist perspective is to expect the impossible. Hardy resisted many of the assumptions of Victorian society and hoped to enable change; as such, he created strong, atypical women characters whom he consciously constructed to challenge societal expectations. But Hardy also treated his women characters as embodiments of nature. As such, they must be Other, forever on the parameters of culture. But to say that is not to say anything new. As Cixous and Clément write, "[T]he sorceress conceives Nature, and woman, the periodic being, takes part in something that is not contained within culture" (8). Within Hardy's schema, I see woman as identified with nature, the body, gesture, the earth itself. Many writers, of both genders, articulate their women characters in these terms. As the debate over essentialism rages within feminist theory, it is crucial to remember that for some theorists not merely literary characters but all women can be perceived in these terms. Again Cixous and Clément, "[W]oman is body more than man is. Because he is invited to social success, to sublimation. . . . Woman, who has run her tongue ten thousand times seven times around her mouth before not speaking, either dies of it or knows her tongue and her mouth better than anyone else" (95). Hardy's basic equation of woman with nature is endemic to Western culture. But his treatment of his women, his understanding of the sexual politics that determine their lives, and his sympathy for their plight set him apart from other Victorian writers. Furthermore, Hardy is a writer who does not attempt to downplay the significance of sexuality to the human totality. Morgan emphasizes Hardy's "commitment to the sexual reality of women," pointing out that he is one "for whom female sexuality is neither to be degraded nor denied" (28). She goes on to claim that Hardy perceives "sensuality, sexual luxuriance and physical self-delight" as the "birthright" of his strong women characters (137).

Furthermore, Hardy's specific use of mythological material to provide a critique of Victorian sexual ethics and gender relations again distinguishes him from his peers. In Hardy, the feminine is typically privileged, while sexism in its many guises is often attacked, an unusual position for a Victorian male to take. This is not to suggest that Hardy's mind set is "feminist" in the late twentieth-century sense of the word. Hardy remains a man of his time in many ways and, as such, accepts some traditional definitions of gender. However, his understanding of the dynamics of power at work in man-woman relationships is remarkable, and his strong championing of the woman, even if his definition of her is at times problematic, is unusual given his circumstances and is deserving of study. Morgan points out how Hardy does not associate certain traits of character with one gender or another (159); in his works, both men and women can be moral, intellectual, capricious, passive, and so on, which again sets Hardy apart from most of his peers. Some of Hardy's goddess figures are not always pleasant, nor do they consistently exercise good judgment. However, they remain sympathetic characters because of the restraints unjustly imposed on them, often by male characters who assume their own superiority. The mythic overtones to the struggles of gender that Hardy documents make up the body of my work. The novels that most directly treat the cosmic confrontation between the Great Goddess and her Judeo-Christian antagonist are the ones I treat at length. However, themes that appear in the works considered his major novels also appear in the other works as well. It is worth looking briefly at these works, focusing on the variations from the major motif and also considering the treatment of the central female character in each.

Desperate Remedies, Hardy's first novel, is not set in Wessex, nor does it share the tone of most of his later work. With it, Hardy attempts to write a detective story, a genre he abandons after what most consider an unsuccessful project. Hardy similarly will abandon the conventionalism that characterizes this early novel. The rustic world that came to be seen as Hardy's hallmark does not appear here. Nevertheless, this early endeavor does share some traits with his more mature work. Even here, the world is in transition: old and new coexist, as they repeatedly do in Hardy's fiction. The folk here have superficially accepted Victorian religion and culture, but yet remain apart from them, informed by older values. Hardy's hostility to Christianity already appears here, albeit subtly; the church that figures prominently in the setting is decaying, and both the narrative voice and the folk of the village speak of it in terms of gloom and death. The folk also reveal some of the obliviousness to the church that will later characterize the rustics of Egdon Heath. Also, a perhaps unconscious hostility on Hardy's part toward the church may reveal itself in his choosing the mode of Cytherea's father's death—he falls off a church he is restoring, while the sun shines merrily on.

Cytherea, the novel's protagonist, is portrayed as a cultured woman who is born of a very sophisticated mother, making her a very untypical Hardy woman. In terms of the configuration of her family, however, Hardy here begins a pattern that he will repeatedly return to in his fiction. With the death of her father fairly early in the novel, Cytherea is all but independent of parental authority figures and is quite capable as such. Hardy also creates a brother, the first of many similar male relatives in his canon, who becomes problematic for the protagonist because of his enshrining of respectability. Hardy's development of Cytherea's brother's character may result from his own inability to envision a young woman so completely independent or from his assumption of a similar stumbling block on the part of his readership; however, it may equally well grow out of his perception of the unfairness endemic to patriarchal culture. As orphaned adult siblings nearly the same age, both intelligent and capable, it would seem that Cytherea and Owen would exist as peers, as equals. However, Owen, a product of a patriarchal culture that validates his maleness at the same time that it denies the agency of his sister, assumes the right to dominate Cytherea, a right the narrative questions in that the structure of the text encourages reader identification with the woman and reader hostility to Owen. The enabling connections among women that repeatedly occur in Hardy's fiction are manifest here in Cytherea's bond with the older Cytherea, who bequeaths her fortune to the younger woman left penniless by her father's death. Essentially, the patriarchal world divests a woman of wealth and power, while a gynocentric world endows her, providing for her security and survival.

In spite of her name, Cytherea cannot be read as a goddess figure, although she shares several traits with the later Hardy goddess figures. She possesses a sixth sense, an intuition, that allows for knowledge beyond what her senses and her intellect can provide. For example, she hears Mr. Aldclyffe die, although she is physically too distant for that to be possible, and she sees the older Cytherea at the moment of her death. The young woman is also physically strong, in spite of her development as a dainty woman, capable of fending off Manston when he attempts to rape her. When she eventually does marry, her marriage is portrayed as a celebration of love and sexuality; the gloomy vision of the human condition that characterizes *Jude the Obscure* is absent in the world Hardy portrays here.

Other recurring Hardyean patterns first appear here. The villain, Manston, shares the satanic associations of such later characters as Fitzpiers and Alec D'Urberville. Like them, he is alienated from nature: his career as an architect removes him from the agricultural community. The male protagonist, whose name, Springrove, aligns him with the bounty of nature and hints of a Pagan past, while an educated, cultured man, nevertheless retains his rural heritage and even owns sheep, prefiguring in some rough way the later Gabriel Oak. Nature also is endowed with agency in ways predictable in Hardy's works. At its most powerful, it sets fire to the inn, allowing for the revelation necessary to save Cytherea from a horrific marriage to Manston. Finally, the role of folklore prefigures the later work; for example, Cytherea changes her wedding date because it falls on a Friday, an indication of bad luck.

Under the Greenwood Tree, the first of the actual Wessex novels, is more typically Hardyean throughout. For the most part, the world Hardy constructs here is contained within myth; history, the "real," intervenes in only trivial ways. Nature here is almost totally benign: the novel is pastoral, and the characters never experience any significant threat, either from nature or from each other. The sense that the old order is disappearing is revealed, interestingly, through what occurs in church: the Mellstock Choir is being replaced by an organ, much to the chagrin of the folk of the community, who now will no longer be able to play their sheep-shearing songs in church. The separation of life into the secular and the sacred, one manifestation of the loss of Pagan consciousness, reveals itself through this incident.

However, throughout most of the novel, Christianity and Paganism coexist in a comfortable balance as they will later do in *Far From the Madding Crowd*; ironically, much of the action of the novel centers around the church and the church choir. As he will do in later novels, Hardy here structures his work around Christian holidays, for example, Dick Dewy first sees Fancy Day on Christmas. However, here the holiday functions without the layers of irony and symbolism that will inform Hardy's treatment of Christian holidays in later works; Hardy's portrayal of a rustic Christmas allows him to show the folk at play and emphasizes the novel's light, happy tone. The folk sense of Christianity is not solemn; they routinely sit in the church drinking ale, singing sheep-shearing songs. Additionally, these folk have not abandoned their Pagan past completely; hence, a giant mistletoe figures significantly in their Christmas celebration, and the witch that Fancy consults for assistance when her father attempts to disrupt her love relationship does a lucrative business. However, in this novel Hardy for the first time makes a religious figure the antagonist of the work; while Parson Maybold is, for the most part, innocuous, as the rival for Fancy's love he figures in opposition to Dick Dewy, with whom narrative—and presumably reader—sympathies lie. Later, Hardy's treatment of the clergy will be far less gentle.

Fancy, the female protagonist, is a very different sort of character from Bathsheba, Eustacia, and Tess. As a schoolteacher, she functions as the bearer of culture to the rural community, and specifically to Dick Dewy, her rural sweetheart whom she marries at the novel's end. Initially, the text suggests Fancy will lead her husband away from his rural heritage; however, by the end of the novel, her meeting him halfway and adapting to folk customs to some degree appears very likely. Hardy works through a "poor man and the lady" motif here, with Fancy inheriting her wealth through a very patriarchal father who is the source of many of the young girl's problems. Unlike most of the later female protagonists, and Cytherea as well, Fancy is never independent within the novel, ruled over first by a loving but somewhat dictatorial father, then jumping into marriage with Dick to escape her home. However, the novel's pastoral tone is not seriously threatened by the father; unlike later vicious fathers, this one can be charmed into compliance with his daughter's plans. Furthermore, Fancy is as bound to her mother as she is to him, making this world appear less blatantly patriarchal.

While Fancy strikes the reader as cute rather than darkly beautiful, rather manipulative at times, and ultimately weak, she is the first of the Hardy women characters to have the thick dark hair that will later characterize Hardy's goddess figures. Interestingly, however, Fancy herself is distressed by her hair, wishing it were lighter, more in keeping with Victorian standards of prettiness. Fancy is also the first of the Hardy women to reveal a healthy sexuality, although the entire issue of sexuality is much more understated here than it will be later in Hardy's canon. The young woman deliberately wears muslin dresses to church, in spite of the scandal she causes by what some consider her inappropriate appearance, and on her wedding day, which is a joyous culmination of the novel's pastoral mode, she betrays a delightful eagerness for what the night will bring.

Dick Dewy, Fancy's beloved, is again a good man associated with nature. Unlike Springrove, Dewy is completely rustic, working as a tranter in the agricultural community. Like the later nonrustic male characters, though, his sexuality is weaker than that of the woman he loves: through most of the novel, he lives at home with his parents and is not particularly eager to marry.

Hardy's next novel, *A Pair of Blue Eyes*, is the first novel to end tragically and to reveal a more complex, threatening world. Hardy for the first time links societal structure, and particularly its patriarchal foundation, to the destruction of the human spirit, played out upon the body of young, winsome Elfride Swancourt. Throughout the work, Elfride develops relationships with four men, each one more socially prominent than the one before, and each one sapping her of more of her strength and vitality; at the end of the novel, Elfride, now Lady Luxellian, is buried in her husband's family vault, the victim of a patriarchal culture and a father obsessed with social advancement. Significantly, Elfride's first suitor, who dies prior to the novel's beginning, is a rustic lad; his absence from the work suggests the impossibility of returning to the prelapsarian state, to the world of *Under the Greenwood Tree*. This world is not nearly so pleasant, nor so rustic. Elfride's father is not one of the folk but rather the area's rector, the representative of the Christian, patriarchal world to the folk he serves. While Rector Swancourt loves his daughter, takes pride in her intellectual achievements, and allows her an amazing amount of freedom, he is also a spiteful man who is self-conscious of and unabashed about his extreme snobbishness, making no attempt to mask the social criteria by which he judges a person's value. The Hardyean motif of the religious figure as antagonist is immediately apparent; Hardy also establishes very clearly the ties between Christianity and classism. In this work, the antagonistic male relative and the antagonistic clergyman, both standard figures in Hardy's canon, fuse into one. Elfride's mother is dead, allowing the girl no access to a gynocentric world even in her own home. Like the rustic love, the bond with the mother, the Ur-Goddess, exists in the past, in prehistory, only as memory.

Generally in the novel, primarily through the figure of Rector Swancourt, Victorian Christianity appears in an unfavorable light. The folk over whom he presides resemble those of *The Return of the Native*, although lacking their active Paganism; these rustics snooze through the sermon when they go to church and repeatedly claim that religion leads to madness. Hardy also repeats a trope that appeared in *Desperate Remedies*, in which the church building itself is sinister; here a church collapses, killing a woman with its debris.

Elfride, the central character, initially appears radically different from the Hardy goddess-women, resembling Fancy Day more than any other Hardy woman, but lacking even that character's spunk and defiance. One cannot, for example, imagine Elfride seeking out a witch to help her deal with her father, partly because of her own timidity, but also because her world is so far removed from Fancy's mythical Wessex that no witches could exist in it. However, traces of the future women characters appear in her, and, unlike Fancy, Elfride spends significant amounts of time in nature, often riding her horse. Interestingly, she often writes as she rides, revealing the confluence of the natural and the cultural within her. Hardy frequently describes Elfride in natural terms, but the images are usually diminished and suggest nature having been tamed—a colt in a harness, a rabbit in a hutch. Considering how bound she is by her tyrannical father, the images are appropriate; however, they also reveal how the folk of the area view nature in general, as bound, controlled, manipulated by the human. However, nature remains a viable force here, repeatedly functioning to protect Elfride and thereby emphasizing the bond it shares with the girl. It conveniently causes the church to fall on the maniacal Mrs. Jethway, Elfride's sworn enemy, and it induces Henry Knight, the novel's "villain," to slip on a rock and fall over a cliff. Elfride, however, intervenes, saving his life and allowing for her own destruction, suggesting nature's limited scope in this fallen world.

Petite Elfride also possesses a surprising strength, which she demonstrates most clearly in this scene; she is able, through the agency of the rope she makes by shredding her undergarments, to pull Henry back over the edge of the cliff. Furthermore, she possesses some of the intuition with which Hardy endows his goddess figures; in one of her early encounters with Henry, she experiences a premonition of his fall from the cliff. She also sees a vision of Mrs. Jethway, the woman who is determined to destroy her in a confused desire for revenge for her son's death. Finally, in this most patriarchal of novels, Hardy begins what will become a standard motif with him, his privileging of matrilineal descent. Elfride inherits her wealth and her position in society from her dead mother; for all her father's obsession with bloodlines, his is unimpressive, his social advancement effected by his two marriages.

Henry Knight, the man most directly responsible for Elfride's death, is a typically Hardyean villain. Obsessed with knowledge and the intellect, he is a cultured snob who by profession is a book critic. Like his counterparts in the other novels, he knows little of nature, his only interest in it academic. Like Angel Clare and Clym Yeobright, he possesses no sexual vitality, having lived celibate his entire life by choice and having decided never to marry. In this novel Hardy for the first time probes both the dynamics of sexual relationships and patriarchal attempts to define women's sexuality. Hardy states several times that Elfride and Henry's problems stem from the inequality between them, an inequality that results from Elfride's enculturation into a system that denies women agency in their relationships with men. Hardy is not subtle in pointing out that Elfride's routinely obeying Henry, instead of resisting him when his demands are ridiculous or run counter to her own plans, weakens her to the point where Henry can make her his victim. Nowhere in Victorian literature can I think of a more sensibly argued case for equality between the sexes; Hardy clearly understood the premise of "Power corrupts." Hardy's clearsightedness appears again in his discussion of Henry Knight's obsession with Elfride's "innocence." Knight, a precursor of Angel Clare, is even more exacting than Hardy's scholar-turned-farmer will be, demanding not only that Elfride be a virgin but also that she never have kissed anyone else. However, Hardy is unambiguous in his discussion of Henry's rationale; the critic cannot abide the thought that a woman be capable of judging his abilities as a lover. Patriarchal obsession with feminine chastity suddenly appears in a new light, appearing to have little to do with virtue and much to do with male insecurity and male desire for power.

Elfride's second suitor, Stephen—the first one to actually appear in the novel—functions as the "good" suitor here. In many ways, he resembles Edward Springrove from *Desperate Remedies*; like his earlier counterpart, Stephen has been educated, but also like him, he returns to his home, still desiring rustic simplicity. Elfride's happiest times in the novel occur with Stephen, when the two roam about together in nature; such scenes suggest that were these two to marry, they would have a happy life together. Stephen, however, befriends Henry Knight and is the cause of Elfride's meeting him. Having entered the patriarchal world, Stephen is contaminated and indirectly contributes to Elfride's death.

Several other motifs appear here that resurface in later works. While the novel is not set among the folk the way, for example, *Under the Greenwood Tree* is, the folk that are introduced here are a vital, living bunch, many of whom take on individual personalities, prefiguring the folk of Weatherbury and Egdon Heath. Hardy reveals them to be the force holding the community together, the ones doing the necessary work, while the Rector Swancourts and the Henry Knights do nothing beyond make problems. Hardy also locates part of the work in London, where he paints a bitter portrait of city folk, particularly emphasizing the artificiality of the city women with their makeup and wigs; later, Hardy will routinely use such cosmetic devices as semiotic indicators of narrative disapproval.

The Hand of Ethelberta, Hardy's next novel, is the first of a short series of fairly forgettable works, in which Hardy experimented with genre and discovered what he could and could not—and would and would not—do. Interestingly, however, Ethelberta can be considered the first of the Hardy goddess figures. Furthermore, myth figures significantly here. The folk regard Ethelberta as a witch, prefiguring Eustacia in her alignment with Paganism, and by the end of the novel, Ethelberta has triumphed in a sacrificial act in which she functions both as the Great Mother and as Persephone in the underworld. Briefly, the story involves Ethelberta's need to find a husband before her inheritance runs out. The novel opens with Ethelberta, a young widow, on excellent terms with her wealthy mother-in-law, until the younger woman begins publishing some of her writing, an act the older one considers disrespectful to her dead son's memory. When Ethelberta points out that she has been three years a widow and that she is now coming back to life, the old woman abandons her, claiming her daughter-in-law owes fidelity to her dead husband. Ethelberta had, prior to the quarrel, achieved the Victorian ideal: she is socially prominent, incredibly wealthy, and has the best possible husband in the world—a dead one, incapable of making sexual demands on her or abusing her. The narrative, however, emphasizes the unnaturalness of Ethelberta's situation, as well as the injustice of the dynamics of power that exist between the two women.

Throughout this novel, Hardy appears very cynical, especially about marriage and the status of women in society; however, his "cynicism" may actually be level headedness, the result of his bitter awareness of the conditions his society produced, and his unsentimental gaze that refused to look away from the social reality he saw. Once Ethelberta begins her active husband-hunting, the narrative voice becomes especially bitter about the courtship and marriage practices of the Victorians, a bitterness that will culminate in *Jude the Obscure* and Hardy's decision to abandon fiction writing. Conventional Victorian courtships, in which couples were carefully chaperoned and therefore had no opportunity to become acquainted with each other, are mocked, most particularly in the scene in which Neigh, Ethelberta's most repulsive suitor, assumes that Ethelberta "has" to marry him after compromising herself by walking with him unchaperoned in a garden one afternoon. The narrative voice also accepts the economic necessity for women like Ethelberta to make good marriages, but refuses to mitigate the unsavoriness involved in contracting oneself—and specifically one's body—to another; romance is not permitted to taint the picture. Ethelberta does not love her wealthy husband, and she has no romantic illusions about marriage overall. She perceives the institution as predicated upon a power struggle that is essentially political, and thereby is able to survive a fallen world. The novel suggests that for a woman to survive the patriarchy, she must beat it at its own game. Ethelberta's decision to marry an old rich man whom she knows she can manipulate allows her to provide financially for a horde of younger siblings; however, she does so without experiencing the guilt and grief that mark Tess's similar decision. Even so, Hardy marks Ethelberta's decision as a sacrificial act through a scene in which the young woman rides a donkey shortly before her wedding, an allusion to Christ's entry into Jerusalem prior to his crucifixion. Such a use of Christian myth occurs again in *Tess of the D'Urbervilles*, in which Hardy repeatedly draws parallels between Tess's life and that of Christ to point out her divine nature.

Although she is not nearly so memorable a character as the later goddess figures, Ethelberta shares much with them. She is the first completely independent Hardy woman, even though both her parents are living. However, she makes her own decisions and in many ways is the authority figure to them, as well as to the many children they have produced. The family structure revealed here resembles that of the Durbeyfield family without the squalor; Ethelberta's family is not socially prominent (her father is a servant), but they are never in danger of starvation or of displacement from their home. Another parallel with *Tess of the D'Urbervilles* occurs in the development of Ethelberta's relationship with her younger sister Picotee, which, like the Tess and Liza-Lu dyad, as well as the two Cythereas, allows Hardy to explore a woman divided into two selves—one forced to negotiate the cultural world, the other remaining in the unfallen world. Here, the goddess figure is not destroyed by culture but rather assimilates into it, her sacrifice allowing her younger sister to a large degree to avoid the patriarchal world and to marry the man Ethelberta herself has loved, just as Tess bequeaths Liza-Lu to Angel before her death.

Ethelberta shares other traits with the Hardy goddess figures as well. Repeatedly, she is described as being a prophetess, possessing gifts of second sight, as have all the Hardy women characters. She becomes the inheritor, ruling, by the novel's end, the lord's manor with an iron hand. As in the cases of the other goddess figures, nature sympathizes with her and she is identified with it. In the opening of the novel, she transforms from static, lifeless character to movement and life when a hawk and duck fly by. Nature also comes to her defense when she decides to marry. In an almost humorous scene, Ethelberta's father, brother, former lover, and future brother-in-law—in other words, the combined forces of the patriarchy—all tear madly across the countryside to stop her marriage to Lord Mountclere, only to be thwarted by rugged weather on every hand. Nature, accepting Ethelberta's sacrifice of self, will not allow the marriage to be halted. Like the other goddess-women, Ethelberta—and Picotee, her natural counterpart as well—is sexually aggressive, strong, and happiest when she is in nature, although she is most often shown in exile in the city. Before her sacrificial marriage, Ethelberta takes her family to the seashore for an extended vacation, allowing herself one final opportunity to be independent in nature before her journey to the underworld. Given the fallen world presented here, no alternatives are allowed her. She may either rule in hell or serve in heaven, and like Lucifer, she is too proud to do the latter. Ethelberta's world exists purely within history; the mythic world of *Under the Greenwood Tree* is unavailable here. The young woman has no recourse to an alternative set of values, to a place apart from the patriarchal. She must, then, provide for and educate her siblings if they are to survive in a world that is no longer agricultural, that values formal education, and that is obsessed with class consciousness.

The male characters in this novel figure in predictably Hardyean ways. The characters of whom the narrative voice does not approve are alienated from nature and in some cases share the satanic allusions of Alec D'Urberville and Edred Fitzpiers. Christopher, who is a good enough man, but who must come to accept the fact that he may not marry Ethelberta, cannot distinguish one tree from another, Hardy's litmus test of who is one with nature and who is not. Neigh, who is appropriately named, given his negative character, is much more sinister; his interactions with Ethelberta are paralleled by his relationship with nature. This completely citified man is revealed to own some land on which he keeps horses which he mistreats. Hardy signifies Neigh's evil nature by attributing satanic qualities to him, for example, the man's supernatural knowledge of Ethelberta's journey. Neigh is also almost completely sexless, predictably, given Hardy's treatment of him as removed from the natural. Even Mountclere, whom Ethelberta marries in this fallen world in which no good choices exist, is alienated from nature even though he lives in the country. The male relatives function as they often do in Hardy, as the source of the female protagonist's problem. It is a man who disinherits Ethelberta after her mother-in-law reinstates her into her will, and Ethelberta's brother Sol will not help her escape when she learns the truth about her husband's mistress. The patriarchal assumption of their privilege over women makes these men a source of antagonism for Ethelberta.

Christianity plays a less significant role here than in most of the other works, and no clergymen appear in the novel. The folk, however, share the belief of the folk in *A Pair of Blue Eyes* regarding religion and madness. Also, Hardy creates one of his brilliant, weird, illogical characters—Christopher's sister, the aptly named Faith, who becomes more and more religiously fanatic as the novel progresses, eventually becoming a fixture in a museum basement, poring over religious ruins as life passes her by. Faith serves no function in terms of the novel's action; her location in the basement, dead to the world, must be read as a comment on people whose faith turns them away from life, nature, and human interaction.

Ironically, while the mythic Wessex is not glimpsed in this novel, Hardy's self-conscious use of myth is stronger than it often is in the other works. What this work shares with other works in Hardy's canon is the movement from the present to the primitive past: Christopher must journey out of London to a rural area to find Ethelberta. Her familial structure calls attention to the dual worlds she must negotiate. Her father enables culture, living not with his family in the country, but rather working as a butler in the city. In the country, Ethelberta's mother rules the family; if the prelapsarian world does not obtain in this work, women's empowerment nevertheless does. However, myth returns through Hardy's allusion to Orpheus and Eurydice. Christopher, a musician, journeys to the underworld to retrieve his love, only to learn that she chooses to remain there; he returns to the world to win her human counterpart to be his wife and to continue living.

This novel is perhaps most significant for its treatment of issues of class; it shows a greater social consciousness than the other early works do, particularly in its sympathetic discourse on manual laborers. Hardy portrays the effect of the mass relocation of agricultural workers to London, where their lives and identities disintegrate as a result of a rigid societal structure and their separation from the natural. The narrative provides a symbolic commentary on the relationship of the classes through its depiction of Lord Mountclere's house, with its phony facade. His "ancestral" home is all newly constructed, lacking rootedness in the past, while the servants' quarters occupy the authentic manor of the past. Hardy here uses architecture to validate the lives of the working classes at the same time that he points out the superficiality of the higher classes.

There is little to say about *The Trumpet-Major*, Hardy's attempt to write a historical novel. In attempting to locate his work in a historical rather than a mythical past, Hardy's style becomes artificial and uncomfortable; the novel is, for the most part, forgettable, as are its characters. Nevertheless, the work shares a few traits with Hardy's other novels. The protagonist, Anne, lives in a close, warm relationship with her mother, her father having died previously. Hardy's vision of the historical past includes a sense of the family core being the mother-child dyad, a point that will again be raised in discussion of *Jude the Obscure*. Within the novel, Anne finds a father figure in Uncle Benjy, who also dies, leaving her both independent and wealthy as his beneficiary. Like the later Hardy women, she is sexually aggressive, although only toward the end of the novel; she appears to grow into her sexuality rather than innately to live it. She is also strong enough to fend off a man who attempts to rape her, and she lives in nature, her last name appropriately being *Garland*. In this novel, Hardy again explores the natural woman/cultural woman split, although here Matilda, the bearer of culture, is the more sexual of the two and possesses the dark thick hair of the nature goddesses; however, she also wears makeup and is deceptive, Hardy's recurring characteristics of cultural women. Matilda is developed as the fallen woman, but redeems herself in a heroic act that deconstructs the artificial duality that determines a woman by her sexual behavior.

The novel lacks the strong sense of the sacred that pervades most of Hardy's work. However, narrative hostility for organized religion reveals itself in one scene in which a noisy, swearing carter interrupts a church service. However, this world is not particularly Pagan, in spite of its removal to the past and the miller's faith in omens. If anything, this is the world of fairy tale, with three suitors, a fairy godmother, a meeting with the king (which is in no way connected with the overall structure of the work), and a magical inheritance. However, the fairy tale elements serve no narrative function, which adds to the sense of the novel's weakness.

The unsuitable suitors in the work are, as usual, removed from nature, and one is extremely passionless. All three have abandoned their rural heritage to become soldiers, but the one Anne eventually marries returns to his earlier life. The narrative opposition to the rootlessness of a military life that characterized *Far From the Madding Crowd* recurs here, and in many ways Derriman, the suitor who tries to rape Anne, recalls Sergeant Troy in his contempt for women and his general seediness.

While *A Laodicean* is not a particularly strong novel, it, like *The Hand of Ethelberta*, remains interesting in light of the overall pattern that I see governing Hardy's works. This text explores a world in transition, signified initally by an ancient castle with a telegraph wire leading into it and a new clock, the reminder of time passing, on its grounds. The old way of life has been penetrated by the new. The owner of the castle is not descended from an old family, but rather is a young girl, the daughter of an engineer, and thereby aligned with the cultural half of Hardy's equation, who is attempting to recreate the past. Like Sue Bridehead, the past she longs for is the historical one, and all her journeys back—one of them an almost literal one, to a medieval village—lead her to versions of the patriarchal present. Perhaps it is with this novel that Hardy himself begins to realize that the past for which he is nostalgic does not exist within a historical context.

Paula, the protagonist, is characteristic of Hardy's women characters. She is completely independent, both of her parents being dead. She lives with an aunt, although perhaps it is more accurate to say that the aunt lives with her, since while the two women respect and love each other, their relationship is not hierarchical and the aunt does not presume to control Paula. Interestingly, though, this matriarchal bond served to save Paula from her father's religious fanaticism, since when she was a girl, only the aunt's intervention prevents Paula from becoming involved with her father's evangelical sect. The incident highlights the connection between Christianity and the patriarchy, and sets the feminine in opposition to both. Paula, like some of Hardy's other protagonists, is independent psychologically as well; she is not particularly seeking a lover, although much of the plot revolves around her romantic entanglements. Here, however, a more interesting relationship is the one between Paula and her companion Charlotte deStancey. On the one hand, Hardy again explores a strong woman/weak woman pairing, with Charlotte obviously the weaker of the two. Eventually she joins an Anglican sisterhood, an act which makes her Paula's antithesis, signifying her turning her back on life, as religious involvement in Hardy often does. However, the lesbian overtones to the friendship recall the several other erotic encounters between women in the Hardy canon—the two Cythereas and Grace and Felice come to mind—as does Sue Bridehead, who is often discussed as possibly lesbian. Hardy is clearly fascinated with the subject, but his depositing of Charlotte in a nunnery suggests his equal discomfort with a situation which he on the one hand treats as natural and on the other hand as something incomprehensible.

Paula, for all her wealth and power, is not developed as a goddess figure. She is likable and strong, but since she cannot find her way to a Pagan past, she is locked into history, where women are not perceived as goddesses. She is, however, a strong woman who commands her household capably. She is the one who inherits, as Hardy's women characters often do, revealing, I believe, Hardy's desire for women to possess social and economic agency. Modern though she is, nature is sympathetic to her, turning the day dark and threatening when Captain deStancey, the wrong suitor, comes courting. Like the goddess figures, Paula acts on instincts/intuitions which are essentially wholesome, thereby saving herself both from baptism into the sect and from an infelicitous marriage with deStancey.

Paula's well being is threatened by three men, one a relative, one a suitor, and one a satanic figure whose role in the novel can only be seen as emblematic. The relative, Uncle Abner, attempts to force Paula into a bad marriage, as antagonistic male relatives in Hardy's canon routinely do. He is a type of satanic figure himself, mysteriously appearing and disappearing as Paula's strength waxes and wanes. The suitor, Captain deStancey, recalls several other Hardy villains; he is a soldier who not surprisingly is alienated from nature. The narrative emphasizes the unwholesome effects of his life style by contrasting him with some of the folk who are the same age as he: they appear young and hardy, he old and tense. The third man, Dare, is a mysterious, sinister figure who ultimately destroys Paula's castle, her link with the past, thereby forever locking her in culture. Unlike characters such as Eustacia and Tess, however, Paula has one good suitor as well, George Somerset, who, in the opening pages of the novel is blessed by the rays of the setting sun. He is the first character introduced in the novel; the reader moves with him through the underbrush that leads to Paula's castle, a gynocentric world where a woman rules. George's experience with Paula's world results in his abandoning his earlier habit of drawing churches, substituting domestic scenes as his chosen topic for his art, an indication of his leaving behind the values of the patriarchal world.

Hardy's using a detail such as George's decision to stop drawing churches ties in with the novel's overall blatant hostility toward Christianity. The churches again are in decay here, literally and symbolically; Paula's first act within the novel is to refuse baptism in one. The scene is significant in that the baptism would presuppose a beginning, to the novel, as well as to Paula's life in Christ; however, Paula refuses the rite, choosing to make her own beginning, although doing so means quite literally denying the patriarchy, since her dying father's last wish was that she undergo the ritual. Hardy, I believe, understands that for Paula to retain her autonomy and independence, she must refuse the connection to the church. Mr. Woodwell, the minister who hopes to add her to his flock, figures through part of the novel as yet another spiteful clergyman, but he is rendered ineffectual and poses no real threat to Paula's power once she makes it clear to him that she has claimed her own agency.

In *Two on a Tower*, Hardy creates another independent woman, but one whose choices in love are more restricted than are Paula's. Viviette is independent and wealthy as a result of an onerous husband's death. Slightly older than most of Hardy's female protagonists, she represents the goddess figure whose worshipers reject her in favor of science. She shares with the other goddess figures the thick dark hair and the sexual aggressiveness one would expect, but she is more cultured than they, resembling in her life style Felice Charmond in *The Woodlanders*. However, Viviette's happiest time within the novel is her rustic honeymoon with Swithin, indicating that her ties with nature have not been severed. Viviette and Swithin respond to the world from positions of polar opposition: where she sees magic and wonder, he finds scientific explanations. Her sense of intuition is so strong that she experiences a vision of the child she does not yet know she is carrying; he is so immersed in the scientific, the rational, that he cannot see people around him and comes to feel invisible and insignificant. His obsession with science, which leads him to abandon her and eventually destroy her, parallels modern humankind's rejection of magic and the Mother Goddess in favor of a new doctrine.

Hardy here again uses the strong woman/weak woman dyad that recurs in his works; its treatment here recalls the Eustacia-Tamsin pairing in *The Return of the Native*. In this case, Tabitha, the weaker woman, is also one of the folk, attuned to nature herself, functioning as a nonmythical Viviette. Swithin, the narrative leads one to believe, will eventually marry Tabitha, the diminished version of the woman he essentially kills, a Liza-Lu instead of a Tess.

Swithin, though he is one of the folk, wants nothing more than to escape his rural past. He has estranged himself from nature, seeing it only through a telescope, at great distances. That movement away from his heritage and his essential self destroys Viviette, who loves him in spite of the threat he poses to her. Swithin, however, is not the only man in the novel dangerous to Viviette. The usual collection of hostile, treacherous, patriarchal figures again appears here, this time in the guise of a husband, a brother, a bishop, and her lover's uncle. Significantly, while Viviette is dead by the end of the novel, so are they all with the exception of her brother; Hardy seems to understand that some representative of the patriarchy must survive in a work that shows one world view gaining ascendancy over another. Two of these men, the brother and the lover's uncle, possess the kind of uncanny knowledge and sense of timing that characterize the Hardyean satanic antagonist.

Significantly, the novel begins in Advent, the Christian time of waiting for renewal; Viviette's world is a dark one, but the light she awaits cannot be the Christian one, as the narrative makes clear through her encounters with the village minister and the bishop, both portrayed as joyless opposers of the life-force. The folk here do not interact much with these clergymen, choosing rather to celebrate their lives and their sexuality freely. They live in the mythic past, but Swithin pulls Viviette into history, with predictable results.

Hardy uses the concept of the goddess differently in *The Mayor of Casterbridge*, focusing on the triple aspect of the goddess: maiden (Elizabeth Jane), mother/sexual woman (Lucetta), and crone (Susan). The three interrelate throughout the work, mysteriously appearing and disappearing to undo Michael Henchard, to the point where doubt is cast on their actual existence as separate characters. Susan, as she meets Michael in the ruins, appears to be a ghost; her appearance in Casterbridge after so many years, as well as her mysterious disappearance so quickly after she is sold, adds to the impression of her as supernatural. Similarly, Elizabeth Jane's fluidity in adopting fathers, which raises questions about her own identity, makes her mysterious, as does Lucetta's timely inheritance from an aunt/fairy godmother/matriarchal connection. Matriarchy is generally stressed here, especially through the strong mother-daughter relationship Hardy depicts, as well as through the doubt that is cast on the verification of paternity. The patriarchy is represented through Michael Henchard, the eventual town mayor who assumed the right to own—and sell—his wife and daughter. As such, he is yet another of Hardy's antagonistic male relatives, but he at least dies in the final pages of the text. This novel locates itself in part in a mythic world, where the three-part goddess, nature incarnate, avenges the crime committed against her. The supernatural is woven into the work; the fair that Michael Henchard cannot find again, the sailor who mysteriously takes Susan and the child away, the weather prophet, all are taken for granted here.

However, as is usually the case in Hardy's work, the mythic here exists simultaneously with the historical world. The folk here have fallen out of their former world and hence no longer possess the joy or spirit of the Weatherbury or the Egdon folk. With their lack of spirituality and their bleak lives, they give the novel an almost naturalistic feel. While they live in nature and take their living from it, they experience no real sense of its existence. Michael Henchard's spiritual emptiness, which allows him to sell his wife, is echoed in them, and the retaliation nature takes in the form of the three-part goddess mirrors the retaliation nature takes against them in making their lives devoid of meaning. The one man who escapes that wrath is Donald Farfrae, who is blessed by nature, taking on the sort of supernatural qualities of a Gabriel Oak or a Diggory Venn. Nature acts in Farfrae's behalf, causing, for example, his exhibition to be successful while Henchard's gets rained out. Nature also is portrayed as sympathetic to Susan and Elizabeth Jane, as one might expect. Their bleak little apartment is always warm and sunny, continually receiving nature's benediction. Initially, nature had attempted to extend its benevolence to Michael Henchard, sending a bird to distract him when he first contemplates his immoral act, but he foolishly seeks out the path to his own destruction.

Hardy's last novel, *The Well-Beloved*, resembles *The Mayor of Casterbridge* in that its protagonist is male. Jocelyn Pierston is a familiar Hardy figure; he has abandoned his rural past, which he attempts to reclaim even as he desires the cultural world accessible to him as an artist. Like Angel Clare and Clym Yeobright, Jocelyn is a sexless man who can only love the spiritual, completely repulsed by the physical. He believes he is searching for the ideal woman, but his true desire is for Psyche, pure spirit, since in patriarchal fashion he has identified purity with the spirit and therefore cannot accept a whole woman.

What makes the novel especially interesting is the shimmering of the uncanny that characterizes most of Hardy's works, that here reveals itself in the woman, or rather the women, that Jocelyn loves. Hardy presents a series of three women—all named Avice—each the daughter of the Avice before her; at various times in his life, Jocelyn is in love with each Avice, and each comes to represent a different fusion of nature and culture. The original Avice possesses both in equal balance; her daughter, who is often discussed as a sprite, a witch, or a troll, and who resembles most, especially in her strength, the Hardy goddesses figures, is aligned almost purely with nature, while the third Avice, interestingly the dark-haired beauty of the three, is almost completely identified with culture. Since Jocelyn functions as the focalizer for the narrative, the three Avices never take on any existence outside of his perception of them; as a result, they are not fully developed characters within the text. But the matriarchal structure of the three, whose husbands assume virtually no importance in the text, as well as the matrilineal bequeathing of the family fortune recall other Hardy novels. Also, the difference between the second and third Avices suggest the strong woman/weak woman dyad that Hardy frequently treats. Predictably, the Avice who functions as the bearer of nature is strong and capable, while the other is not.

One other woman figures significantly—Marcia, with whom Jocelyn lives as a young man and marries as an old one. Marcia possesses many traits of the typical Hardy woman character. Her living with Jocelyn without the sanction of marriage suggests she has not assimilated Victorian sexual values. Furthermore, she is a very independent woman who resists being bound to any man. However, Hardy's treatment of her is perplexing in some ways. His recurring association of the culturally assimilated woman with artificiality, especially through her wearing of makeup, appears here as well; when Marcia reappears in the text after many years, she looks far younger than Jocelyn because she has learned how to alter her appearance cosmetically. However, to please him, she abandons her habits to become by the end of the book actually ugly; Jocelyn, who has come to distrust beauty because it is physical, is happy with his wife's appearance. Since this is the only work in which Hardy's female protagonist actually ages,[2] it is difficult to know how to read Hardy's development of Marcia.

While *The Well-Beloved* is not set in Wessex, it does locate itself on an island that participates in the Pagan, mythic realm, which Hardy blatantly contrasts with the city in which Jocelyn lives for most of his life. The folk of the island resemble the Wessex folk in their zest for life and in their sexuality. The narrative voice repeatedly calls attention to an island custom that encourages a young man and woman to live together before they marry; Marcia and Jocelyn's arrangement might be inappropriate in the eyes of Victorian society, but it is conventional behavior in their homeland. Nature here is portrayed with less agency than is typical for Hardy, but it does enable Jocelyn and Marcia's initial encounter by distracting Jocelyn from the first Avice, whom he idealizes much as Angel Clare does Tess.

Taken as a whole, Hardy's works can be seen to explore similar themes repeatedly; the variations occur as the author comes to clarify his thoughts and focus his vision. Hardy situates his works between the mythic and the historical, the ideal and the real, one foot in never-never land, the other solidly in England. It is for that vision that readers continue to read Hardy and that vision that distinguishes him as a writer.

NOTES

1. Much excellent material is available on this subject. Of particular interest might be Fraser Harrison's *The Dark Angel*, Leonore Davidoff's "Class and Gender in Victorian England," and Anna Clark's "The Politics of Seduction in English Popular Culture, 1748-1848."

2. Susan in *The Mayor of Casterbridge* also appears as an old woman, but one might argue that the female protagonist of that work is actually Elizabeth Jane, the maiden side of the crone. Viviette, the "older" woman in *Two on a Tower* is only twenty-eight at the novel's opening and in her early thirties when she dies.

2

Far From the Madding Crowd: And Nature Saw What She Had Done, and It Was Good

It is very likely that a great deal of Thomas Hardy's continuing popularity, especially with readers who do not routinely read Victorian literature, results from the complex and powerful women characters he created. In the ongoing debate over whether male authors can create believable women characters or not, Hardy's women often spring to mind as examples of intelligent, psychologically believable characters who have been created by a writer not only sympathetic to the situation of women in Victorian society but also surprisingly understanding of the subtle dynamics of sexual politics. Bathsheba Everdene, around whom *Far From the Madding Crowd* revolves, is the earliest example of such a character. In the earlier novels, although the central female characters are lovely and charming, they remain in many ways the traditional heroines of Victorian literature. Cytherea Gray, Fancy Day, and Elfride Swancourt strike the reader as girl-women (sometimes just girls, actually) surrounded by loving but possessive families, and very caught up in the social fabric of Victorian convention. Interestingly, what these young women share with the more memorable Hardy women, such as Bathsheba and Tess, is age. Hardy routinely creates "women" characters who by contemporary standards would be considered girls, teenagers not assumed capable of making life choices for themselves. His one "older" woman, Viviette from *Two on a Tower*, is only twenty-eight. Admittedly, women often married in their teens in Victorian society; even so, Hardy's fascination with women so young, particularly considering the sorts of responsibilities and choices he attaches to his characters, is interesting. On the one hand, we could read these characters, who are also unusually sexually passionate for characters in Victorian novels, as early Lolitas and Hardy's interest in them as prurient. However, the strength and self-determination with which Hardy has endowed his characters are not qualities one attaches to a Lolita. Rather, those qualities enable a reading of these characters in terms of cultural myth. Hardy's major women characters, beginning with Bathsheba, can be seen as variations of a pattern that sets Hardy apart from his contemporaries, most especially in the portrayal of female characters. In telling Bathsheba's story, Hardy is scripting a cosmic drama that echoes the great myths that inform western, if not global, consciousness.

Far From the Madding Crowd is, of course, the first of what have come to be called Hardy's "Wessex novels." Andrew Enstice claims, and many would agree, that this novel treats Wessex as a kind of Eden rediscovered ("The Fruit of the Tree of Knowledge," 11). While I am not completely comfortable with the Eden parallel overall, it certainly is the case that the world Hardy portrays here is one of innocence and wish fulfillment, of regeneration and life. But if this is Eden, the angel with the two-edged sword has dozed, and Adam and Eve have been readmitted after the fall.

What marks this pastoral world as unique is its integration of nature and humanity. As much as is possible for Hardy to do and still tell a story, he presents nature and humanity not as separate or at odds with each other but rather as bound together in a unified, synthetic relationship. Hardy's agenda appears to be to present a world in which culture—not in its larger definition as the language, religion, and customs of a people, but rather in its more connotative sense of being the codified rules of behavior that allow for a hierarchic categorization of people and activities— intrudes as little as possible.[1] The world Hardy presents is one in which, as Enstice points out, the focus remains on the out of doors, with very few scenes taking place in interior space (*Landscapes*, 49). For the most part, in this version of Wessex, we see life, whether it be plant, animal, or human. Gillian Beer argues convincingly that Hardy tries to find a place for the human in the universe of his fictions that is neither "unrealistically grandiose, nor debilitatingly reductive" (249). His narrative necessarily must deal with people and their situations, but Hardy takes pains not to foreground the human too much, but to reveal it as a part of the texture of the greater whole. An undifferentiated state, the fusion of the human and nature, is, of course, necessary for any concept of an Eden; what distinguishes Hardy's vision of the ideal is his refusal to romanticize nature (and all that it encompasses, including the human). For the most part, Hardy sketches nature as only rarely destructive, which lends an idyllic quality to Weatherbury. Nature in this work functions to stave off the encroachment of the cultural, for example, when the workhouse is covered in lush, beautiful ivy. However, Hardy can accept—and celebrate—nature in its totality, not averting his eyes from what some would call the destructive aspects of nature. This is nowhere so clear as in the scene when Gabriel Oak's dog drives the sheep into the chalk-pit. Hardy focuses on Oak's sorrow for the pain of the sheep (even as he acknowledges that his purpose in raising them was ultimately to slaughter them) as well as on his grief at his financial and social loss. But very unsentimentally, he also portrays the kindhearted Oak shooting the overly diligent dog even after the narrative had allowed the reader insight into the dog's thought processes. The situation Hardy presents is one in which no blame can be attributed to anyone or anything. In a natural state, such random acts of death and destruction are commonplace, a fact society (ours and Hardy's) has difficulty grasping. John Paterson, addressing such a societal consciousness, claims that, for Hardy, reality was not limited to human endeavors and human creations, but grew out of the author's understanding of the totality of nature. Paterson goes on to point out that while Darwin's findings destroyed the Romantic understanding of nature as benevolently identified with the human community, what resulted was a sense of nature as possessing an "integrity" and an "independence of man" that allowed for a renewed and enlarged sense of awe and wonder ("The Continuing Miracle," 140–141). However, in *Far From the Madding Crowd*, such independence rarely occurs. The Wessex folk are so attuned to the natural cycle as to be indistinguishable from it, and the major characters take on mythic roles that recreate and embody those natural cycles.

While Bathsheba's story is foregrounded in the novel, it is woven over the texture of the lives of the folk here, who live out their lives in an endless cycle that for Hardy represents true stability. As George Wing points out, "Hardy's regionalism, then, in one of its identities, means without any indication of atrophy, staying put, existence through generations in one spot" (84) and adds, "[I]n Hardy's world, change often means loss" (86). The world of Weatherbury is static without being atrophic because it has escaped from time, from history, into myth; it exists as a place at odds with the historical, antithetical to it. The narrative approval evident in the passages describing the folk suggests that Hardy has portrayed this prelapsarian society as possessing the values he himself holds, but values that challenge and threaten Victorian society. When he claims that the folk are "as hardy, merry, thriving, wicked a set as any in the whole country" (77), we sense not only a celebration of the folk through the first three words, but a unity that includes the fourth term. The text suggests that the folk would not be nearly so hardy, merry, and thriving, were they not so wicked, which raises questions about the nature of their wickedness, the suggestion being that while the folk might be considered wicked by a culture that itself is attenuated and infirm, that wickedness is coexistent with their lust for life, which is what allows them to survive. Similarly, these folk do not assume the same implications of gender as Victorian society does. While they initially are skeptical about Bathsheba's managing her farm herself, once she begins doing so effectively, they defend her. They see no need for her to marry; as Henery Fray says, "I don't see why a maid should take a husband when she's bold enough to fight her own battles, and don't want a home" (181), by no means an appropriate statement for a Victorian man to make, since it so obviously expresses his admiration for such a "maid." The folk furthermore possess open and healthy attitudes about sexuality that contrast with those of Victorian society. Their admiration of Cainy Bell's grandfather for creating a new species of apple through grafting is in no way injured by the fact that he "used to bide about in a public-house wi' a 'ooman in a way he had no business to by rights" (250). They value his understanding of nature, which allows him to produce something both useful and aesthetic, and they ignore his disregard for convention, which they consider less significant than creating a new species of apple. They also completely understand Bathsheba's sexual passion for Troy; as Matthew Moon astutely says, "[M]aids rather like your man of sin" (253).

Initially, the novel does not overtly appear to be infused with the mythic. The

Bathsheba of the opening chapters lives with an aunt and performs routine agricultural duties seemingly detached from any real sense of community. Like Fancy and Elfride before her, she seems very young and uncertain, even as she toys with Gabriel during his feeble attempts at courtship. However, Bathsheba's introduction to the novel allows us to read these early chapters as indicative of Gabriel and Bathsheba's social development. When Gabriel first sees Bathsheba, she is alone, perched atop a wagonload of household goods, the driver having been sent to retrieve the tailboard of the wagon, which had been jolted free. As she waits, she unwraps a mirror and gazes at herself, obviously delighted with what she sees. The scene has often been commented upon, particularly because of its innate voyeurism; George Wotton, for example, comments how a recurring motif in Hardy's work is that of women constituted by male gaze (127). However, alternative readings can also be made. Marjorie Garson discusses Bathsheba's associations with the goddess Venus (34), whose iconic attribute is the mirror, from which the symbol for woman evolved. If we think of the goddess as identified with nature, the scene reveals nature aware of and pleased with her own creation.[2] Rosemary Sumner contrasts Bathsheba's "simple vanity and delighted enjoyment of her own appearance" with Boldwood's obsessional fear "that he is fading away" (54). Bathsheba's acknowledgment of her face in the mirror functions as an affirmation of her self, which gets at an earlier reading of the scene that suggests it reveals Bathsheba's vanity. In the patriarchal injunction against a woman's admiring herself one can trace the attempt to deny a woman her selfhood, not to mention her right to her own pleasure. It is not surprising that "vanity" is almost exclusively a trait associated with women; men are rarely accused of it, regardless of how much self-pride they display.

We can also read the scene through Lacan's concept of the mirror stage, which he describes as producing in a very young child the same sort of glee Bathsheba experiences at her specular image. He sees such a gaze as indicating the child's sense of its integrity of self, its lack of knowledge of any other that would determine the parameters of its existence (2). In these terms, Bathsheba can be seen, then, as woman-unto-herself, as woman not yet aware of herself as the object of the gaze, or of the presence of the other. The social is not yet developed in her. She exists like a very young child, with the aunt/mother as her only companion, not yet involved with her peers, not in any real way constituted by society at large. Were the trajectory of the novel to continue in this way, we would have another version of *Under the Greenwood Tree*; however, Hardy's project here is different. He pulls Bathsheba and Gabriel into a universe where they are allowed to transcend what is human and take on mythic overtones, Bathsheba as an agricultural goddess and Gabriel as her consort. That movement from what we might see as the historical, the day-to-day "reality" of a poor Victorian farm girl and a struggling young farmer, to the mythic is significant in Hardy's career as a novelist. His most known work—*The Return of the Native, The Woodlanders, Tess of the D'Urbervilles*, and *Jude the Obscure*—begin with the mythical world well established; *Far From the Madding Crowd* is the site of the creation of that world. Interestingly, this is also what many scholars consider the first of Hardy's "major" novels; Hardy's mythical world is not only a very comfortable one for him, but one that is very appealing to his audience. It is what sets him apart as a novelist.

But *Far From the Madding Crowd* differs from Hardy's later mythic novels[3] in its ending. Here the goddess figure is not destroyed by a Christian-identified figure, nor is she pulled into the historical world. Nor for that matter is the mythic world destroyed; we end with a sense of the natural cycle continuing and with the folk still attuned to it. In Weatherbury the reader encounters the Pagan world that so often exists in Hardy's Wessex. It is this Pagan world to which Hardy alludes when he speaks of the "Dryads . . . waking for the season" (154) in terms of the totality of nature coming alive again after the dormancy of winter. Not surprisingly, the natural world with its Dryads is set in opposition to a "noisy city," which is made to look vitiated and insignificant compared to the majesty which is nature. Nature's work, the work of the folk, becomes sacred work in the Pagan world revealed here. Hardy's description of the sheepshearing barn, a lengthy passage which essentially compares the building to a church, fosters the idea that what occurs in that barn is holy work, that the yearly ritual involving the animals is a part of the continuing cycle of birth, growth, and death that is celebrated in Paganism.

In the later novels, the Pagan elements will be enhanced and Christianity will function as a destructive force; however, here the Pagan and the Christian exist harmoniously. In the lush spring in which Gabriel and Bathsheba initially fall in love, we learn that "God was palpably present in the country" (175), apparently at peace with the Druids who are awakening simultaneously. Even the Weatherbury man of the cloth, Parson Thirdly, is portrayed as an admirable man, unlike the typical Hardyean ecclesiastic figure, who is arrogant, pedantic, cowardly, and generally foolish.[4] Matthew Moon describes him as "as good a man as ever walked" (252), and the text reveals him to be modest and gentle. The folk here are, for the most part, sincere in their Christianity and even nature's priest, Gabriel Oak, prays and sings in the church choir. However, hints of the antagonism that will later appear so predominantly surface here at times. Gabriel Oak, as his name would suggest, appears to have integrated both Christianity and Paganism into his nature. However, when he initially describes Gabriel, Hardy writes:

> On working days he was a young man of sound judgment, proper dress, and general good character. On Sundays he was a man of misty views, rather given to postponing, and hampered by his best clothes and umbrella; upon the whole, one who felt himself to occupy morally that vast middle space of Laodicean neutrality which lay between the Communion people of the parish and the drunken section—that is, he went to church, but yawned privately by the time the congregation reached the Nicene creed, and thought of what there would be for dinner when he meant to be listening to the sermon. (41)

The weekday Gabriel, as presented here, is a much more likable fellow; his churchgoing in many ways resembles that of Tess—he is there in person but hardly in spirit.

One technique that Hardy repeatedly uses throughout the Wessex novels is to make the most Christian of the rustics the butt of the jokes of the others, as happens here in the character of Joseph Poorgrass, whose first name recalls the earthly father of Christ and whose last name suggests his separation from nature and his lack of fertility. While poor Joseph is not nearly so cowardly or so humorous as some of his later counterparts, most obviously Christian Cantle in *The Return of the Native*, he nevertheless shares some of their traits. He frets about the morality of those around him, most particularly of Bathsheba's late father, who, to stay faithful to his wife, had to pretend she was only his sweetheart and not someone he was honor-bound to love. Furthermore he frequently spouts aphorisms which make him look foolish, for example, when he first meets Gabriel and carries on at length about how the folk should "feel full o' thanksgiving" that Gabriel is a moral man who plays "merry tunes" instead of "ba'dy songs" on his flute. He goes on to claim that "for our wives' and daughters' sakes we should feel real thanksgiving" (101). As the most Christian of the group, Joseph is the one who accepts most readily the patriarchal concept that the sexuality of the wives and daughters must be co-opted by their male kin, that women lack agency where their own sexuality is concerned. But even Joseph is looser with his Christianity than his later counterparts will be. He reveals his lack of familiarity with the scriptures, as well as his nonchalance about their sacredness when, in the process of trying to find the book of Ephesians, he exclaims, "Tis nothing but Corinthians and Thessalonians in this danged Testament" (169).

In alluding to Christianity in the text, Hardy writes that it has "suffered . . . mutilation at the hands of time" (176), indicating the religion may have at one time benefited humankind but that it has outlived its usefulness, and has become, in Hardy's term, "worn-out" (177), an ironic term to describe a religion newer than the Paganism to which Hardy at least unconsciously subscribes. He explains himself by adding, "The defense and salvation of the body by daily bread is still a study, a religion, and a desire" (177). The Pagan perspective, bonded as it is to nature, does not exist in time and therefore cannot become "worn-out," whereas Christianity, whose central myth involves the intersection of the mythic with the historical, must necessarily exist in time and therefore can be subject to its ravages. Furthermore, Christianity has becomes associated with the cultural to the point where the two can no longer be separated; one of the folk suggests as much when he comments, "what with the parsons and clerks and school-people and serious tea-parties, the merry old ways of good life have gone to the dogs—upon my carcase, they have!" (313).

The Pagan-Christian struggle that is so central to Hardy's later work becomes apparent in Bathsheba's similarities to Tess and Eustacia, the two other major goddess figures in Hardy's work. As we would expect of mythic figures, all three women are extremely beautiful, in Bathsheba's case so much so that at least three men instantly become obsessed with her, causing one to immediately abandon the woman he loves and another to go mad, suggesting that her beauty is not of the mere mortal quality, but rather belongs in the world of fables. As Susan Beegal points out, the story of "an unusual, beautiful woman courted by three men" is an archetype

(108), pointing the way to a mythic reading of the work. Significantly, Bathsheba is the first of the dark-haired Hardy women—he emphasizes her "ropes of black hair" (58), playing her against the Victorian stereotype that identified fair hair with purity and ideality. He further distinguishes Bathsheba from the cultural ideal by claiming that her "beauty [belonged] rather to the demonian than to the angelic school" (170). This break with tradition is obviously deliberate; Hardy is creating a woman who will challenge the Victorian definition of a woman as weak, prim, and chaste, rather than, like Bathsheba, strong, capable, and sexual.

Of Bathsheba's strength the text leaves no doubt. Both the devices of the plot and Hardy's rhetoric make it clear that Hardy perceives Bathsheba to be an extraordinary woman. For example, Hardy emphasizes the boldness of Bathsheba's decision to function as her own bailiff by pointing out that "The men breathed an audible breath of amazement" (112). The effect of the sentence is to leave the reader "amazed" at the daring of this young Victorian woman; when, then, she proves herself extremely capable in her new position, managing her farm efficiently, trading in the exclusively male Corn Exchange, and walking nightly around her land to insure that all is in order, she appears even stronger and more atypical than she would had the narrative not emphasized the peculiarity of her decision. Later, after Bathsheba has become infatuated with Troy, her midnight drive to Bath, obviously not typical behavior for a Victorian woman, receives narrative attention when the text's focalizer, in this case the servant Maryann, assumes the mysterious figure who glided into the barn must have been a gypsy, since a "woman was out of the question in such an occupation at this hour" (239). On this same ride, Bathsheba proves herself capable of taking a rock out of the shoe of a lame horse, to the amazement of the men who overtake her. After her marriage, the horrendous storm provides another look at Bathsheba's courage and resourcefulness, as she unflinchingly mounts the hayrick again and again, even though the lightning is a "perfect dance of death" (279). However, she also reveals her moral courage when she admits to Gabriel, her friend but also a man who feels free to criticize her and who had warned her against Troy, not only that her new husband is irresponsible but also that her motives for marrying him were confused ones. That same strength of character appears when she opens Fanny Robbin's coffin to ascertain Troy's infidelity and later again when she herself washes and dresses her husband's corpse, causing the surgeon to exclaim, "Gracious Heaven—this mere girl! She must have the nerve of a stoic!" (405). Again, the rhetoric emphasizes Bathsheba's extraordinary abilities, ones that enable a mythic reading of her as superhuman, as goddess, a reading supported by a random comment made earlier by Bathsheba's servant Liddy, who describes her mistress as "almighty womanish" (230). The "almighty" can of course be read colloquially; however, the more usual religious connotations of the word are precise, given Bathsheba's goddess-like power.

Bathsheba's association with the Great Goddess occurs in another instance as well. Hardy's reference to her as the Queen of the Cornmarket links her to a tradition in which the goddess functions as the Queen of the Corn and of the harvest. One of her functions associated with the corn is the sacrifice of the corn king, literally the cornstalks that are harvested to provide food for both humans and animals; in ritual the sacrifice was reenacted symbolically through the death, either literal or figurative, of the priest. The goddess herself never dies, but at the death of the corn king, her consort, already bears within her womb (the earth) the seed of the next consort (the new corn crop). While Bathsheba does not sacrifice any of her lovers in the work, the cycle she enacts with the three of them can be seen as alluding to the eternal return of the goddess. The powerful image of her bearing Troy's dead and bleeding body on her lap recalls the stricken goddess, sorrowing for the lover she has had to slay to ensure the survival of the planet.

While Bathsheba's goddesslike strength is difficult to overlook, initially her sexuality may appear less significant, especially since Hardy's treatment of it is much less blatant than is the case with Tess or Eustacia. However, a closer look at the character of Bathsheba reveals the same powerful levels of sexuality that mark the women in Hardy's later novels, although, as Richard Carpenter shows, here the sexuality is often displaced (340), which demands a careful analysis of language and imagery if we are to trace its trajectory through the novel. Her name itself is a first indication of how Hardy intends us to view her. Her first name, which significantly is prebiblical, aligning her with the mythic rather than the historical, means "voluptuous" or "daughter of satiety," while her last name means "wild one" (Caless, 10–11). Both names are apt. However, while Hardy could not assume readers would seek out such meanings, he could know for certain that they would immediately call to mind the biblical David's mistress, a woman of such beauty, sensuality, and power that she leads the Judaic king essentially to commit murder.

Bathsheba's sexuality is established early in the novel, when, astride a horse, having rejected as ridiculous the sidesaddle propriety demanded of women riders, she drops back upon the horse and rides fully extended upon the horse's back. The association of horses with sexuality in the subconscious has been frequently discussed, and while Hardy could not anticipate the lengths to which Lawrence would later go to make such associations obvious, he does locate the start of Gabriel Oak's obsession with Bathsheba in this scene, indicating some recognition of the sexuality implicit in Bathsheba's ride. However, Hardy distinguishes Bathsheba's natural sexuality, which is one with the sexuality inherent in the animals she tends, from the contemporary cultural sense of that word. He stresses that "Had she been put into a low dress she would have run and thrust her head into a bush" (55), indicating that Bathsheba's response to any societal notions of turning her into a sex *object*, as opposed to naturally sexual, would be a retreat to nature.

In an age when modesty was seen as a requirement for a novel's heroine, Hardy creates a woman who enjoys male attention and is piqued when she does not receive it; yet her lack of modesty does not result in either death or disgrace, but rather in marriage and fulfillment, indicating narrative approval of her behavior and attitudes. Throughout the novel, Bathsheba acts in ways inappropriate for a Victorian heroine. When she rescues Gabriel from the hut in which he is nearly asphyxiated, she suggests he hold and kiss her hand; when, in response to such behavior, young Oak comes courting and is mistakenly turned away, Bathsheba runs after him shouting, "hoi, hoi," oblivious to any Victorian sense of feminine propriety. Later, when she manages her own farm, she enjoys the attention she receives at the Corn Exchange, where she is the only woman present, and it is her ire at Boldwood's ignoring her that leads her to send the valentine which triggers his obsessional behavior and subsequent madness. But it is in her encounters with Troy that we see Bathsheba at her most blatantly sexual, not just aware of the effects of her beauty and power on men, but physically aroused and passionately responsive herself.

In the well-known "The Hollow amid the Ferns" chapter, the swordplay replicates the sexual act in a space that must be identified as feminine space. If Bathsheba as goddess is herself the landscape, the hollow amid the ferns into which Troy descends is the vagina; what follows is a description of Bathsheba's pleasure, her orgasm:

> In an instant the atmosphere was transformed to Bathsheba's eyes. Beams of light caught from the low sun's rays, above, around, in front of her, well-nigh shut out earth and heaven all emitted in the marvellous evolutions of Troy's reflecting blade, which seemed everywhere at once, and yet nowhere specially. These circling gleams were accompanied by a keen rush that was almost a whistling—also springing from all sides of her at once. In short, she was enclosed in a firmament of light, and of sharp hisses, resembling a sky-ful of meteors close at hand. (216)

After this encounter, Bathsheba is all but driven mad by the conflict between her body and her mind. In her hysterical argument with Liddy over Troy's character, her erratic mood swings, her lashing out in anger, her tears, all result from her knowing that Troy is reprehensible but knowing equally well that she cannot resist him. She is led to marry him not because of love but rather because of sexual attraction, her body's assertion of its desire for pleasure.

If Bathsheba's actions are inappropriate for a Victorian heroine, Hardy has revealed her thoughts to be equally scandalous. Her acceptance of the sexuality of other women strikes the reader as particularly anomalous for one of her time, yet Bathsheba twice defends women who have chosen to be sexually active. Early on in the book, she is visibly annoyed with Henery Fray, when, in response to her question about Temperance and Soberness Miller, he calls them "Yielding women—as scarlet a pair as ever was!" (114). Bathsheba, in addressing the women, makes it clear that what concerns her is the nature of their work on her farm; their private lives, their sexual behavior, is irrelevant to her. Later, even though she is pained by the knowledge of Fanny Robbin's pregnancy, what hurts her is the discovery of her husband's dishonesty toward her. What she feels for Fanny is pity and what might be called love. She brings the coffin of the young girl into her house for the night and bedecks it with flowers in an attempt to comfort the spirit of the neglected girl. Never does she reveal any sense of indignation at Fanny's behavior, even though Victorian culture would have expected such a response. Her attitudes about marriage are equally inappropriate for a Victorian heroine, as Hardy knew. From Gabriel Oak's proposal on, Bathsheba reveals her distaste for marriage, and while women characters in other novels may have claimed as much, they for the most part do not share Bathsheba's sexual nature. It is not men Bathsheba objects to; rather she does not desire the limitations imposed by a husband. As she tells Oak, "whenever I looked up, there he'd be" (67). Like Tess later, Bathsheba loves the romance and sexuality that accompany courtship. When she tries to explain to Farmer Boldwood that she sent the valentine innocently and playfully, she says, "Yet each of those pleasures was just for the day—the day just for the pleasure" (234), a radically *carpe diem* attitude for a Victorian woman. Her attitude about marriage strikes one as weirdly informed by contemporary feminist ideology. Hardy writes, "She had never taken kindly to the idea of marriage in the abstract as did the majority of women she saw about her" (303). She "fancied there was a certain degradation in renouncing the simplicity of a maiden existence to become the humbler half of an indifferent matrimonial whole" (303). Bathsheba's having resisted culture's indoctrination about the glories of matrimony again sets her apart from the norm. She functions as the goddess-unto-herself, she who gives herself where she pleases but cannot be bound against her will.

However, the goddess' collision with the forces of the patriarchy, here represented by Troy and Boldwood, cause her to regret her sexual nature and lead her to feel guilty for claiming her own pleasure. Once she has renounced her independent state and entered into marriage with Troy, who immediately assumes control not only of her but of her servants and her fields, she begins to be diminished, unempowered. The text tells us that "[u]ntil she had met Troy, Bathsheba had been proud of her position as a woman" (303). Such pride, however, is unacceptable in a woman in a patriarchal state. It challenges the accepted definition of "woman," just as Bathsheba herself has been a challenge to all accepted norms, not merely in her sexuality but in her independent life style and in her strength. The men, seemingly rivals but unified in their attempts to possess and control Bathsheba, inculcate her with culture's message—that the feminine state and female sexuality are sources of shame, not pride—until Bathsheba is ready to commit Sue Bridehead's "fanatic prostitution" and marry Boldwood, not out of love or even out of sexual desire, but out of a sense of duty. At this point in the novel, Bathsheba's mythic stature is least evident, and she most resembles the typical Victorian heroine, bound and oppressed by culture.

However, the overarching mythic structuring of the novels enables Bathsheba to regain her power and her will to choose her consort. Throughout the novel, Bathsheba is associated with nature in ways that allow a reading of her as nature embodied, as the Great Goddess. In the early, pre-Weatherbury section of the book, the girl Bathsheba works side by side with her aunt, tending livestock and specifically assisting at difficult births, enabling the natural process. The two women agricultural workers who are matrilineally related recall Demeter and Persephone. Later, when Hardy moves the novel from the "realistic" world in which it opens to the mythical, cosmic world that makes up a majority of the work, Bathsheba's association with the natural is even more strongly stressed. Her change in dress is one device Hardy uses to emphasize that association. Initially, she appears in a crimson jacket, which, like Troy's military uniform, contrasts with the landscape, setting her apart from it. By the end of the novel, Bathsheba appears most often in a green riding habit, wearing nature's color as she herself embodies the natural cycle of the year. Therefore, in the spring, a glorious and beautiful Bathsheba works closely with Gabriel during lambing; also in the spring, Bathsheba sends Boldwood the unfortunate valentine, nature's message to a celibate man, who is mysteriously forced to respond. In the later spring, as the natural world is becoming more fruitful, more blatantly sexual, Bathsheba discovers passion through her meeting with Sergeant Troy, whom she marries toward late summer, as the natural world begins to die. In October, when the Pagan world celebrates the ritual of Samhain, the recognition of the goddess' mourning for the loss of her consort, Bathsheba learns of Troy's affair with Fanny and retreats from sight, devastated and shrunken, spending the winter "as if she were now a dead person" (356), a phrase that recalls Persephone in the underworld, removed from the earth. After Troy's murder and Boldwood's madness, which occur in the winter, Hardy tells us "Bathsheba revived with the spring" (411). Within her life she enacts the rhythms of the natural year, becoming the visible embodiment of nature.

To further enable that association, Hardy writes nature as responding sympathetically to Bathsheba's plight. For example, when she sets out to meet Troy immediately after a thunderstorm, we are told the storm "had refined the air, and daintily bathed the coat of land, though all beneath was dry as ever" (231); the condition of the land parallels Bathsheba's state—her renewal is only superficial. No life-giving rain has fallen; no rebirth is occurring in either the land or in Bathsheba. Nor can it, while she is associated with Troy, who, having rejected the mythic world of Weatherbury to enter the historical (and specifically political) world of the military, here functions as the representative of a world antithetical to the world represented by Bathsheba. However, once Bathsheba is caught up in Troy, she becomes oblivious to the natural world. Hardy describes a scene in which the contrast between a lyrically beautiful description of nature (238), one of the most beautiful passages in the novel, and Bathsheba's unmindfulness of the scene emphasizes Bathsheba's alienation from the natural world she embodies—and hence her alienation from self. Her indifference becomes so great that she honeymoons with Troy during the crucial harvest time, ignoring the fieldwork that will provide the food necessary to survive the winter. After her marriage, the weather remains "dry and sultry" (269), echoing her realization that her match was an unfortuitous one, based purely on passion, but lacking the nurturance necessary for survival. On the evening of the party celebrating the marriage, nature acts out Bathsheba's repressed anger at Troy's dismissal of her and her dismay at her marriage in a storm of unbelievable force and destructiveness. Hardy describes the universe as "infuriated" (279) and presages the death and confusion that will follow the ill-fated union by describing the lighting as a "perfect dance of death" with "forms of skeletons . . . in the air, shaped with blue fire for bones—dancing, leaping, striding, racing around, and mingling together in unparalleled confusion" (279). Bathsheba, as nature embodied, acts unnaturally in aligning herself with Troy; hence nature must also act unnaturally, and in the midst of the storm lets out an unearthly shout that reminds one of the horrible birds from the north in *Tess of the D'Urbervilles*. Significantly, though, the rain holds back until Bathsheba and Gabriel, working together, have secured the hayricks; Hardy emphasizes the peculiarity of the rain's delay by having Gabriel, who repeatedly demonstrates his extensive and even uncanny knowledge of the patterns of nature, comment, "I cannot understand no rain falling" (280). Later, when Troy wounds Bathsheba by revealing his love for Fanny, a love he visibly demonstrates by arranging countless flowers on her grave, nature again vents Bathsheba's repressed fury in the form of another storm that, with the aid of a gargoyle, a Pagan representation, washes away with a vengeance all the efforts of Troy's labor. Her anger spent, Bathsheba replaces the flowers the next day, and they remain in place.

Bathsheba's fusion with nature reveals itself further in a scene that initially strikes the reader as incongruous. After Bathsheba learns the full extent of Fanny's involvement with Troy and must confront the fact that her new husband does not love her, in her emotional agony she flees the house and retreats to nature. She decides that "it seemed better to be out of the house than within it" (322). The typical—or perhaps stereotypical—response of a Victorian heroine would have been to retire to bed and stay there, curtains closed, firmly ensconced within the house. Bathsheba instead seeks refuge in a dismal swamp, a malignant site appropriate to her despair. Hardy's description of the area again points to the fusion of woman and landscape; however, Bathsheba is blind to the hideousness of the site, affirming, "I shall not come indoors yet—perhaps never" (331). Like Tess when she hides in the leaves to escape the boorish men, Bathsheba innately understands that interior space is equated with the civilized and the patriarchal; there, men can harm her. Outdoors she is free and safe; she grieves, and the earth echoes her grief in its deformities, but Troy has no access to her there.

In his discussion of Bathsheba and nature, Peter Casagrande sees the unity of the two but refers to nature as "defective nonhuman nature" (52). If the human is equated with the cultural, then certainly nature as Hardy treats it must be read as non-human, since it figures in opposition to culture. However, claiming it is "defective" reveals an essentially sentimental view of nature. Bathsheba's occasional acts of capriciousness and willfulness mirror nature's refusal finally to be controlled or restrained. For this reason, Bathsheba, as well as Eustacia in *The Return of the Native*, functions more powerfully as a representation of nature than does Tess, whom Hardy felt compelled to present as moral. At times unreasoning and impulsive, Bathsheba and Eustacia echo nature in its amorality. Judging that nature as "defective" or immoral is essentially fruitless; however society chooses to regard nature, it remains a force that must be dealt with on its own terms. As Nor Hall writes: "Law, before it is hatched, is held deep within the body of the Mother (Earth or Nature). Her laws, the way-she-lays-it-down, are primitive or basic. . . . Unlike the great changing law of the Father, which is based upon consciousness of self, property, and others, the Mother's laws are those of unvitiated nature"(40). However, while Hardy clearly identifies Bathsheba with the natural world, he does not implicitly link her with Paganism as he will later do with Eustacia and Tess. The world Bathsheba inhabits is simultaneously Pagan and Christian, but she seems oddly neither. Perhaps Hardy had not yet grasped the connection between Christianity and the repression of women, or perhaps he simply was unwilling to fly in the face of convention, as he later will do repeatedly. Nevertheless, while Bathsheba is associated with the Great Goddess and with the landscape, the cycle of Pagan rituals that will inform the later novels is absent here. Virtually the only manifestation of such rites appears, ironically, in the scene involving the Bible and key divination, an act for which witches (i.e., often women adhering to Pagan ways) were brought to trial in Scotland (Firor, 45). Divination in and of itself is not acceptable within Christianity; one gets the sense that the ritual evolved as a way of mitigating the sorcery involved in the process, sanctioning the act by involving the Bible in it. The scene functions to further reveal Bathsheba's attitude toward Christianity, or at least toward its holy day. When Liddy expresses some hesitation about dabbling in magic on a Sunday, Bathsheba replies, "What's right week days is right Sundays" (128), revealing a lack of compulsion to honor the Christian Sabbath.

Many of the patterns that are repeated in the later Wessex novels trace their roots to *Far From the Madding Crowd*. Like many other women characters in Hardy, Bathsheba is an heiress; however, the later heiresses tend to come to their wealth through maternal relatives, which sets up a matriarchal, matrilineal subculture within the novels.[5] Bathsheba inherits through a dead uncle. So while, like many of the other Hardy women, she is freed from an immediate patriarchal family structure,[6] she nevertheless rises to her position through an extension of the patriarchy, which associates her with the cultural, historical world. However, Hardy stresses her separation from that world by calling attention to her problems with language. She tells Boldwood, "It is difficult for a woman to define her feelings in language which is chiefly made by men to express theirs" (376). If we see speech as linked with culture, Christianity (the *word* made flesh), and the patriarchy, her discomfort with it associates her with the opposite—nature, Paganism, and matriarchy, where gesture, the act, takes primacy over the word. Interestingly, Bathsheba tells Troy that she stopped learning French verbs at the time of her father's death; this particular language, which bears the implicit signification of culture, becomes bound up with the idea of the father and, by extension, the patriarchy. Troy attempts to court Bathsheba in French, aligning him with that tradition.

Hardy's rhetoric in one instance appears to challenge the dichotomy he otherwise establishes. When Bathsheba hears of Troy's love for Fanny, she lets out a cry that Hardy calls the "Τετελεσται" of her union with Troy (327). The words, "It is finished," recall, of course, Christ's words on the cross, which might initially indicate an association between Bathsheba and Christ. However, given the rest of the novel, it seems more likely that Hardy is playing with the idea that he develops more fully in the character of Tess, whose life can be read as a Pagan inversion of Christ's life, which stresses her divine nature at the same time that it focuses attention on her separation from the Christian tradition.

Several of the motifs that run through the later novels appear here in a somewhat mediated form. One pattern that Hardy explores repeatedly is that of a goddess-identified woman courted by two men, each in differing ways antithetical to her nature. Here, Troy and Boldwood can be read as identified with patriarchal culture, although Hardy does not make those identifications as pronounced as he will do later. Troy, for example, might initially be seen as identified with the mythic past rather than the historical present, particularly given the Hellenic associations of his name.

However, other details of the text alienate him from the mythic and bind him firmly within culture. We learn, for example, that Troy has *two* fathers; he is "a doctor's son by name . . . , and . . . an earl's son by nature" (196). The patriarchal bond is doubly emphasized here, while the nobility of the one father and the education of the other function to distance Troy from the agrarian society of Weatherbury. Although Troy claims Weatherbury as home, he is portrayed as ill-suited for life there. His ineptness at agricultural work, for example, when he attempts to hive the bees, juxtaposes him not only with Gabriel Oak but also with Bathsheba herself, who does not merely manage her farm but engages skillfully in farm labor. Troy's love for Fanny with her golden hair, the emblem of the cultural ideal, serves to link him with stereotypical societal values, and his career in the military, as Brooks shows, points out his "rootlessness," his opposition to "a way of life rooted in seasonal ritual" (169). In addition, Hardy discusses Troy in language that dissociates him from the sense of a past that gives identity and self-knowledge:

> He [Troy] was a man to whom memories were an incumbrance, and anticipations a superfluity. . . . His outlook upon time was as a transient flash of the eye now and then; that projection of consciousness into days gone by and to come, which makes the past a synonym for the pathetic and the future a word for circumspection, was foreign to Troy. With him the past was yesterday; the future, to-morrow; never, the day after. (197)

This description, in addition to calling attention to Troy's shallowness and flightiness, also marks Troy's distance from the natural world, which is essentially timeless, moving in an eternal cycle rather than progressing in a linear fashion. In the later novels, Hardy elaborates on the idea that germinates here, so that characters not rooted in a sense of past repeatedly appear as unlikable and destructive.

Troy's separation from nature appears in other instances in the text as well. The aforementioned hiving of the bees, which makes his arms ache, is one such example. Troy's expertise in the sword exercise indicates that he possesses physical strength and agility; however, Hardy's making Troy incapable of routine agricultural work emphasizes his incongruity in an agrarian setting. Dress functions similarly. In describing Bathsheba and Troy's clandestine meeting, she is unified with the natural setting amid the ferns, whose "soft, feathery arms [caress] her up to her shoulders"

(214). Troy, on the other hand, is described as "a dim spot of artificial red" (214), highlighting his obtrusiveness upon the natural. Interestingly, in the early section of the novel, Bathsheba also appears in red; however, Hardy's narration integrates her with the natural in a way that never occurs with Troy. After calling attention to her "crimson jacket," which "painted a soft lustre upon her bright face and dark hair," the narrative voice points out the "myrtles, geraniums, and cactuses" amid which she sits on the wagon, describing them as "fresh and green" and claiming they "invest" the scene "with a peculiar vernal charm" (44). Essentially, Bathsheba in crimson functions as the geranium flower, the bloom of color arising from the leafy greenery. Phrases such as "soft lustre" and "vernal charm" contrast strongly with words such as "dim" and "artificial" in the description of Troy, so that in the one instance the crimson becomes identified with nature and in the other instance is antithetical to it. Finally, one other scene deserves comment. After Troy plants the flowers on Fanny's grave, as Horne points out, "some force—numinous and ironic and powerful—seems to work against Troy" (47). That force is nature, working in a way reminiscent of the Old Testament god rejecting the sacrifice of the murderous Cain. If, as Horne suggests, Troy's work with the flowers is his attempt "to beautify the earth" (48), nature's response indicates that only through Bathsheba, the vegetation goddess, can the earth be beautified. Once Troy rejects her, his life is never again beautiful or productive; when he reappears after his symbolic death, the text becomes oddly surreal and we see the once-proud military man traveling with a pathetic little circus as a makeshift actor. The scene shimmers with the uncanny in a way that suggests Troy has achieved a sort of personal hell.

Mythically, hell is an appropriate place for Troy, since his archetype within the text is Satan, as many critics have suggested. Much in the text aligns Troy with the biblical archfiend, but what muddies the issue is Hardy's frequent use of what have come to be called "Mephistophelian visitants." Even Gabriel Oak achieves satanic status in one scene, when his aerial view of Bathsheba is compared to "Milton's Satan first [seeing] Paradise" (51). However, in this instance the comparison appears to have been made more to emphasize Bathsheba's beauty than to suggest anything destructive in Oak's character. Not so with Troy. Not only does Hardy continually emphasize Troy's red clothing,[7] but he also focuses attention on actions that encourage the reader to view Troy as malevolent. In one scene, he describes Troy as "[rising] from the earth" (225), creating the image of a devil ascending from hell. Brooks sees Troy's behavior at the wedding feast, where he coerces the rustics to drink, as evidence that he possesses "the devil's power to distort human dignity" (170). Merryn Williams discusses Troy as an early working of Alec D'Urberville (131), another of Hardy's satanic figures. The two are distinguished, however, by Alec's alliance with Christianity (e.g., becoming an itinerant preacher), which Troy does not share. Here, Troy attempts to pass himself off as a devout churchgoer, when in fact he does not attend. Interestingly, it is Bathsheba who uses Troy's argument to convince Oak of Troy's goodness when she herself is never portrayed as attending church and in fact is surprised to discover that Oak sings with the choir. Hardy's ambivalence about Christianity as a signifier is evident here. On the one hand, Bathsheba's disinterest in churchgoing cannot be seen as a critique of her, since the narrative voice encourages a favorable reaction to her. On the other hand, Oak's attending church speaks well of him, and were Troy to attend as he claims to do, the reader would be forced to reevaluate his character. By some of the later works, Hardy's ambiguity will have largely diminished. The sense that comes through later, that Christianity is destructive of the feminine, really does not appear here. Troy himself is portrayed as very mysogynistic, for all his sexual attraction to women, if not because of it. Admittedly, his attitudes about women and sexuality can be seen as evolving from the Judeo-Christian concept of women and femininity, although the text does not emphasize the connection between the two. Troy's sexism is societally constituted and societally endorsed. Hence Troy regards women as "other," as a subfield of the human, and decidedly as inferior. Furthermore, women for Troy are not individual human beings but rather are a composite body made up of identical, interchangeable members. Hardy writes: "He [Troy] had been known to observe casually that in dealing with womankind the only alternative to flattery was cursing and swearing. There was no third method. 'Treat them fairly, and you are a lost man,' he would say" (199). Troy's entire agenda in his interaction with women is the acquisition of power, either through psychological violence or through sexual game-playing, both time-honored methods of treating women in a culture that affirms male supremacy. Troy also accepts society's notion that class and sexual behavior determine a woman's worth. For example, when he first meets Bathsheba, in the dark lane late one night, he asks if she is a woman, but quickly amends his phrasing, substituting "lady" for "woman." Significantly, Bathsheba erases the distinction by saying, "It doesn't matter." At his own wedding party, Troy prefers the company of men to women and sends the women, including his bride, home, indicating his sense that women function merely as trivial ornaments but cannot be true companions for him. Furthermore, Troy has inculcated the Judeo-Christian notion that women are seducers, betrayers of the pure soul of man. He twists logic, in ways, however, that have strong historical precedent, to even blame Bathsheba for his own infidelity to Fanny, claiming: "If Satan had not tempted me with that face of yours, and those cursed coquetries, I should have married her. I never had another thought until you came in my way" (327). Throughout Troy's relationships with both Bathsheba and Fanny, his primary desire is for domination; Troy has readily assimilated the cultural tenet of male supremacy and female submissiveness. Specifically in his dealings with Bathsheba, the power he wields is always symbolically linked to the phallus. In his first encounter with her, it is his phallic spur, tangled in her dress, that binds her in a situation that symbolically replicates the sexual act. The aforementioned erotic scene in the ferns revolves around Troy's sword, another phallic signifier; Troy's demands that Bathsheba stand still and the physical danger she experiences suggest rape more than seduction. Peter Coxon comments on Troy's afterward slicing off a lock of Bathsheba's hair as indicating that "his sexual domination and her submission are complete" (104). Susan Beegal similarly associates Troy's sexuality with death, claiming, "The iridescent, world-obscuring blue of the sword in the air and the fresh luxuriance of the fern-pit are undeniably sensual and attractive. But the scene's real excitement depends on the sword's capacity to deal death" (113). The culmination of the sword exercise is, of course, the running through of the caterpillar that has crawled onto Bathsheba's bosom. The scene serves to align the sexual with death, an association that is commonplace in cultural, and specifically, Christian, thought, but one at odds with the Pagan view of sex as life-affirming and life-giving. But Troy's sexuality destroys what it touches: Fanny, who dies along with her and Troy's child; Bathsheba, who never conceives a child with Troy; even the luxurious fern pit, which turns hideous and becomes the site of contagion. As Beegal so accurately states, "Contact with Troy has turned the novel's feminine space, and Bathsheba's perception of her own sexuality, into a 'loathsome, malignant thing'" (114), a perception the Judeo-Christian tradition has continually foisted upon women. Furthermore, Troy's love for Fanny is much more visible once she is dead. While she lives, Troy's encounters with her are marked by a struggle for dominance; dead, she must remain totally passive, allowing Troy, who shares in his culture's hatred of the empowered woman, to fully love her.

Bathsheba's attraction to a man like Troy presents a problem for some readers. However, when one considers Bathsheba's choices within the novel, her behavior becomes more plausible. The only Weatherbury men introduced in the text who are in any way Bathsheba's peers in terms of education and social standing are Troy and Boldwood. Furthermore, Troy is the only man in the novel who acknowledges his own sexuality, albeit in destructive ways. However, perhaps even more significantly, with this novel Hardy begins what will become a pattern in the three major novels; in no one of them does he allow the male protagonist to marry a virgin. Tess, Eustacia, and Bathsheba all have sexual encounters with experienced, sexually conscious men before they marry Angel, Clym, and Gabriel. Hardy's radical move accomplishes a great deal. It allows him to challenge the Victorian notion that virginity becomes the defining standard for morality in a woman; one might argue convincingly that his agenda in writing *Tess of the D'Urbervilles* is precisely to attack that position. Further, it reveals Hardy's awareness of the dynamics of sexuality in culture. Hardy comes to understand that for many men, the taking of a woman's virginity becomes a sign of their possession of or power over the woman.[8] By creating scenarios in which his women characters experience the sexual act prior to their marriages with the major male figures, Hardy equalizes the power between the lovers more. Finally, on the mythic level, the sexually experienced woman functions more readily as an embodiment of the Pagan vegetation goddess, since one quality cross-culturally associated with the goddess is sexuality and, specifically, freely choosing sexual partners for short-term encounters.

In seeking out a sexual peer, Bathsheba understandably considers Troy before Boldwood, who functions both as Troy's opposite and also his counterpart. Whereas Troy is a sexual libertine, Boldwood is celibate, and in many ways completely asexual, having for years been oblivious to the many women who have sought to court him. His being a farmer would suggest an attunement to the natural world, yet his own life in no way echoes that world since, at forty, he remains a bachelor. When he first becomes aware of Bathsheba, Hardy compares him to Adam upon first seeing Eve, an appropriate statement to make of a youth but hardly one fitting of a man well into middle age. The edenic allusion further reflects Hardy's sense of the inappropriateness of the biblical myth in the timeless world of Weatherbury. The dynamics of power between Adam and Eve revealed by the Genesis account are not endorsed by Hardy. Hardy's narrative further serves to identify Boldwood as essentially at odds with Bathsheba, in that he is linked with the cultural rather than with the natural. For example, Hardy in one instance describes Bathsheba as lighting up Boldwood's eyes as the moon lights up a tower. The moon with which Bathsheba is associated is natural; the tower is manmade, artificial. Throughout his courtship of her, Boldwood acts in socially appropriate fashion for a Victorian gentleman in that he suppresses any sort of physical desire or passion for Bathsheba;[9] however, the absence of such desire indicates that what Boldwood perceives as marriage is not the coming together of two people who love and desire each other, what one might call a natural union, or a union growing out of nature, but rather the culturally endorsed notion of a man taking as possession an ornament, a pretty little trifle to sometimes be proud of and sometimes ignore. In his initial proposal to Bathsheba, he makes no mention of love or passion, but simply lists his assets and announces, "I want you as my wife" (159).[10] He brings neither playfulness nor a sense of joy to the courtship, treating the matter almost purely as a business proposition, as his language reveals when he speaks of their upcoming marriage as "[a] mere business compact, you know, between two people who are beyond the influence of passion" (397). After his arrest, it is discovered that Boldwood has purchased elegant dresses and jewels, all of which he has labeled "Bathsheba Boldwood." His act can be read as the patriarchal man's desire to apparel his possession in finery which will attest to his wealth and to label her with his name, much as he would brand a calf.

On one level, of course, Boldwood must be viewed simply as mentally defective. However, in his courtship of Bathsheba he is living out the Victorian ideal, playing by the rules that society endorses. He acknowledges no sexual desire for Bathsheba, nor does he view her as a peer or a companion. Rather he perceives himself as her protector and provider, which puts him in the position of authority and her in a position lacking agency. In speaking of what her life will be like after their marriage, he promises she will be protected and be entirely free of any concerns for their livelihood; he will hire a man to take over Bathsheba's agricultural duties. That a capable, independent woman would not deem it an honor to relinquish the role she has chosen for herself never occurs to him.[11]

While Boldwood is Troy's antithesis in matters of sexuality, what the two men share is their contempt for women. Troy's disregard of women is immediately apparent, from the very first scenes with Fanny, when he enjoys tormenting her about their presumed upcoming marriage. However, initially it may appear harsh to describe Boldwood's feelings for women, and for Bathsheba in general, as contemptuous. What becomes apparent, though, is that he consistently ignores Bathsheba's requests; when in obvious distress she begs him to leave off the courtship, he consistently demands more and more privileges with her, oblivious of her wants or needs. He perceives himself as superior to her and as rightfully dominant over her, just as Troy does. Furthermore, Boldwood, like Troy, is aligned with death. The grotesqueness of his Christmas party stems from the fact that the festal and the celebratory are alien to him. His persistent overtures to Bathsheba, and his inability to see the inappropriateness of his behavior, cast him in the role of some aging Pluto attempting to lure Persephone to the underworld. His murder of Troy further links him with death, even as it points out the synthesis of their characters, since, in essence if not literally, the two men kill each other.[12] Hardy's mythic Weatherbury cannot survive the presence of such men, who are essentially parasitic, presuming a superiority of rank, wealth, and gender rather than of productivity or usefulness, nor will it allow "heretics" who have abandoned the service of nature for culture.

The tragedy of the later works stems from the fact that Hardy's female heroes, Tess and Eustacia, are forced to choose between versions of Troy and Boldwood, both equal in their potential for destruction; Bathsheba, in the green world of Weatherbury, is allowed a third option, a man suited to her, a counterpart—Gabriel Oak. Very few male characters in Hardy are truly admirable in the way that Oak is. From the first paragraph of the novel, in which his smiling face is described as "a rudimentary sketch of the rising sun" (141), his benevolent presence hovers over the action of the novel, guiding it, blessing it; if Bathsheba's archetype is that of the agricultural goddess, Gabriel is her consort, the agricultural god.

Gabriel's bond with nature is foregrounded throughout the novel. He can read nature like a book, telling time by the stars, predicting weather accurately. But in the shift from the novel's opening setting to the more primitive, ahistorical locus of its development, Gabriel's role changes, enlarges to include a mythical dimension; he begins to function as nature's high priest, her chosen one. His abilities far transcend those of typical farmers. His ability to make sundials, to save the bloated sheep, to receive a "direct message from the Great Mother" (272) mark him as sacred, as does his function as "a kind of midwife to nature" (Beegal, 117) who delivers lambs as well as harvests.

As nature's priest/divine incarnation, it would seem that Gabriel need embody a kind of natural sexuality, parallel to Bathsheba's; on a superficial reading, however, he appears almost asexual. The problem stems from accepting a societally constituted definition of sexuality, one that reinterprets Troy's rapaciousness as sexual rather than merely as the desire for dominance which it is. Beegal's brilliant discussion of Gabriel's sexuality shows how, while both Troy and Gabriel are associated with phallic objects, Troy's objective correlatives are the sword and the spur, objects that wound and kill, while Gabriel's are the sheep shears, the trochar, the marking iron, the ricking rod, and the flute (117), all of which are essential to the life of the farm. Comparing Troy's sword exercise with Gabriel's sheepshearing in their implicit sexuality, she adds: "Unlike the sword-exercise, the sheep-shearing is neither deathly nor ultimately despoiling. Instead, the images are of birth, renewal, and cleansing. The newly shorn sheep arising from its fleece is described as Aphrodite, the newborn and naked goddess of love, rising from the sea" (118). In performing his act of service, he at once serves Bathsheba, nature, and the Great Goddess, all of whom are interchangeable.

Associated as he is with nature rather than with culture, Gabriel responds to the world intuitively, often acquiring knowledge intuitively as well. From merely touching Fanny's wrist, he understands that her heart beats "with a throb of tragic intensity" (87) and feels "himself in the penumbra of a very deep sadness" (88). In his work, his intuition guides him, allowing him to rick the hay in the dark "entirely by feeling with his hands" (277). This privileging of intuition over reason makes him unique among Hardy's male characters and frees him of the vision of the ideal that haunts and destroys men such as Angel Clare and Clym Yeobright. In his interactions with Bathsheba, Gabriel comes to love her fully, aware of her imperfections but accepting of them as coexistent with her intelligence, her beauty, and her spiritedness. His clear-sightedness allows the possibility of a lasting, meaningful love relationship; he allows Bathsheba full expression rather than imposing on her a preconceived notion of the feminine.

If Gabriel does not share a societal notion of gender inequality, neither does he accept a hierarchy of class. Although when he moves to Weatherbury he has lost his wealth and is economically at least on the same level as the folk, the ease with which he mingles with them indicates that he feels no sense of superiority based on education or talent. At the end of the novel, when he has once again acquired wealth, Gabriel shows obvious delight when the Weatherbury folk come by to celebrate his marriage to Bathsheba and refers to them as "old friends" (424). He judges people as individuals, according to their character and values rather than on the basis of wealth and status.

Given Hardy's flattering portrayal of Gabriel, Bathsheba's initial refusal to marry him becomes problematic. However, the Bathsheba and Gabriel that exist in the pre-Weatherbury section of the book are both immature and naive; both have much to learn about human nature and about themselves. Critics are fond of discussing Bathsheba's vanity and triviality in the beginning of the work, but Hardy takes glee in making Gabriel look not only trivial but downright ludicrous when he goes courting Bathsheba for the first time. Gabriel does not simply polish his watchchain and don his best clothes; he also oils his hair until it is the color "of guano and Roman cement," resembling "mace round a nutmeg, or wet seaweed round a boulder after the ebb" (63). Gabriel may be the novel's hero, but in this scene he appears neither sensible nor attractive. Nor does he actually court. Even though he has only ever spoken a few words to Bathsheba, he proceeds to rattle off a list of his assets and talents and assumes that she will consent to marry him. When she sensibly tells him that she does not love him, he retorts, "But I love you—and, as for myself, I am content to be liked" (67). His answer is that of an immature adolescent who has no concept of what marriage entails. When Bathsheba, by way of testing him, suggests he would be wiser to marry a widow with money, he admits that he has considered the idea. At this point, Gabriel shares Victorian society's conflicted definition of marriage as both a financial arrangement and a social discourse, a view that Hardy consistently challenges in the Wessex novels.

Shortly after Bathsheba's rejection of Gabriel, he loses his flock and with it, his wealth. On the mythic level, the hero is being subjected to a series of tests by nature, the intent being to teach him what is required of love before he can win his heart's desire. Significantly, Bathsheba, the embodiment of nature, leaves the neighborhood at about the same time that the sheep die; the two acts can be read as the same act, as nature's withdrawing herself from Gabriel, as her demand that he seek her elsewhere. Hardy makes clear that these losses strengthen Gabriel by referring to ordeals that have the potential to destroy, but if survived, are the basis for fortitude and calm assurance. A second act of nature reunites him with Bathsheba. Traveling through the countryside, he encounters a wheat-rick on fire, and, unconcerned with whose it is or what he may or may not stand to gain, he becomes the major force in saving the crop. Having proven himself, he finds himself face to face with Bathsheba, who has been transformed from a simple country girl to the mistress of the manor, the queen of this mythical universe. Clearly, a fairy tale motif governs here. Once he recognizes his love, he asks to serve her, not as a bailiff, but as a lowly shepherd. Having asked the right questions, a necessary part of any quest, Gabriel finds himself not only employed by the woman he loves, but working side by side with her in a state of virtual equality. Although he nominally serves her, his power is made clear in the scene in which she must beg him to come to save her sheep. The two exist in a complementary relationship that revolves around the life and work of the farm. As they work together, Gabriel experiences true happiness; Hardy states "that his bright lady and himself formed one group, exclusively their own, and containing no others in the world, was enough" (178).

Gabriel's next test comes in the form of the rivals Troy and Boldwood. Since it is necessary for the questor to learn humility, Gabriel loses Bathsheba to both of the other men. The myth of the Great Goddess becomes significant here. It is necessary for Bathsheba to be sexually involved with some other man, since one aspect of the goddess is her right to sexual self-determination. Hardy does not allow Gabriel the option of even unconsciously considering Bathsheba his property because of societal notions of sexual possession. In the later novels, the women's initiatory experiences will occur with lovers rather than husbands, which is mythically more appropriate; however, in this earlier work it appears likely that Hardy chose to take liberties with the myth to guarantee reader acceptance of Bathsheba. However, he nonetheless structures the work so that both the folk and the reader assume for several pages that Bathsheba has taken Troy to her bed without marrying him. Hardy's narrative ploy allows him to essentially have it both ways. Bathsheba retains her respectability, but the reader is left with the sense of her as sexually free.

Gabriel's response to Bathsheba's marriage is to remain devoted to her, even to the point of risking his life to save her hayricks while the dissolute Troy sleeps off his drunken stupor. If, as the goddess figure here, Bathsheba and the crop are one, in saving the hayricks Gabriel is in essence saving Bathsheba. Financially the case is obvious: Bathsheba would have lost the farm had the crop been lost. However, on a psychological level, Gabriel's devotion and assistance allow Bathsheba to survive her grief and despair, on some level aware that the farm will effectively be maintained and that when the time comes to seek out a friend, she will have one.

Gradually, because of his service, Gabriel regains his wealth but retains his modesty. Along the way, he matures from the naive young man of the pre-Weatherbury section; one indication of his maturity, of his inner integration and wholeness, is what could be called his move toward androgyny. Hardy stresses that after Gabriel has become a man of means again, "he lived in no better style than before, occupying the same cottage, paring his own potatoes, mending his stockings, and sometimes even making his bed with his own hands" (357)[13] Repeatedly throughout the Wessex novels, the male characters Hardy posits as positive or moral, such as Gabriel and Giles Winterbourne in *The Woodlanders*, routinely do what some would call "woman's work."[14] On some level, Hardy reveals an understanding that gender inequality, like class inequality, is a function of society, and therefore does not belong in his vision of Eden.

Gabriel's maturation also reveals itself through a new understanding of love. From the man who had once told Bathsheba, during a proposal of marriage, that whether she loved him or not was inconsequential, since he loved her, Gabriel has changed into a man who, in discussing Bathsheba's possible marriage to Boldwood, says, "The real sin, ma'am, in my mind, lies in thinking of wedding wi' a man you don't love honest and true" (379–80). The love shared by Bathsheba and Gabriel is honest and true; what she feels for him is not mere infatuation or sexual desire, but "the genuine friendship of a sister" (304). By emphasizing the brother-sister nature of Gabriel and Bathsheba's love, the text replicates the many myths of the goddess in which her consort is also her brother, and the two exist as equals in their rule, much as Gabriel and Bathsheba share the management of the farm. Once these two recognize their feelings for each other, Hardy celebrates their love in one of the most beautiful passages of any of his novels, a passage that reveals Hardy's understanding of what is required for love to flourish:

> They spoke very little of their mutual feelings; pretty phrases and warm expressions being probably unnecessary between such tried friends. Theirs was that substantial affection which arises (if any arises at all) when the two who are thrown together begin first by knowing the rougher sides of each other's character, and not the best till further on, the romance growing up in the interstices of a mass of hard prosaic reality. This good-fellowship—*camaraderie*—usually occurring through similarity of pursuits, is unfortunately seldom superadded to love between the sexes, because men and women associate, not in their labours, but in their pleasures merely. Where, however, happy circumstance permits its development, the compounded feeling proves itself to be the only love which is strong as death—that love which many waters cannot quench, nor the floods drown, beside which the passion usually called by the name is evanescent as steam. (419)

In discussing Bathsheba's marriage with Gabriel, Brooks talks of the failure of "high romance," her characterization of Bathsheba's relationship with Troy, and the acceptance of "prosaic reality" (167). The disruption of the romance is significant to Hardy's agenda, given the genre's bond with Christianity and culture; therefore, he uses the elements of the quest to celebrate not the romantic but its opposite. To further stress the story's dissociation from that tradition, Hardy scripts the ending to involve Gabriel's making a matrilineal move into Bathsheba's house. Even though by this time both are equal in terms of land and wealth, and metaphorically in terms of self, the house they live in is Bathsheba's; Gabriel accepts the bounty of nature and lives off of it. There is no more affirmative ending in Hardy.[15]

Far From the Madding Crowd ends with the Pagan world fairly intact, existing with but not necessarily threatened by the Christian/cultural world of history. Bathsheba and Gabriel, nature goddess and nature god, marry with Hardy's blessing. Nothing taints their union. Joseph Poorgrass may quote Hosea that "Ephraim is joined to idols" (424), upon hearing of the marriage, but even he is not emphatic in his criticism. The idol Hosea refers to, the goddess Ashtaroth, one manifestation of the Great Goddess, belongs in Weatherbury. The book ends out of time, safe from history, in a world where sheep may safely graze, and shepherds and shepherdesses may love with a love "which many waters cannot quench, nor the floods drown."

NOTES

1. Marlene Springer points out how even Hardy's choice of a title for the novel reveals his "juxtapos[ing] the superior natural world against the civilized" (58).

2. We are reminded of Shug Avery's discussion of God-as-all, including nature, in Alice Walker's *The Color Purple*:

> But more than anything else, God love admiration.
> You saying God vain? I ast.
> Naw, she say, not vain, just wanting to share a good thing. I think it pisses God off if you walk by the color purple in a field somewhere and don't notice it. . . .
> You ever notice that trees do everything to get attention we do, except walk?
> (178–179)

3. I use the term "mythic" with some hesitation, since myth figures significantly in many of the later novels that have not achieved tremendous renown (*Two on a Tower* and *The Hand of Ethelberta* come to mind immediately). However, those works tend to retain a solid basis in the historical world—much like the opening chapters of *Far From the Madding Crowd*—that is lacking in such works as *The Return of the Native* and *Tess of the D'Urbervilles*, which may explain why the books have been virtually overlooked. Hardy is at his most impressive as a writer when the mythic comes into play. Without it, his prose can seem over-grandiose, inflated.

4. The list of such clerical men is long and ranges in rank from the lowliest parson to a bishop. Usually, at least one religious figure per novel comes off badly, but the most hateful include Rector Swancourt in *A Pair of Blue Eyes*, Mr. Woodwell, the Baptist minister in *A Laodicean*, the bishop in *Two on a Tower*, and Richard Phillotson in *Jude the Obscure*.

5. Actually, Hardy begins this pattern in his first novel, *Desperate Remedies*, in which

Cytherea comes to her wealth, not through her father, whose death leaves her impoverished, but through Miss Aldclyffe, who functions as a sort of Terrible Mother in the novel. In *A Pair of Blue Eyes,* Elfride's claim to position is inherited from her mother, while her father comes from a line of outcasts and strays. By the time Hardy writes *Tess of the D'Urbervilles*, he reverses this pattern, having become hostile to classism. Tess inherits her beauty and her bond with nature matrilineally. In *The Return of the Native*, while Eustacia has no wealth, she has descended from a matrilineal line, her father having taken her mother's name and home. In *The Mayor of Casterbridge*, Lucetta inherits through an aunt, and in *The Well-Beloved*, Avice inherits through her mother.

6. Seven of the fourteen novels feature heroines who are independent of any parents (Cytherea—*Desperate Remedies*; Bathsheba; Ethelberta—*The Hand of Ethelberta*; Eustacia—*The Return of the Native*; Paula—*A Laodicean*; Viviette—*Two on a Tower*; Sue—*Jude the Obscure*). Three other novels show women in adult, supportive relationships with their mothers (Anne—*The Trumpet Major*; Elizabeth Jane—*The Mayor of Casterbridge*; Avice—*The Well-Beloved*). The other four novels feature plots that revolve, to varying degrees, around problems created by the heroines' fathers (Fancy—*Under the Greenwood Tree*; Elfride—*A Pair of Blue Eyes*; Grace—*The Woodlanders*; Tess—*Tess of the D'Urbervilles*).

7. In itself, the association with red is not damning. For example, in *The Return of the Native*, the enigmatic Diggory Venn's redness is stressed throughout; while the color serves to set him apart from the folk and hints at his preternatural powers, it does not associate him with Satan.

8. Hardy deals most blatantly with this subject in *A Pair of Blue Eyes*, in which Henry Knight openly admits to wanting a woman who has never been kissed so that she cannot compare and evaluate his abilities as a lover.

9. If we consider the house as a metaphor of the self, Hardy's description of Boldwood's parlor, presumably the heart of the house and the man, becomes significant. There "everything that was not grave was extraneous" and "the atmosphere was that of a Puritan Sunday lasting all the week" (132).

10. Interestingly, Gabriel's initial proposal to Bathsheba takes much the same form, underscoring the notion of marriage as having less to do with shared affinities than with merging assets. However, through the course of the novel, Gabriel comes to acknowledge the need for love, if not for physical desire.

11. Susan Beegal accurately points out, "The marriage Boldwood offers [Bathsheba] is one of entombment, of suffocation" (110).

12. Boldwood is sentenced to die for his murder of Troy; however, the sentence is commuted for reasons of insanity. Nevertheless, narratively, Troy's murder removes both men from the novel at the same time and can be read as a symbolic mutual destruction.

13. Marjorie Garson speaks of Oak's "feminine" qualities, specifically referring to his work as midwife and nursemaid to the sheep, as providing him with "stability and maturity; indeed, it is his solidarity with the Great Mother which is the basis of his own inner unity" (29).

14. Of course the androgyny works both ways in Hardy; hence Bathsheba is equally capable in a "man's world," as her dealing in the Corn Exchange, her sheep shearing, and her midnight patrols of the farm amply demonstrate. Morgan writes, "Hardy's greater heroines are not, in his original conception of them, confined to a domestic domain beside the proverbial hearth but are persistently recalled to the world of men and work. There is no sphere, in Hardy, designated women's realm" (59).

15. Not all critics view the ending so positively. Rosemarie Morgan, for example,

focuses on what she sees as Gabriel's obsession with money and social advancement and sees the novel as revealing a "progression away from rustic innocence and sylvan idylls toward a distinctly bourgeois capitalistic existence" (41). Her position is one that I find hard to share, considering Hardy's language in describing the love between Bathsheba and Gabriel. Rather, I agree with Susan Beegal that this novel is Hardy's "fullest treatment of a rare, ideal love, written when Hardy . . . still believed in both the existence of such love and the possibility of fulfilling it." (110).

3

The Return of the Native: And Nature Said, "You Are Dust, and to Dust You Shall Return"

Of the major women characters in Hardy's Wessex novels, Eustacia Vye in *The Return of the Native* presents the greatest critical problem. Although Hardy's admiration for her is obvious to most critics, to some it remains inexplicable. They share Leonard Deen's claim that Hardy "makes her more impressive than she has a right to be, considering her age and sex and the apparently frivolous nature of her desires" (120). While the sexist nature of Deen's remark is immediately apparent, many critics—some feminist ones among them—see Eustacia as spoiled, childish, willful, self-pitying, and, in short, anything but admirable. However, an alternative reading of Eustacia's character presents itself if we look at the text's mythic implications and consider why the beautiful, pastoral setting of *Far From the Madding Crowd* has been transformed into a nearly barren, mean landscape.

Hardy is scarcely subtle in his associations of Eustacia with divinity, at the same time that he presents her as a frustrated woman living out an empty existence on Egdon Heath. But as I have argued, Hardy's ability to infuse ordinary reality with mythological overtones is his particular genius. One could argue that *The Return of the Native* is an alternative version of *Far From the Madding Crowd*. Ian Gregor points out how the original version of *The Return of the Native* closely resembled the earlier novel, with Thomasin playing Fanny's role, Venn replacing Oak, Wildeve figuring as Troy, and, of course, Eustacia functioning as the Bathsheba figure (*Great Web*, 79). In the final version of the text, Venn, like Oak before him, is associated with the out-of-doors and possesses abilities beyond those of the folk, seemingly by virtue of association with the natural. Both Troy and Wildeve are indecisive philanderers who prey upon women. However, Eustacia initially appears to be a far different sort of character than Bathsheba. Whereas Bathsheba effectively manages a farm, Eustacia wanders the heath aimlessly. While Bathsheba is, for the most part, cheerful, optimistic, and content with her life, Eustacia suffers from depression and is dissatisfied with and alienated from her surroundings. If, however, we consider the archetype of the Great Goddess, we can argue that the two women each embody a different aspect of that divinity. Whereas Bathsheba, for the most part, is identified with fertility and regeneration, Eustacia, as Jean Brooks points out, appears as a Persephone figure (184). As such, we must consider her as nature at rest, fallow, empty, and we must understand that fallowness and death are inevitable parts of the cycle of nature, although ones that modern readers, often themselves estranged from the natural, see as somehow problematic, as requiring mending.

Textual support for the Persephone reading is ample. If we recall the myth, Persephone is kidnapped by Pluto and forced to reign as his queen in the underworld, where she pines away, longing for light and beauty and a reunion with her mother in the world of the living. Eustacia also inhabits a realm of emptiness and loneliness. After the death of her parents, she is pulled from the glittering society of Budmouth to reside on the sparsely populated heath, where she has no friend and no peer. If one considers nineteenth-century notions of class hierarchy, one can see that she would be regarded as a "queen" compared to the folk of the heath and would not be expected to consort with them. Furthermore, like Persephone, she is associated with death, from her first appearance in the text, rising mysteriously out of the Rainbarrow, which is, after all, a burial mound. Clym's first and only textually recorded present to her is a funerary urn that, in Christian Cantle's terms, contains "real skellington bones" (213). Hardy refers to her as both "Queen of Night" (93) and "queen of the solitude" (42), and emphasizes the fact that she always dresses in black (contrasted with Bathsheba, her counterpart, in her green riding habit). Significantly, although she is sexually involved with two men during the course of the novel, and has been lovers with Wildeve for some time prior to the novel's diegetic time, she never bears a child. As the embodiment of death, loneliness, and fallowness, she herself is not fruitful, again paralleling her archetype, Persephone. In their discussions of the frequently quoted "Queen of Night" chapter, critics cite the lines in which Hardy refers to Eustacia as a "model goddess," but "not quite a model woman," often ignoring what follows:

> Had it been possible for the earth and mankind to be entirely in her grasp for a while . . . few in the world would have noticed the change of government. There would have been the same inequality of lot, the same heaping up of favours here, of contumely there, the same generosity before justice, the same captious alternation of caresses and blows that we endure now. (93)

In archetypically representing the Great Goddess, Eustacia is identified with a religious viewpoint that is accepting of the natural processes of life—birth and sexuality certainly, but also death, decay, and sterility, themselves as essential to the continuation of life as fruition and generation. In creating Eustacia and Egdon Heath, Hardy reveals that his view of nature is essentially nonsentimental. Although he is well aware of the beauty of nature, as he revealed in *Far From the Madding Crowd*, in the later novel it becomes clear that he understands equally well nature's destructive and terrifying aspect, as well as perceiving that the beauty and the destructiveness are inextricably linked. In creating a figure who essentially must represent a nature deity, Hardy needed to encompass nature in its totality. Eustacia and Bathsheba, read as each other's shadow side, function in the same way as do the two landscapes of these novels—Egdon Heath is the reversal of Weatherbury. *The Return of the Native*, then, as Brooks points out, explores the "elemental myth that presents man's painful predicament in relation to a demonic landscape of barren earth, isolating wind, stormy water, and creative/destructive fire" (198).

Eustacia and Bathsheba, then, both function as nature goddesses tied to a land from which each in her life in the body is undifferentiated. However, the two landscapes represented by these women are radically different. The timeless character of Weatherbury is altered here. Although the heath may initially appear to be a more primitive place, simply because of how rugged life there is, history informs Egdon, removing it from the mythic, and placing it solidly within nineteenth-century England. In the earlier novel, although Bathsheba runs off to Bath to meet Troy, the Bath that we narratively experience, through the words of Cainy Bell, is a fairy tale place whose residents "never need to light their fires except as a luxury, for the water springs up out of the earth ready boiled for use" (251). Aside from that city, Weatherbury appears to exist off a geographical grid, removed from commerce, politics, fashion, art. By contrast, the residents of remote Egdon are familiar with Budmouth (even the otherworldly Diggory Venn knows a woman there who requires a companion), contemplate emigrating to America, and plan vacations in Paris. The novel is much more grounded in a specific geographical setting in a specific century, the result of which is a corruption of the mythic which manifests itself in the character of Eustacia, the embodiment of the heath. We are told she has lived for a while in Budmouth, in the world of art and fashion, a world of which she has grown enamored, at the same time as she has grown increasingly dissatisfied with her role in the natural realm. She has become a reluctant nature goddess, desirous of embracing a world that by its very essence is hostile to all she represents. For example, she denies knowing of any Druidic stones existing on the heath, preferring to speak of the boulevards of Paris. When Clym becomes a furze-cutter, she resents his dressing in the clothes of a worker and doing fieldwork. While she is not materialistic per se, she begins to long for the material goods that money could buy her. Even more important, she loses faith in her own nature and invests Clym with the power that he will ultimately turn against her. She wants someone to "deliver her soul" (155)—in other words, to transform her from what she essentially is—and she loses so much of her own perspective that she views Clym as "scarcely incarnate" (350). Eventually she accepts Clym's values to the point of seeing herself as a "sinner," an indication of how far she has lapsed from the Pagan values she initially embodied. In Eustacia's transformation we see the transition from myth to history, to a time when a land and a people consciously separate themselves from nature, beginning to perceive it as "other." Whereas in later novels, Hardy will suggest the historical encroaches upon the mythical and coerces change, here he implies that to some degree the adherents of the old ways are dissatisfied with accepting nature on its own terms, choosing rather to accept values at odds with what they represent. Since the goddess figure herself no longer accepts the world view she represents, the switch in values appears inevitable: myth will of necessity collapse into history.

Although Eustacia can be seen as representing a different aspect of the Great Goddess than Tess and Bathsheba represent, she shares traits with them. Like them, she is a dark-haired beauty who exercises power over men. Like them, she does not fit the Victorian ideal, being "full-limbed and somewhat heavy" (93) rather than slim-waisted and delicate. Similarly, her strength and courage are epic in a time when societal stereotypes insisted women be frail and weak. We are told she has never once in her life been ill, an odd circumstance in a time when femininity was virtually equated with illness, but in a mythic context, a hint at her divine nature, and again, a quality she shares with Tess and Bathsheba. Furthermore, like them she roams around freely and comfortably at night, regardless of the weather; Hardy tells us, "Her extraordinary fixity, her conspicuous loneliness, her heedlessness of night, betokened among other things an utter absence of fear" (80). Repeatedly in Hardy's works, the ability to feel comfortable at night indicates a character at home in nature, while the characters who are afraid of the dark or who lose their way at night are those alienated from the natural. In virtually every novel, one or the other situation occurs.

Eustacia's strength manifests itself psychologically as well; she can admit to her former lover that her marriage is a disappointment, and that her plans to escape the heath through it have failed. She remains calm and controlled when Clym goes berserk, tearing into her letter box like a madman; even when he becomes violent with her, she remains silent, refusing to dignify his rage by responding to it. Finally, when she realizes that the world contains no place for her, she stoically chooses death rather than compromise her character.

Eustacia also resembles Bathsheba in terms of family structure; both are independent of parents, although Eustacia does live with her grandfather until her marriage to Clym. But in a pattern typical of Hardy's major women characters, Eustacia is not in any way controlled by Captain Vye. Hardy tells us, "The old captain's prevailing indifference to his granddaughter's movements left her free as a bird to follow her own courses" (172). As Andrew Enstice claims, Captain Vye functions in the novel as "little more than a device" (*Landscapes*, 87) to placate Victorian audiences, who could not have accepted such an outrageous heroine without some parental figure, regardless how supernumerary.[1]

In creating Eustacia, Hardy allowed himself to create a more blatantly sexual figure than either Bathsheba or Tess. Her name, which Hardy specifically changed when he redrafted the novel and which means "rich in corn" or "fruitful," ties her sexuality to nature, to the life-force (Caless, 15). His physical description of her stresses her sensual/sexual nature: "[Her] mouth seemed formed less to speak than to quiver, less to quiver than to kiss. . . . Her presence brought memories of such things as Bourbon roses, rubies, and tropical midnights; her moods recalled lotus eaters and the march in 'Athalie', her motions, the ebb and flow of the sea; her voice, the viola" (94). Eustacia herself is very aware of her sexuality and acts upon it. She feels no guilt for her love affair with Wildeve; in spite of censorship, Hardy has her claim that she has given herself to him and speaks of belonging to him "body and soul" (88). Nor does she apologize for what her contemporaries would have considered her libertine attitudes. Hardy reveals her desire for sexual fulfillment by claiming she longed for "passionate love more than for any particular lover" (96). She is realistically aware that love of the loftier sort "would sink simultaneously with the sand in the glass" (96), and, like Tess, would prefer her courtship with Clym to continue as an event in itself, without necessarily leading to marriage. Furthermore, the text points out that she is unimpressed with "fidelity in love for fidelity's sake" (96), an attitude antithetical to Victorian notions of propriety and respectability. She is oblivious to what people may think or say about her, as unconcerned about gossip "as a goddess at a lack of linen" (120). The simile is apt; if gossip does not disturb this goddess figure, neither does sexuality or physicality. We are told she holds "in indifference all things honoured of the gods and of men" (357), indicating her contempt for all patriarchal values.

While most critics readily recognize Eustacia's sexual nature, Leonard Deen feels that Eustacia's disguising herself as a man for the mumming indicates that she "wants to alter her essential human condition, to change her sex" (124). His contention is absurd. Eustacia's frustration, at times, with her position as a woman stems from the societal limitations placed on that role. Her "essential human condition" is not the problem, since the societal definition of what is female—helplessness, weakness, hysteria—is in no way essentially female. The mumming scene suggests, rather, that for Eustacia to approach Clym, the embodiment of the patriarchal male, she must disguise her true femaleness, or risk intimidating or repelling this virtually passionless man who claims "my body does not require much of me" (199), and whose response to the passion roused by courtship is distress, which he feels the need to "cure" (220) through marriage.

If Eustacia's sexuality to some degree distinguishes her from Tess and Bathsheba, her association with the natural world identifies her with them. Hardy's introduction of Eustacia begins with the landscape from which she is initially indistinguishable; the text reveals how she completes the landscape with her physical being:

> Without it, there was the dome without the lantern; with it the architectural demands of the mass were satisfied. The scene was strangely homogeneous, in that the vale, the upland, the barrow, and the figure above it *amounted only to unity*.
>
> The form was so much like *an organic part* of the entire motionless structure that to see it move would have impressed the mind as a strange phenomenon. (41; emphasis mine)

To add to the effect, Hardy writes that Eustacia's sigh mingled so completely with the natural sounds of the heath "that its beginnings and ending were hardly to be distinguished" (82). As Gregor claims, she is "an integral part of the universe she inhabits—at one with the body of the Heath" (*Great Web*, 107); Brooks argues similarly, claiming of the heath that Eustacia "share[s] its primal vitality and indifference to others" (188). Both heath and woman are stern and unforgiving, desolate and empty, interchangeable with each other. It is appropriate, then, that, until her infelicitous marriage to Clym, Eustacia almost never appears indoors. We learn that Wildeve has never seen the inside of her house, indicating that their love affair has appropriately occurred outside, in nature. After her marriage, however, Eustacia more and more frequently appears indoors in what for her, as a nature divinity, is alien space. Whereas Bathsheba and Tess retreat to nature during their times of crisis, Eustacia, in what could be read as an indication of her co-optation by culture, remains indoors, out of her element, emerging only to die there, and then choosing, significantly, not to die by some manmade device, but rather by merging with nature in the form of water.[2]

Hardy emphasizes Eustacia's bond with nature through his use of what is critically known as the pathetic fallacy; he makes nature respond sympathetically to Eustacia's plight throughout the novel. Diggory Venn's attempt to overhear a conversation between Eustacia and Wildeve is thwarted when the wind comes up to muffle their voices. When Eustacia first tries to see Clym, who will ultimately be the cause of her destruction, nature, in the form of fog and rain, intervenes to prevent their meeting. Heavy rain appears again on the day that Clym sets out to select the pathetic little house in which he intends Eustacia to live after their marriage. During the first few days after their marriage, while Eustacia is happy, the otherwise dreary heath is described as "gorgeous." But once the marriage proves unfulfilling, the horrible heat and dryness set in, echoing Eustacia's inability to be renewed and indicating her lack of sexual fulfillment, a frustration which leads her across the heath to attend the dance at which she reencounters Wildeve. The night she dies, the life-giving rain falls once again, which both equates her death with the renewal of the earth and but also suggests that nature weeps for the loss of her own.

Eustacia's identification with nature adds to the sense of her Paganism, which Hardy emphasizes throughout the novel. Giordano points out that Hardy associates her "with pre-Christian paganism by placing [her] on an ancient Celtic barrow, or burial ground" ("Eustacia," 506). Similarly, Paterson describes her as identified "with a world not yet touched by the spectral hand of Christianity" ("Introduction," 116). Eustacia's association with ancient Pagan sites and objects, such as the Rainbarrow and Druidic stones, lend support to his idea, as do the Pagan rituals that appear repeatedly throughout this novel, which opens with Eustacia and the folk engaged in observing such a Pagan ritual—the lighting of the balefire.[3] Significantly, Eustacia's fire is the biggest one of all, and is removed from the others, indicating both her kinship with their shared Pagan mentality as well as her essential difference from the other folk. The Mummer's Play in which Eustacia takes part is a debased form of yet another early Pagan ritual (Firor, 203); not accidentally, Eustacia plays the role of the Pagan, who, in the Egdon version of the play, is defeated by the Christian, an act that encapsulates the entire action of the novel. The gipseying on the heath is not simply a contemporary dance to relieve the monotony of fieldwork but what Firor calls "the nearest approach to the primitive orgiastic May rites" (138)—in other words, the remnants of the celebration of the Beltane Sabbat, in which the sexuality of the land and its inhabitants is affirmed. Eustacia participates in the gipseying at a time when her relationship with the Christian Clym has become stagnant and nonfulfilling, and emerges from it with "a new vitality" (283), indicating that the regenerative powers of the ritual have not been vitiated. Overall, Pagan ritual so pervades the novel that Jarrett comments, "The year and the day which is the span of all but the short final book of *The Return of the Native* is measured out and punctuated by ceremonies that are pagan survivals and celebrations of life (167). The "year and the day" is also significant in being the standard reckoning of time within Paganism, a year being equivalent to thirteen lunar months, or 364 days, the extra day necessary to keep solar and lunar systems synchronized.

Further emphasizing Eustacia's link with Paganism is Hardy's depiction of her as a witch. In discussing the novel's Pagan sense, Paterson claims that Eustacia comes to represent a pre-Christian consciousness existing in a world incapable of comprehending alternative forms of belief; her encoding as a witch simultaneously encodes her as an opponent of Christianity ("Introduction," 116). Paterson's sense of the witch is accurate as far as it goes, but it overlooks the even more significant point that a witch is a priestess of the Great Goddess, a celebrant of a religion that held sway before the advent of Christianity. Persephone, Eustacia's mythic archetype, is sometimes called "the Queen of Witches." The Egdon folk take Eustacia's witchcraft seriously, and in spite of her distress at Susan Nunsuch's attack in church, the young woman consciously adopts the role, wearing black clothing, carrying an hourglass, and dispensing crooked sixpence. Her frequent nocturnal ramblings further enhance the image, the night and the moon both associated with witchcraft. Hardy's rhetoric in describing her relationships with Wildeve and Clym is deliberately chosen to perpetuate the image of the witch. After she initially summons Wildeve with her heath fire, his words suggest he has come against his will, "in obedience to [her] call" (91); he complains, "You give me no peace. Why do you not leave me alone?" (88), suggesting her powers are supernatural. After the gipseying on the heath, we are told Wildeve responds to the "spell that she had thrown over him in the moonlight dance" (300), and a furious Clym talks of having been "bewitched" by her eyes. Language such as this reinforces the sense of Eustacia's being a witch and further serves to sever her from both Christianity and Victorian society. That separation is also emphasized by Hardy's associating Eustacia with a matriarchal past. Her father adopted her mother's name when they married, which creates a sense of matrilineal descent. In addition, when Hardy introduces the figure of Eustacia, he writes that she seemed "more interesting, more important" (42) than the "boys and men of the neighboring hamlets" (43). Stressing the maleness of the others calls attention to and prioritizes Eustacia's gender and aligns the heath with feminine space.

While Eustacia is narratively described in language and associated with images antagonistic to Christianity, Hardy goes further in creating her character openly opposed to the religion. Whereas Bathsheba is indifferent to Sundays, Eustacia hates them, desecrating them by humming Saturday night ballads (presumably bawdy ones) on them. The text states that "Had she been a mother she would have christened her boys such names as Saul or Sisera in preference to Jacob or David, neither of whom she admired" (97). After her one attempt at churchgoing results in Susan Nunsuch's sticking her with a needle, she simply refuses to go again, without the least sense of guilt or loss. Finally, her readiness to consider suicide reveals a non-Christian set of values, one in which suicide is no sin. Her actions and attitudes support Paterson's claim that the novel celebrates "a wisdom older than Christianity and fundamentally at war with it" (*Making*, 141).

As in the cases of *Far From the Madding Crowd* and *Tess of the D'Urbervilles*, that war rages most strongly because of love. Like Tess, Eustacia loves men who ultimately destroy her. At first glance, however, Wildeve seems a fitting counterpart to Eustacia; he participates in the Pagan rituals with her, he is certainly not Christian in any orthodox sense, and his last name suggests ancient, Pagan ways. However, such superficial characteristics aside, Wildeve is no Gabriel Oak. For all his roaming about at night and his lovemaking in the wild, Wildeve is estranged from nature. Like all the characters Hardy distances from nature, Wildeve is afraid to walk the heath at night, frequently stumbling when he does. He is uncomfortable in the presence of the heath-croppers, the wild ponies indigenous to the heath, who are noticed but virtually ignored by most of the Egdon folk. To stress his alienation from the natural even more, Hardy makes him by profession an engineer; he has studied how to control nature, to use it for humankind's ends. Credited with tilling "Wildeve's Patch," one of the few areas of the heath that have been domesticated, he appears in this instance blatantly in opposition to the natural, since the Egdon folk live off the heath without cultivating it but rather by cutting the furze that grows on it. Furthermore, he wants Eustacia to come away with him to America, to a new world, to abandon their roots, the connectedness with the land which has produced them.

Paralleling Wildeve's separation from the natural is his identification with the cultural and the Christian patriarchy. His counterpart in *Far From the Madding Crowd* is not Gabriel Oak but Sergeant Troy, with whom he shares a basic contempt for women. Wildeve, we are told, regards himself as a "lady killer" (70); his trifling with both Eustacia and Tamsin is ample evidence of his living up to his self-concept. After the birth of his and Tamsin's child, a servant mentions that he "is twanky because 'tisn't a boy" (334), indicating his acceptance of the patriarchal notion that boy-children are more significant than girl-children and, by extension, that men are superior to women. Furthermore, after Eustacia's unhappy marriage, he tells her that she "rightly belonged" to him, basing his presumption on the patriarchal attitude that sexual involvement with a woman, specifically with a virgin, gives a man power over her. After his death, the contrast between his corpse and that of Eustacia stresses the dichotomy between them. She is smiling and dignified, at home in nature at last; he looks weary, his fingers "worn and scarified in his dying endeavors to obtain a hold on the weir-wall" (393). Even to his death, he reaches out toward the artificial, the *man*made.

Although Eustacia ultimately rejects Wildeve as a lover, her choice in his stead is even more problematic and even more antithetical to the natural world to which Eustacia is bound. Clym Yeobright, like Angel Clare, represents modern consciousness, Hardy's grim projection of where the human species is headed. The author's dismay at what Clym represents becomes apparent in the passage describing his world-weariness:

> In Clym Yeobright's face could be dimly seen the typical countenance of the future. . . . The view of life as a thing to be put up with, replacing that zest for existence which was so intense in early civilizations, must ultimately enter so thoroughly into the constitution of the advanced races that its facial expression will become accepted as a new artistic departure. . . . Physically beautiful men—the glory of the race when it was young—are almost an anachronism now; and we may wonder whether, at some time or other, physically beautiful women may not be an anachronism likewise. (190)

Paterson indicates that in the novel as it now stands, Clym is more genteel than he was in the Ur-version of the text (*Making*, 34). Hardy has acted to clearly distance Clym from the Egdon folk and their values. In spite of Clym's desire to return to Egdon, he repeatedly reveals his alienation from the way of life of the folk there. He has rejected his father's profession, farming, which would bond him with nature, to become a diamond merchant, a profession that can exist only in a status-conscious society; Hardy could scarcely have found two other professions more antithetical to each other, or more clearly representative of the duality he is interested in exploring. When Clym returns, his intent is not to return to the old way of life but rather to change it—his desire is to start a school, to civilize a people whose belief in witches, folk remedies, and Pagan ritual appalls him. When, for example, Clym hears of Susan Nunsuch's Sunday morning witch hunt, he does not consider the sort of power Eustacia must wield to evoke such a response, but rather reaffirms his sense of mission to educate the masses, asking of his mother, "Do you think I have turned teacher too soon?" (201).

When it comes to women, Clym readily accepts the teachings of the patriarchal culture he has embraced. He blames Tamsin for having been jilted on her wedding day, claiming she has "mortified" (181) him and his mother, not considering either Tamsin's grief or her lack of agency in the incident. In his rage with Eustacia, he claims he could be more understanding of her if only she were "contrite" (347), if she were to grovel before him, indulging his sense of superiority. When Eustacia is reported missing, Clym's only worry is that she may have committed adultery, the "worst a wife can do," (378) in his words, allowing patriarchal pride to obscure concern for human life. His sense of superiority to the Egdon folk, even after he has worked as a furze-cutter among them, is revealed when, in response to Tamsin's raising the possibility of marrying Diggory Venn, he responds, "You might marry a professional man, or somebody of that sort" (411). As Jean Brooks maintains, the physical blindness he suffers is symbolic of his greater blindness: "He is blind to the reality which is in the heath, himself, his mother, Eustacia, and the 'Egdon eremites' he had come to teach how to bear it" (186).

For all of Clym's talk of loving the heath, Hardy nevertheless presents him as removed from nature. The name of his home, Bloom's-End, hints at the mythic action of the novel, the destruction of the natural by the cultural. That home is, significantly, situated on the very edge of the heath, not actually a part of it, but rather in a place of transition, between the mythic world of the heath and the historical world that encompasses it, a metaphor for Clym himself. In describing the white picket fence of Bloom's-End, Hardy compares it to "white lace on velvet," an image strikingly incongruous in the world Hardy creates here, but one that works to identify the house and its inhabitants with a world removed from the one in which the Egdon folk reside. When Clym strolls on the heath, the text says that he does not hear its "stir of resurrection" (214); in addition, the heath oppresses him because "it gave him a sense of bare equality with, and no superiority to, a single living thing under the sun" (230). Clym's need to believe in his own social and intellectual superiority, to exist in a hierarchy, again aligns him with the cultural consciousness Hardy is writing against in the Wessex novels.

However, while Clym lives on the heath, he undergoes a subtle transformation, at least temporarily. After a short time at home, a time spent primarily in the company of Eustacia, the nature divinity, he is rejuvenated, becoming physically more healthy, less pale, less stressful. As Jean Brooks points out, during this time Clym reenters Eden through his abandonment of his class consciousness, which allows him to experience direct contact with the earth, a process that revives and strengthens him (187). However, after the death of his mother, Clym once again retreats from nature and loses the paradise it could have offered him, choosing the promise of the Christian paradise after death instead.

A part of Clym's inability to deal with nature on its own terms is his own attenuated sexuality. His obliviousness to sensuality, which he reveals when he says, "my body does not require much of me. I cannot enjoy delicacies; good things are wasted upon me" (199), precludes his ever being a deeply sexual person. Even when he is obviously attracted to Eustacia, he at the same time very methodically considers how she can help him in his mission. If anything, the passionate love he comes to feel for her distresses rather than pleases him; he says, "There is only one cure for this anxiety, dearest—you must be my wife" (220). He completely ignores her astute, prophetic answer: "Cynics say that cures the anxiety by curing the love" (220). Very shortly after his marriage to the incredibly sexual Eustacia, a time filled with lovemaking and great intimacy, he chooses to begin staying up late at night with his books. One can see in his actions the attempt to separate himself from the sexual, to retreat from the bond he is establishing with his wife. His obsession with scholarship very quickly leads him to a state of virtual blindness, which, as Mary Ellen Jordan points out, "suggests self-punishment for sexual indulgence" (112). We must also not forget that blindness in literature often has been read to represent symbolic castration, which in this case can be seen as Clym's desire, as a means of escape from a situation which is uncomfortable and indeed antithetical to his nature. Although Clym is never portrayed as vital, as potent, for a brief time during the courtship he experiences passion; however, after his marriage, his subsequent blindness, and Eustacia's death, Hardy writes, "Every pulse of loverlike feeling which had not been stilled during Eustacia's lifetime had gone into the grave with her" (402). Completely devoid of sexual impulse, he exists in a state at odds with the natural, unwilling even to participate in his only surviving relative's wedding, choosing rather to sequester himself in his room to write a sermon.

That choice comes as no surprise, given, as Paterson accurately claims, that Clym's "allegedly advanced views only thinly disguise the Christian champion" ("Introduction," 116). Throughout the novel, Clym is associated with Christian figures: John the Baptist, who is sent to prepare the way for a new order, St. Paul, the most woman-hating of the New Testament figures, and most significantly, Christ himself. Clym appropriately first appears on the scene at Christmas and ends the novel an itinerant preacher, shortly before his thirty-third birthday. As a child, Clym was widely recognized for his knowledge of the Bible; the association with the boy Jesus teaching in the temple is apparent here. His mother's words on his return from Paris—"what there is for him to do here the Lord in heaven knows" (194)—suggest both his relationship with God the Father and his mission on the heath. The nature of that mission becomes clear after his marriage to and destruction of Eustacia. As they are pulled from the weir, Clym returns to life, having triumphed over the natural—embodied in Eustacia, who stays dead—and therefore, like Christ, his archetype, having upset for all time natural law. As he himself says, "I cannot die" (394). Yet death is an integral part of the natural cycle, necessary if there is to be life. So Clym, as the novel ends, is unable to participate in either life or death. He lives a barren, ascetic life, living in two mean rooms, served only by *Christian* Cantle, unable "to remain in the presence of enjoyment" (403), the living embodiment of the conquering "pale Galilean," to quote Swinburne. But as Swinburne's poem indicates, the Galilean's conquering has left the world "gray"; the victory of Christian consciousness over Pagan, the novel suggests, is ultimately a loss for all humanity. However, within the fictional world of Egdon, Hardy allows for a reprieve. Whereas *Far From the Madding Crowd* ends with the Pagan world intact, and *Tess of the D'Urbervilles* with it completely destroyed, *The Return of the Native* ends with the seeds of the destruction planted, but with nature still allowed a final moment of glory. Clym/Christ will eventually prevail; history has been written. Rosemarie Morgan claims that at the novel's end, the Egdon folk's "capacity for renewal cannot be guaranteed" (82). Citing Johnny Nonsuch and Christian Cantle as examples, she argues that Egdon's younger generation "exemplify an etiolated life wholly alien to the vigorous, turbulent, enduring heights overreaching them" (82). However, Hardy chooses to move the emphasis away from such characters and away from Clym's ascetic emulation of Christ to focus on Tamsin's Pagan, life-affirming celebration of the sexual. The maypole ritual, a Pagan celebration of the act of sex in which the phallic pole is bedecked with flowers, significantly brings Tamsin and Diggory together. Their subsequent marriage is the focal point of the Egdon folk, who have forgotten Clym's existence in their celebration of one of the oldest of human rituals.

Given Eustacia's association with Persephone and Clym's identification with Christ, it becomes immediately apparent that a relationship between the two is untenable. The text foreshadows the outcome of the collision of the two when, at their first introduction to each other, Clym wounds Eustacia with a rope, a symbol of bondage. Later, he destroys her completely through marriage, which, while it can represent a celebration of the sexual, can also in its patriarchal sense represent another form of bondage. Hardy's development of the book's several marriages hints at both interpretations. In the case of Wildeve's marriage to Tamsin and Clym's marriage to

Eustacia, both events are associated with the church; particularly in the former case, the predominant mood is one of gloom and, significantly, of alienation from community. Four people gather in a church, where a priest, through his words, forges a union that creates "man and wife", that is, human and possession. The ritual, if it can even be called that, in no way is a societal recognition of a rite of passage from childhood to adulthood, from self to integration with another. In the case of Tamsin's second marriage, the primary association with the marriage is the maypole, the Pagan element, and the marriage itself "occurs" not in the church but in the rowdy celebration that follows the ecclesiastical element, when, through their horseplay, the Egdon folk affirm the sexuality of the new partners and welcome them as a couple to the community. In the latter case, marriage functions mythically, appropriate to Hardy's ending in which the complete overthrow of the mythic has not yet occurred, and appropriate for Tamsin and Diggory, themselves identified with the Egdon folk and their Pagan ways. In the earlier cases, marriage functions as the historical institution, a tool of patriarchal culture, which is appropriate given that the grooms involved, Clym and Wildeve, are themselves the embodiments of that half of Hardy's cosmos.

However, Eustacia and Clym's marriage is problematic in other ways as well. In addition to their being archetypal antagonists representing mutually exclusive world views, Eustacia and Clym marry for reasons that guarantee failure. Clym assumes marriage will relieve him of the distress of passion and will provide him a helpmate in his mission to educate the Egdon folk. Eustacia marries because her boredom is great and her choices are limited. Realistic about their love's inability to last, she marries Clym because, in the isolated world of the heath, she has no other suitors. Hardy writes, "She had loved him partly because he was exception in this scene, partly because she was determined to love him, chiefly because she was in desperate need of loving somebody after wearying of Wildeve" (166). Furthermore, Eustacia becomes somewhat misled by Clym because she cannot read him accurately. Aligned with nature—and by extension, with intuition—as she is, she prioritizes gesture over language, while Clym, the bearer of culture, does the reverse. The implications of gender become significant here. Hélène Cixous addresses the communication of women when she writes: "[I]t's with her body that she vitally supports the 'logic' of her speech. Her flesh speaks true. She lays herself bare. In fact, she physically materializes what she's thinking; she signifies it with her body" ("Laugh," 881). If she speaks in language, "her word almost always falls on the deaf, masculine ear, which can only hear language that speaks in the masculine" (Cixous and Clément, 92). Hence Eustacia trusts Clym's gestures, assuming that the same economy of signification applies to him as to her, but those gestures are false, while he relies on her words, which are not always true. As she tells him, "You deceived me—not by words, but by appearances, which are less seen through than words" (348). Clym's gestures to Eustacia during their courtship suggest he is a passionate man; however, as the representative of the modern spirit, Hardy has constructed him with an attenuated sexual sense. The marriage these two have contracted will never be capable of sexually fulfilling Eustacia, who represents the antithesis of the modern spirit and as such embodies sexuality, specifically women's sexuality, unrestrained by patriarchal culture's attempts to co-opt it. Clym and Eustacia then function as polar opposites, the collision of the Pagan and the Christian.

Clym is not, however, the only character in the novel aligned with a Christian, patriarchal world view. His mother is also removed from the Pagan, from a world of feminine empowerment, and accepts Victorian values regarding gender and social class. Hardy's pattern of aligning unlikable, destructive characters with Christianity in some way comes into play again in the development of Mrs. Yeobright's character—he emphasizes that she is a curate's daughter. Although narratively, her father's career does not figure into the work, Hardy's calling attention to it allows him again to link Christianity with classism, as he also does in characters such as Rector Swancourt in *A Pair of Blue Eyes* and the Clare family in *Tess of the D'Urbervilles*. Because Mrs. Yeobright presumes that her father's position is somehow socially significant, she had "once dreamed of doing better things" (60) than marrying a farmer, and she has retained her classist notions, considering herself socially superior to the Egdon folk. One of her objections to Clym's courtship of Eustacia is the young woman's family, which she does not consider socially adequate, and she initially discourages Diggory Venn's suit of Tamsin for the same reasons. Clym's resigning his position as a diamond merchant dismays her, even though his following that career would keep him geographically far removed from her. Her constant pushing Clym toward material "success" reveals, as Anne Mickelson points out, her "acceptance of the protestant ethic which gives holy sanction to progress, self-improvement, and accumulation of wealth" (52), values Hardy does not endorse. Although she herself is a woman, she accepts cultural (i.e., patriarchal) definitions of gender, and allows herself and other women to be limited and defined by men, as she reveals when Tamsin and Wildeve's marriage cannot take place because of a legalistic technicality; Mrs. Yeobright considers the matter "disgraceful" and Tamsin "ruined." Similarly, she considers Eustacia's freedom in roaming about unchaperoned scandalous. She accepts the patriarchal good girl/bad girl duality and, in the typical "blame the victim" mentality that such a duality fosters, faults Eustacia for being attacked by Susan Nunsuch, claiming, "Good girls don't get treated as witches even on Egdon" (202).

Given her values, her separation from nature comes as no surprise. Like all the characters Hardy dislikes, she is afraid to walk on the heath unaccompanied by Tamsin or one of the rustics, and she disapproves of Tamsin's solo journeys across it by night, even though the world Hardy has created is one free of burglars, rapists, and murderers. But even more important is Mrs. Yeobright's relationship with her own sexuality and with sexuality in general. Although she was widowed at a young age, she never remarried, but rather chose celibacy without expressing any regret at her decision. Like her son, the demands of the flesh appear to be very weak in her. As a result, she cannot comprehend a healthy sexuality in others. Out of touch with nature as she is, she, as Brooks claims, "ignore[s] the primitive power of the cosmos in her 'civilized' desires" (184). She calls Clym "unnatural" for falling in love with Eustacia, seemingly unaware that what Clym is experiencing is the epitome of the natural and that her own state is the unnatural one. Hardy makes a point of excluding her from both Tamsin's and Clym's weddings; like Clym later, she is out of place at a celebration of sexuality and fruitfulness. Her death further emphasizes her distance from both the natural and the Pagan and is appropriately ironic—she is killed by the bite of an adder on the heath. The symbolic power of the snake, which represents wisdom, sexuality, and significantly the fusion of the two, comes into play; Mrs. Yeobright, who all her life resented what was natural and sexual, is ultimately destroyed by that life-force.[4]

In this novel, unlike in *Far From the Madding Crowd*, the Pagan/Christian conflict is central to the work.[5] In the opening chapter, "A Face on which Time makes but Little Impression," Hardy writes that the "untameable, Ishmaelitish thing that Egdon now was it had always been. Civilization was its enemy" (35). However, in this novel, Christianity is very implicitly tied to civilization, from the opening chapter on. Hardy speaks of a "division in time" (33) separating the heath from the world around it, the world that figures here as the historical world. The glory of the heath begins at dusk and develops into the night, a time usually associated with sin and death in Christian terms, but a time of celebration and ritual in Paganism. Hardy goes on to describe the heath as "a place perfectly accordant with man's nature—neither ghastly, hateful, nor ugly—neither commonplace, unmeaning, nor tame" (35). Hardy's underlying assumption about human nature is not a Christian one; within Christianity, the human is seen as tainted by original sin and is therefore ugly and hateful apart from the grace of God. In the Pagan world view, the human and the natural are essentially one and the same, just as, in Hardy's description, the heath and human nature mirror each other. Within the novel, however, the days of such a world view are numbered. Hardy presages the apocalypse, claiming that the heath is awaiting "one last crisis—the final overthrow" (34); that crisis comes with Clym's triumph over death, the point at which nature is overthrown. For some critics, however, the novel's end is affirmative; Brooks writes:

> [t]he transformation of Eustacia into Clym (on the tumulus) has replaced the dark
> winter with summer afternoon, isolation with relationship to man and the lower species,
> and the self-absorbed unconscious drives of nature with hope of redemption through
> man's consciousness of the roots from which he sprang. (194)

With the change in consciousness that Brooks cites, humankind comes to perceive nature as "other." A consciousness of self necessarily demands a comprehension of that which is not self, which indicates the loss of the primal unity that typifies a prelapsarian consciousness. Once self is perceived, all that falls outside the parameters of what constitute self to some degree functions in opposition to the self. Division occurs. The human sets itself against nature; the former perception of the human as inseparable from nature is lost. With that loss comes also a loss of the sense of the world as sacred; if the human exists in antagonism with the forces of nature, clearly it will not perceive those forces as holy. The fall into such a consciousness is what Hardy mourns, and what Clym triggers within the novel.

For the folk of the novel, who live out their lives bound to nature and who have retained their Pagan roots, the old world remains prominent.[6] In speaking of living on the heath, Enstice writes: "[T]he process is one of struggle and hardship, success and failure being as the blossoming and decrease of the annual ferns. Men live in a natural balance as old as the heath itself" (*Landscapes*, 81). That natural balance is evident in the lives of the folk; their lives are obviously hard, although Hardy narratively deemphasizes their struggle, but the folk live fully, experiencing both joy and sorrow. Hardy reveals them to be possessed of a knowledge lost to the world that exists in antithesis to the heath, an ability to know the earth as their home, to understand that they and it are not self and other, but essentially one. That unity leads to an acceptance of life and death, a satisfaction that Clym, with his world-weariness and his drive for progress, can never know. Their understanding reveals itself in their language. Shortly before a person dies, the folk describe that person as "looking for the earth" (76), indicating a sense that earth, not heaven, is their final home and revealing an absence of fear at the prospect of death. The prevalence of nature in the novel, according to Enstice, is further "strengthened by the lack of prominence given to buildings" (*Landscapes*, 76) in the text. It is rare in the novel for the folk to appear in their homes. These people virtually live on the land; as one says "we be out of doors in all winds and weathers" (194). Enstice goes on to claim:

> [I]t is here, in *The Return of the Native*, that Hardy gives the clearest exposition of the thread running through all his Wessex novels, of Man as part of a landscape. There is no justification of the situation, or philosophical abstraction of its relevance to Man; merely a statement of fact, that the earth has borne Man, and still bears him, in a harmony of past and present that needs no explanation. (*Landscapes,* 82)

Grandfer Cantle is Hardy's best example of the result of a life lived in such a harmony with the natural. An old, old man, he retains "a light boyish step" (399), revealing him to be strong and sound, a far cry from his diminished son, *Christian*. He mentions that he is never lonely on the heath, nor could he be, given his complete integration with it. He cannot understand how Mrs. Yeobright can die from the bite of an adder, since, as he claims, "[I]f I had been stung by ten adders I should hardly have lost a day's work for't" (316). Although he will eventually "look for the earth" himself, while he lives, he does so fully, dancing wildly through the dying heath fire in an act that typifies the way he has lived his entire life.

Hardy's inherent approval of the Egdon folk and their values pervades the book; those values, however, are at odds with those of Victorian society. But as Bryant Wyatt points out, "In this scheme of justice it is irrelevant whether characters are good or bad in conventional terms," adding that the folk "suffer no retribution for acts we would call immoral, simply *because*, it would appear, they are in harmony with the ageless natural order" (56–57). The immorality Wyatt alludes to is difficult to see; the folk are very moral, although they are significantly not Christian. Hardy presents several conversations in which the folk discuss what Paterson calls "their instinctive distrust of the church" ("Introduction," 117). Even on Christmas, the folk do not attend services. Hardy emphasizes the fact that the Egdon folk who do observe the holiday most typically do so by drinking mead with each other at home. The rituals the folk celebrate in community are those that affirm the rites of passage of their own lives and of the seasons of the earth. And they do that by dancing. As one explains: "You be bound to dance at Christmas because 'tis the time o' year; you must dance at weddings because 'tis the time o' life. At christenings folk will even smuggle in a reel or two if 'tis no further on than the first or second chiel" (50). As they dance through the dying embers of the heath fires or around the flower-bedecked maypole, they, in Paterson's words, "celebrate a vitality older and stronger than Christianity" ("Introduction," 117). Hardy writes that at the times of their celebrations, "Paganism was revived in their hearts and the pride of life was all in all" (281).

But even among the folk, some have abandoned the Pagan ways. The most obvious such case is the aptly named Christian Cantle, the whimpering little coward who is terrified of the heath, and of the night, and of ghosts and devils. Significantly, Christian can find no woman to marry him; the folk refer to him as a "wether," a castrated ram, recognizing his impotency. They understand his state to be psychologically unhealthy, claiming, "You'll have to lie alone all your life; and 'tis not to married couples but to single sleepers that a ghost shows himself when 'a do come" (54). In their gentle teasing, the residue of their true beliefs appears, as is often the case with humor. They understand that "lying alone" leaves one restless and disturbed. But having abandoned the old ways, which celebrate life in all its forms, to take up a religion that celebrates virginity and chastity, Christian must be content with his lack of vitality.[7] It is impossible that Christian's name is accidental; like Bunyan's Christian, who on his journey represented the journey of all Christians, so Hardy's Christian can be seen as his representation of where Christianity can lead.

If Christian embodies what the future holds for the folk, Diggory Venn, the mysterious reddleman who haunts the heath, emerging from and disappearing into it, recalls their past.[8] Venn is even more attuned to and identified with nature than the other folk are. While they are rarely shown in their houses, he does not even own a house; he routinely camps on the heath in a wagon that is so completely unified with its surroundings that it appears almost to appear and disappear at random. In his development of Venn, Hardy follows a pattern that recurs through his novels, that of portraying those characters who live close to nature in heart and body as learning her secrets and coming to a greater understanding of all of life than do those characters who live at a remove from nature. Venn's patterns of thinking reflect his intimacy with nature, the landscape, as in this example, when he ponders:

> To do things musingly, and by small degrees, seemed, indeed, to be a duty in the Egdon valleys at this transitional hour, for there was that in the condition of the heath itself which resembled protracted and halting dubiousness. It was the quality of the repose appertaining to the scene. This was not the repose of actual stagnation, but the apparent repose of incredible slowness. (40)

The passage is reminiscent of a similar one in *Far From the Madding Crowd* in which Hardy writes that Gabriel's "special power, morally, physically, and mentally, was static" (49). Like Gabriel Oak, Diggory Venn exists in a privileged relationship with nature which informs the way he thinks. For example, Venn rejects Victorian notions of propriety when he refuses to condemn Tamsin as "ruined" simply because her marriage to Wildeve was thwarted by circumstance;[9] he very sensibly asks, "[W]hy should her going off with him to Anglebury for a few hours do her any harm?" (122). Not surprisingly, then, it is Venn who asks Tamsin for permission to plant the maypole, the symbol of the eternal renewal of life, in her yard, an act that brings her and, to some degree, the Pagan world back to life after the cataclysm occurs.

But Gabriel Oak and Diggory Venn do not function as interchangeable characters. Gabriel in all his benevolence can readily be seen as nature god/nature's priest. Venn lacks Gabriel's benevolence and his mythic stature, but takes on a supernatural and even a sinister quality that is absent from Gabriel.[10] While Gabriel's power springs from an exceptionally astute knowledge of nature, Venn's abilities are not so easily explicable. For example, Diggory can see at night and can not only hear conversations at a great distance but also at times, it appears, thoughts, as in the scene when Eustacia asks him how he knows of Wildeve's plans to come to the Rainbarrow; he responds, "I heard him say to himself that he would" (175). Furthermore, as Bailey points out, the folk are talking of ghosts when he first appears to them (1150), and his constant appearing and disappearing—once mysteriously in a fireplace—lend him a ghostly air that Gabriel never possessed. The best example of his otherworldliness, however, occurs during the uncanny dice game that he orchestrates on the heath by the light of thirteen glowworms. The significance of the number is inescapable and adds to the otherworldliness with which he often shimmers. Brooks suggests that Venn's archetype is Loki, the Nordic fire-god usually associated with mischief and craft (184). Reading him as such provides insight into his antagonism toward Eustacia. If he were the nature god figure of the novel, she would be his natural counterpart. However, the narrative never develops the two as peers; rather Venn is paralleled with Tamsin, who shares his Pagan spirit but lacks Eustacia's mythic grandeur.

What Venn does share with Eustacia becomes apparent in Brooks' description of him as "not so much a 'Mephistophelian visitant' of the Christian era as a primitive fire daemon capable of good or evil" (192). Hardy's view of nature as a balance of what naively would be called good and evil is reflected in both their characters. Enstice points out that in this novel, "There are no lambs to bring hope to this gloom, as they did to Oak's; this is the time of utter darkness" (*Landscapes*, 58). However, times of utter darkness are as endemic to nature as are times of light and fruition. Diggory then, like Eustacia, represents those aspects of nature that are not tamed, not amenable to life, not ordered, but random. Marlene Springer speaks of Venn as "Hardy's vivid personification of his belief in the futility of any attempt to act wisely" (103). Venn does experience the parameters of his will; he can determine the outcome of a dice game, but he cannot consistently bend the will of others to his ways. In that, he inhabits the border between mythic character and literal man. Springer points out how "Diggory is maintained in this tensional state between supernal, archetypal ministrant and realistic, patient suitor throughout most of the novel" (104–5). However, Hardy's development of Venn is consistent with his development of his other mythic characters, all of whom negotiate the world as living beings acted upon by political, economic, and social realities at the same time that they transcend the historical, geographical world to appear as nature goddesses and gods.

Many critics dislike the ending Hardy was all but forced to tack onto the work, especially as it affects the character of Diggory Venn, who gives up his position as wandering reddleman for the more respectable—and less mysterious—one of dairy farmer. However, that switch is significant, given the two worlds, one of which is in the process of being destroyed, that Hardy portrays as overlapping in the novel. The movement in the novel is from the mythic (Eustacia's time) to the historical (Clym's time). At the end of the work, the mythic has disappeared, although its vestiges (in the Pagan celebrations) still continue. If Venn is to survive, he must lose his mythic status, his otherworldliness, to enter history, which is what his life as a pedestrian farmer allows him to do. Presumably, as his skin fades back to white, so do his supernatural abilities. Reddlemen who can see in the dark and can will dice matches to be won belong to a world of witches, fairies, sprites, and gnomes, all of which existed in Britain's mythic past, but none of which has survived in a world dominated by Christian thought and rationalism.

However, within the novel, Venn does find happiness in the new order through his bonding with Tamsin, who, like him, bears the two worlds within her, although she is more firmly tied to the older, Pagan one. Her father also shared her dual nature, playing his clarinet for Pagan club-walkings as readily as he played the bass-viol at church services. Tamsin's introduction into culture has been fostered by Mrs. Yeobright, the curate's daughter who sets herself above the folk and who has raised the younger woman. At times, Tamsin exhibits attitudes typical of Victorian England but illogical to a folk consciousness. After her "disgrace" over the thwarted elopement, she becomes ill and retreats indoors, having accepted her aunt's verdict of herself as "ruined." When the marriage does finally occur, she is ashamed and will invite no friends or family to it, and when she is pregnant, she refers to her condition as an "illness." However, such attitudes are offset by the knowledge she gains from her intimate relationship with nature, which is textually emphasized through language that incorporates images from nature to describe her, for example, her chestnut hair and her doe-like run. The narrative voice's approval of her is readily apparent: witness the scene in which she crawls through the piles of apples and shakes the berries out of her hair, blessed by the rays of the sun which continually seek her out. To further emphasize her bond with nature, Hardy consistently reveals her comfort on the heath, the home which she loves and does not fear.

If Tamsin has learned some Victorian values from her aunt, her association with nature allows her to retain folk values as well. After the "disgrace," it is her experience in the apple loft, in nature, that makes her challenge her aunt's attitudes, which she calls "absurd" and adds, "Now, look at me as I kneel here, picking up these apples—do I look like a lost woman? . . . I wish all good women were as good as I!" (137) After the deaths of her husband, her aunt, and her friend, it is nature that recalls her to life and hope: "The spring came and calmed her; the summer came and soothed her; the autumn arrived, and she began to be comforted" (397). Once she has revived, it is she who courts Diggory Venn and she who insists to Clym that she choose her own husband freely, regardless of her cousin's opinion and of her intended's social class. In not acquiescing to the wishes of Clym, who as her male next-of-kin would, to a Victorian mind-set, be the logical person for Tamsin to regard as a higher authority, Tamsin reveals that she has rejected the Victorian idea that a single young woman cannot be self-governing for an older wisdom that understands that single women have raised children and made their own decisions for millennia.

Hardy's approval of Tamsin reveals itself most in that he chooses her to continue the matriarchy that the novel endorses. She bears the baby Eustacia, who will allow the old ways to continue a while longer, although the child's middle name, Clementine, recalls her uncle, whose nature she will also share. In marrying Venn, who, although he has become a respectable dairy farmer, is nevertheless not as wealthy as she, Tamsin recreates the matrilineal move that characterizes so many of Hardy's novels.[11] Brooks discusses Tamsin's life-affirming aspect, claiming, "Doing simply means marrying for Tamsin" (192). She goes on to cite Tamsin's braiding of her hair according to the significance of the occasion, with the most complicated braid reserved for her wedding day, as an indication of the young woman's acceptance of the cycle of life and suggests that the narrative association of Tamsin with light and music during the braiding scene "impl[ies] a relationship to the earth that has not yet become discordant" (192).

The critical problem remains of how to read the novel's ending, since it was not how Hardy initially conceived the book to end. The changes he made were clearly concessionary on his part. Does integrity demand a reading of the novel that restores the earlier conclusion? I think not. Hardy's revision does not deny the impact of Eustacia's death and Clym's resurrection. Two world orders have collided, and one has been destroyed. Tamsin and her daughter will live out their Pagan lives in a world that will be increasingly alien to them. While Egdon was never Eden, it did at least exist out of time and history, until Clym's messianic presence on the tumulus destroys its mythic status.

With *The Return of the Native* Hardy extends what he begins with *Far From the Madding Crowd*. There he presents a world out of time and space, but one that could be termed, at least in places, sentimentally pastoral. With the creation of Egdon, Hardy seems to be forcing himself to come to terms with nature in all her guises, to accept her sterner aspects as well as her beautiful and benign ones. The world is bleak, but the authorial voice is no less comfortable with it for all that. What Egdon does share with Weatherbury, though, is its mythic sense of time and space. In spite of the maps in the front of many of the texts of the Wessex novels that suggest that Wessex can be superimposed over England, both Weatherbury and Egdon exist off the map and out of time. As the maps reveal, one cannot arrive at Egdon Heath, since if one goes to the place at which it should exist, one will be somewhere else. Hardy's narrative attempts to force that consciousness upon the reader. In the initial description of the heath, Hardy writes that one can survey the land and "know that everything around and underneath had been from prehistoric times as unaltered as the stars overhead" (36). He clearly delights in such a stasis, claiming it stabilizes a mind "harassed by the irrepressible New" (36). Later, he comments that "Egdon was a place which had slipped out of its century generations ago" (197). Such a landscape exists in no Cartesian universe. Gregor complains that the mysterious dice game on the heath occurs "in a never-never land" (*Great Web*, 109), but that is precisely the point. If this world is to be construed as mythic, it cannot be historical as well. Enstice points out how the heath Hardy describes here is made up of bits and pieces of heaths that exist in England, but that Hardy deliberately created it as separate from any extant place (*Landscapes*, 76). The text itself indicates as much. As Diggory Venn crosses the heath, he feels himself "in direct communication with regions unknown to man" (113). Hardy later refers to the heath's existing at the "world's end" (417), another clear indication that he intends this world to exist out of time and space, in myth.

The novel ends with the collapse of the mythic world into the historical one; the apocalypse occurs on the horrible night on which Eustacia drowns herself. That Hardy is aware of the apocalyptic implications of the cosmic struggle occurring is apparent from his description of that night as recalling "all that is terrible and dark in history and legend—the last plague in Egypt, the destruction of Sennacherib's host, the agony in Gethsemane" (370–71). Significantly, each of the "terrible and dark" incidents he relates results in a victory for the patriarchal god. This night is no different. Right before Advent, which brings the Messiah, Eustacia, the embodiment of the old, dies. Even with the obligatory ending, Hardy is able to bring the novel full circle. It ends where it began, on the Rainbarrow, but the nature goddess, beautiful and terrible at once, has been replaced by an ineffectual messiah, preaching to disinterested masses. The overthrow has occurred; history has won, and humanity has lost.

NOTES

1. Bathsheba manages to live without a parental figure, but presumably her position of responsibility in running a farm redeems her in the public mind. While she also meets her lover clandestinely, she is certainly not idle, as Eustacia invariably is.

2. Frank Giordano claims, "In this elemental novel, it seems fitting that Eustacia, represented throughout by fire symbolism, should die by immersion in water" (518). I agree that her death is appropriate, not, however, because of the elements involved but because of the regeneration mythically implicit in a death by water. However, by the end of the novel, the messianic Clym has destroyed the natural cycle and Eustacia cannot be reborn.

3. In her discussion of the Pagan manifestations in Hardy's work, Ruth Firor points out that the lighting of such fires dates back to at least 2000 B.C.E. and predates even Woden-worship (148 and 267), making it probable that such fires were lit in honor of the Goddess rather than of any particular God.

4. As Wyatt points out, the characters "who fail to accept or strive to subvert this natural force, suffer dire consequences," and he specifically cites Mrs. Yeobright, who neither likes nor accepts the heath and therefore receives "her mortal wound in its midst and from one of its creatures" (56–57).

5. Other critics have touched on this matter. Giordano sees the central issue in the novel as "the opposition of pagan and Christian values" (506), and Paterson discusses the "crucial criticism of Christianity" ("Introduction," 115–16) that occurs in the work.

6. Robert Heilman writes, "Though Egdon is at times a savage place . . . , it is also the scene

of ongoing life: virtually all the characters in *The Return* adapt well to it and are even devoted to it" ("*The Return*," 62).

7. Paterson writes: "His physical decrepitude and sexual impotence . . . stand out beside the life-worshipping vitality of Grandfer and Timothy and the rest of that lusty crew. And where he lives in constant terror of the sights and sounds of the savage heath, they, complete pagans that they are, feel perfectly at home in this grimmest of all possible worlds" ("Introduction," 118).

8. Of Venn, Paterson writes that he represents the "nearly demoniacal spirit of fen and forest that had found its last resting place on Egdon" ("Introduction," 117).

9. Admittedly, Wildeve shares Venn's attitude, but Wildeve's perspective can be seen as colored by his desire to reestablish his relationship with Eustacia.

10. While Venn does have a dark side, I have a difficult time understanding Morgan's reading of him as cruel, manipulative, meddling, and sexist (69). Venn's ambiguities notwithstanding, he remains one of the positive figures in the novel and in the economy of Hardy's novel is rewarded by winning the woman he loves.

11. Such a move occurs, of course, in *Far From the Madding Crowd*, when Gabriel moves into Bathsheba's house when they marry, but occurs elsewhere also. Men marry women wealthier than themselves in *Under the Greenwood Tree*, *Desperate Remedies*, *Two on a Tower*, and *A Laodician*. Almost all the other marriages in the novels take place between social and financial equals. The only reversals of this pattern occur in *The Hand of Ethelberta* and *Tess of the D'Urbervilles*.

4

The Woodlanders: And Nature Said, "It Is Finished"

While *The Woodlanders* differs fundamentally from the major heroine-centered Hardy novels, the common thread binding the works is Hardy's exploration of two world—one mythical, Pagan, and nature-centered, the other historical, Christian, culture-linked—existing in tension. Given that shared theme, what most obviously separates *The Woodlanders* from *Far From the Madding Crowd*, *The Return of the Native*, and *Tess of the D'Urbervilles* is Hardy's treatment of the central female character. Grace Melbury, while she is pretty, and at times even charming, never approaches the magnitude of Tess, Eustacia, or Bathsheba. Grace is construed to be a believable character in the mode of social realism; very little, if any, of the otherworldly reflects from her. She is a typical English country girl who has been educated out of her class and whose concerns and motivations, while they are appropriate to one of her age and circumstance, can become annoying to the reader. As Ian Gregor points out, Grace frustrates the reader who "expects a heroine and gets somebody disconcertingly less" (*Great Web*, 155). What makes Grace appear so inadequate is the women characters with whom she is compared. Readers of Hardy's major canon are accustomed to women characters who far transcend typical heroines of Victorian novels to become powerful, archetypal beings who resonate with mythic overtones. Grace, however, is not a goddess figure. The world of *The Woodlanders* is a dying one—this is Egdon after Eustacia's death, Marlott after Tess's hanging. The nature gods have all but been driven off; such manifestations of them as remain become thwarted and attenuated in a world whose loss of faith in them has cost them their power. The primary color associated with *The Woodlanders* is gray; one is reminded of Swinburne's line: "Thou hast conquered, O pale Galilean; the world has grown gray from thy breath."

Although Little Hintock, Hardy's setting for *The Woodlanders*, recalls some of his earlier settings in its remoteness and its isolation, it lacks the mythic status of those other settings. Mythic time has collapsed prior to the novel's beginning or, rather, at the moment of the novel's beginning. Hardy's curious introduction, in which Barber Percomb wanders about the woods lost, seeking Little Hintock, symbolically reenacts the appropriation of the natural by the cultural. The barber encounters a carrier's van, significantly driven by a woman, which takes him to the village proper. The entire scene is mysterious, almost dreamlike, and recalls medieval tales of mysterious ladies who lead lost knights out of the woods, into a higher consciousness, even as it reveals Hardy's knowledge that restrictive sex roles are the product of a leisure class and not integral to earlier, less stratified agrarian communities. The barber, whose career is significant in the same way that Wildeve's career as engineer is important, can be seen as the representative of culture; his profession depends on arbitrary values, as all fashion does. The woman functions as the intermediary between barber-as-culture and woods-as-nature. The reader, also a representative of culture, can reach the village only through the woman as well. Once in the village, deep in the woods—and one must not overlook the archetypal association of the unconscious with the deep woods—the barber and the reader encounter a world poised between nature and culture. However, the intrusion of culture, represented by the barber, overturns the balance.

Hence the world here is a historical one, a world newly born, one in which, as Gregor points out, the community "can no longer cohere," given "the growing necessity of recognizing a world elsewhere" (*Great Web*, 144). The world Hardy creates here is a world removed from possibility,[1] a world wherein the natural cycle that leads to never-ending renewal is replaced by a progression to despair and emptiness. With the foregone death of the goddess, vitality and potency have left the world; that which remains behind is blighted and vitiated, throughout all the realms of nature—human, plant, and animal. Even in the bleak world of *The Return of the Native*, the folk exhibited life, dancing wildly over the heath fires; not so here. The sense of the obliviousness to historical space and time that pervades the earlier Wessex novels is absent here. The community presented here is forced to come to terms with a modern world it cannot comprehend. Mary Jacobus claims that a "reduction of myth to machine haunts *The Woodlanders*. Hardy laments a lost mythology as well as the rape of the woods by rootless predators from the modern world" ("Tree," 116). However, while Little Hintock may lack the mythic status of Weatherbury or Egdon Heath, it remains tied to its own past. Perhaps even more than in the earlier works, Hardy stresses here how a people's roots determine self-definition, how the bond with the past enables the formation of identity and renders life in a fallen state tolerable. As the village—and particularly the road to the village—is introduced, the narrative comments: "The spot is lonely, and when the days are darkening the many gay charioteers now perished who have rolled along the way, the blistered soles that have trodden it, and the tears that have wetted it, return upon the mind of the loiterer"(35). In Little Hintock, the past lives not in that it is recreated in the lives of the folk or through ritual, as it is in Egdon Heath or Weatherbury; here it lives *only* in memory. The aura that pervades the novel is one of nostalgia for an irretrievable past. However, memory provides a kind of salvation here, in that it functions to recall the folk to what they were. For example, in discussing the houses of Little Hintock, Hardy mentions that, because change comes so slowly to Little Hintock, their present occupants recreate the lives of the former residents. Hence the houses "reverberate" with the past, while "the castle and cloister [remain] silent beyond the possibility of echo" (54–55). Hardy's rhetoric here is telling; he contrasts the houses, wherein memory allows an entry into the past, with the "castle" and "cloister," spaces set apart through class and religion, essentially patriarchal space, that here functions as dead space, incapable of echoing with the life it never contained but rather only attempted to suppress. The passage illuminates Hardy's recurrent nostalgia for an edenic past untouched by social class or a modern sense of Christianity. It privileges the personal, the home, what might be termed feminine space.

While the Pagan rituals that characterize such works as *The Return of the Native* are absent here, the folk of Little Hintock cling to some of the principles of an earlier age in their personal dealings. Hardy mentions that "reasoning proceeds on narrow premises" (38) in Little Hintock, a statement borne out by the folks' very literal belief in ghosts,[2] as well as by their assumption that, in business dealings, one's word serves to function as a contract. Giles and Mr. Melbury form "a partnership based upon an unwritten code, by which each acted in the way he thought fair toward the other, on a give-and-take principle" (55). Hardy's admiration for the simplicity and integrity of such a life is apparent. Little Hintock may be bleak and life there may be challenging, but the narrative voice continually privileges its backwoods practices over those of the world beyond, a world that continually intrudes upon and disrupts the society of Little Hintock. As Jean Brooks points out, the folk of Little Hintock have created patterns that allow their rigorous lives to be workable; hence their society is characterized by "lack of ambition; a way of life that remains close to nature while improving on its morality by control, mutual loyalties, respect for others and the sacredness of life; respect for truth; and a long memory that enshrines the transient life in the hero-myths of Hintock"(230). When the outside world impacts upon Little Hintock, some issue of contract, of legalism, is often at issue. The initial intrusion within the diegetic time of the novel, Barber Percomb's venture into the woods to coerce Marty to sell her hair, assumes the form of the backwoods "unwritten code" in that he leaves the gold sovereigns with her with the understanding that she can return them when she comes to market if she chooses to keep her hair; however, Percomb's actions and language make it clear that Marty lacks agency in this matter. Leaving aside the issue of the ethics of dangling the equivalent of three weeks' pay before a woman who is forced to work late into the night to provide for herself and her ailing father, Percomb also threatens Marty with expulsion from her home should she not comply with Felice Charmond's wishes. The economics at work are those of the world beyond Little Hintock, the world from which Felice has arrived; there, contracts exist not "on a give-and-take principle," as they do between Giles and Mr. Melbury, but rather reveal the will to power that determines class structure in the world outside. Those dynamics of power are again revealed in another significant legal encounter with the outside world, the issue of Grace's divorce. While divorce is unknown to the folk of Little Hintock, so is the idea of adultery. When, for example, Mr. Melbury must face the evidence that Fitzpiers has taken a lover, he is stunned. Hardy writes, "In the simple life [Mr.

Melbury] had led it had scarcely occurred to him that after marriage a man might be faithless" (244). However, once Mr. Melbury discovers that divorce is a legal possibility in England, he quickly realizes that Grace's best interests would be served were she to divorce Fitzpiers. In taking a lover, Fitzpiers has broken with the Little Hintock code; his word has proven worthless, and therefore any contracts he has made are rendered null. The divorce presents no moral problem to any of the Little Hintock folk, and no one is scandalized at Grace and Giles' resuming their earlier relationship. However, in the world beyond Little Hintock, the divorce laws do not operate to provide justice for all, but rather serve to empower some, namely, men of social standing, and deny agency to others, specifically women. The law is written to guarantee that power stays in the hands of a few, yet that law is the basis of "civilized" society. Hardy's portrayal of Little Hintock is that of a fragile vestige of the past continually buffeted by the values of contemporary society; with each blow, the community is weakened and the ideals that have served to bestow identity upon the folk are called into questioned.

However, the folk in this novel figure far less significantly than they do in the earlier works.[3] Their loss of status serves to indicate that contemporary values have already begun creeping into Hintock and that, as a result, the lives of the folk are not significant enough to merit narrative focus. These rustics do not lend vitality to the work in the way that Grandfer Cantle and his comrades did because they have no vitality to lend. Having accepted the modern world's assessment of them as insignificant, they, like it, have become, for the most part, attenuated and infirm.

In spite of passing references to Norse mythology, the world depicted here is essentially removed from the Pagan past that informs the earlier Hardy novels. The aforementioned story of the Two Brothers may be seen as emblematic of what has occurred in the life of the village. In the tale, the ghosts haunted Hintock Court until they were exorcised by a priest, at which time they took up residence in a local swamp. Similarly, Christianity nominally dominates the world of Little Hintock, but the old ways exist beneath the surface, submerged, driven out into a natural world that the folk increasingly perceive as hostile and blighted.

Hardy, nevertheless, strikes subtle mythic overtones whenever he writes, and *The Woodlanders* is no exception. As Brooks points out, these scenes, "where human relationships are interwoven with the seasonal movements of woodland work, from planting to felling, [give] the poetic underpattern the resonance of myth where human beings ritually act out their archetypal roles" (222). However, as Jacobus points out, while the seasonal ritual still occurs in this world, "[it] does not bring renewal; [the folk's] *consciousness of change* effects a divorce between man and nature" ("Tree," 122; emphasis mine). The crucial issue here is the consciousness to which Jacobus refers. Within the framework of Hardy's novels, nature itself does not change; what changes is human perception of nature, signaled by narrative focus on differing aspects of nature. If Bathsheba and Gabriel see renewal and beauty, while the Hintock folk see decay and blight, the fact remains that they are observing the same phenomenon. Hardy's novels chronicle human consciousness' changing perception of nature—from a past he mythologizes as having felt a unity with nature, to a time when nature began to be perceived as other, to a present where nature is a force against which the human must struggle and which it must attempt to control. Such a consciousness may best be described as postlapsarian; a fall into disunity has occurred, a fall that severs the human from the greater nature, that leaves the human with a sense of its own lack as well as with a sense of nature as flawed. Such a consciousness will exist in a state of dissatisfaction and eternal longing and will seek redemption outside of itself.

Some critics see the fault as somehow existing within nature itself. Geoffrey Thurley, for example, claims the "Hintock woods enclose a world more stagnant and unhealthy than still and mystical" and goes on to speak of "Nature's ruthlessness and bungling" (106), as if the natural cycle were a human character, subject to praise or blame rather than a phenomenon to which the human community must respond. For the woods to become mystical rather than unhealthy, a transformation must occur within the perceiving consciousness. Ian Gregor similarly considers nature within the novel and addresses what he sees as the novel's exploration of ster-ility—"personal, communal, and located within nature itself" (*Great Web*, 140). Sterility is not, however, in and of itself evil or destructive, but rather is an essential aspect of the natural cycle which reveals itself in both landscape and human life. Seeing nature as consistently sterile, however, reveals more about the perceiving consciousness than about nature itself. But does the narrative voice privilege the scenes of blight and decay in *The Woodlanders*? A careful reading of the texts reveals fewer passages describing stagnation and rottenness than the critical responses would suggest. Hardy's placement of such passages is also significant in terms of the narrative action that occurs around them. Leaving aside scenes in which it rains (and the novel is, after all, set in England), only six passages that can be considered truly grim occur in the novel. Perhaps the most hideous, in which Hardy depicts "the bleared white visage of a sunless winter day emerg[ing] like a dead-born child" (62), occurs only a few hours after Marty has heard of Giles and Grace's informal engagement and in despair has cut her hair. That the day would appear bleak and, significantly, like a "dead-born child" precisely at the time Marty has abandoned all her hopes for a romantic relationship with Giles is narratively appropriate. When Grace must confront her father about Fitzpiers' infidelity, the conversation occurs "beneath a half-dead oak, hollow and disfigured with white tumours, its roots spreading out like claws grasping the ground" (267). The allusion to illness ("tumours") reflects Grace's consciousness that her marriage is diseased; the particular tree upon which the narrative perspective focuses provides a commentary not on nature per se, but on Grace's changing understanding of her husband's character. The woods are described as rotting while Mr. Melbury agonizes over Fitzpiers' treatment of his beloved child; as he walks through the woods, "the sky had no colour, and the trees rose before him as haggard, grey phantoms whose days of substantiality were passed" (254). Essentially, Melbury's depression manifests itself in the absence of color in the landscape, and the trees "whose days of substantiality were passed" are clearly projections of his feelings for Grace. Similarly, as Giles lies dying, Grace looks at the trees and notices that "[at] their roots were stemless yellow fungi like lemons and apricots, and tall fungi with more stem than stool" (339), the malformed growths paralleling Giles' body as he struggles vainly to stay alive.

That this novel, which is located amid lush apple orchards, reveals fewer descriptions of rich apple harvests than of diseased trees indicates the unhappiness and frustration of the principal characters throughout most of the work. Mr. Melbury is torn apart by his conflicting desires to amend a perceived wrong to an old friend and to see his daughter rise socially. Grace wants to be a dutiful daughter, but to do so means she must internalize her own desires and silence her voice. Marty grieves for unrequited love for Giles and is constantly reminded of her plainness. Felice is depressed as a result of her isolation from the human community. Fitzpiers is frustrated by his idealism, continually finding his world limiting and unsatisfactory. And Giles is plagued by monetary woes and the awareness that the woman he loves is socially superior to him and constantly judging him. When characters such as these look at a landscape, they will not be able to see beauty and fruitfulness. The few occasions in the work when nature is described as lush and beautiful occur when Grace is happy. Returning from her honeymoon, having indulged her love of travel and presumably (from the nature description) sexually fulfilled, she looks out over "gardens and orchards now bossed, nay encrusted, with scarlet and gold fruit, stretching to infinite distance under a luminous lavender mist" (204). Later, after the pain of her mismatch is over and she believes she is free to pursue Giles, we learn: "The earth this year had been prodigally bountiful, and now was the supreme moment of her bounty. In the poorest spots the hedges were bowed with haws and blackberries; acorns cracked underfoot, and the burst husks of chestnuts lay exposing their auburn contents" (234).

If human perception determines how nature looks, it also determines what nature means. If this novel, unlike the earlier works, lacks a nature goddess, it is because the kind of human consciousness that seeks out blight and decay does not permit the existence of the sacred in nature. Marty is perceived by the villagers, if she is even seen at all, not as embodying the natural, but simply as a poor woman struggling to survive. Her mythic status has been lost and, with it, the possibility of myth redeeming the world. Jacobus sums up the problem well, claiming, "Subjected to a post-Romantic gaze, Nature reveals the same defects, the same crippling evolutionary struggle, as urban industrial society" ("Tree," 116). The world of Little Hintock is virtually contemporary with the world in which Hardy lived, and both are determined by such a "post-Romantic gaze." As a result, the world is left desacralized, not admitting of mystery and wonder, rendered barren by scientific knowledge and progress.

However, Hardy's relationship with nature is a dialectical one. While he indicates that he recognizes how human perception shapes nature, he nevertheless accepts nature as possessed of its own agency, as working through its cycle regardless of human perception, understanding, or attempted control. In essence, it claims a power apart from that with which humans may have imbued it. Even when humanity has lost faith in the possibility of renewal through nature, nature as Hardy describes it fights back, attempting to force human consciousness to acknowledge her power, her ability to transform life. Brooks speaks of "the stylized ritual of nature's larger purposes working themselves out through character and event" (216) in this novel, to the end that the human becomes subsumed within the greater whole of nature (219).

Although Hardy in the novel portrays what is in many ways a fairly modern world, one in which the folk have abandoned their faith in nature, he nonetheless indicates within the framework of the fiction the sort of past that did once exist. This is perhaps seen best in the incident of John South's tree, which can, of course, be explained away in psychological terms, but which remains powerfully emblematic of the interconnectedness of the human and the natural throughout Hardy's work. In Brooks' brilliant discussion of the scene, she claims that "South's belief in his link with the tree reflects the sympathetic magic that expressed primitive man's sense of kinship with nature" (221), adding that the kinship reveals itself as "a close natural interdependence that can only be broken at great risk" (222). Significantly, John South, the one member of the community who still perceives himself as closely identified with and linked to nature, dies in the course of the novel. His death here, as the Widow Edlin's death in *Jude the Obscure*, transcends the death of one individual, signifying rather the death of a mode of perception, of a mind-set. Brooks goes on to say that Giles' gradual climb up into South's tree, during which he cuts away the branches beneath him as he ascends, "dramatizes the destructive power of modern thought and codes, which cut away the stability of man's roots in nature and the past" (223). Thus it is telling that Giles, the member of the community who is most attuned to nature, possessing some of the mystical understanding that characterized Gabriel Oak, fells the tree. His act replicates the kind of self-destructiveness that attaches to Eustacia Vye's obsession with Paris boulevards in *The Return of the Native*. However, Giles' act grows out of Fitzpiers' diagnosis of South's illness. Marty intuitively understands her father's psychic bond with the tree and provides a context for his seemingly bizarre behavior by pointing out that "Others have been like it afore in Hintock" (133). Fitzpiers, himself oblivious to any bonds to the natural world, cannot see that to cut down the tree is to cut down John South as well. Hence the old man dies, and with him the idea that one can exist in such a complete synthesis with nature that a wound to one half of the equation causes pain to the other.

However, while John South may have possessed a unique identification with nature, the other folk in this novel are not completely severed from the power of the natural. They are still very much governed by the natural cycle in their agricultural existence, a circumstance that distinguishes them from the contemporary world as Hardy envisions it. While they have to some extent lost their ability to be sustained and comforted by what has become for them an unconscious knowledge of their unity with natural processes, they nevertheless retain the instinctive morality that characterizes Hardy's rural folk throughout the Wessex novels. Hardy furthermore portrays the folk as sharing in the health, vigor, and hardiness of the Weatherbury folk, so much so that Fitzpiers complains that his skills as a physician are unrequired in Little Hintock. Hardy's decision to make the irresponsible, lazy Fitzpiers a physician takes on political significance as well in light of the historical tension between Pagan and Christian England. Traditionally, the folk were treated by the village healers, often old wise women known as wicce (from which modern Wicca, the reconstructed religion of the Goddess, also known as witchcraft, takes its name). Long after the Christian church had waged war on Paganism and had consigned to the flames anyone accused of following the old ways, the folk, especially the women, still sought out the healers, particularly when a midwife was needed. As the exclusively male medical profession began to assume dominance, they were particularly determined to abolish female midwives, who were principally annoying because they would render their services free of change. Long after the Burning Times,[4] English midwives could be accused of Witchcraft and forced to pay exorbitant fines, a practice that was instrumental in the demise of midwifery. However, the herbal healers continued their practices, particularly in rural areas, so it is likely that the folk Fitzpiers assumes are so hale and hearty simply know effective herbal remedies for routine ailments.

The world of Little Hintock can be seen, then, as existing somewhere between the mythic time of the earlier novels and Hardy's historical present. While the novel ends grimly for several of the human characters involved, the natural cycle continues apart from the human. The apple trees that Giles planted will grow, their blossoms appearing every spring, followed by the rich fruits of late summer. Giles, in enabling this natural process, lives a life of purpose. To privilege the human over the totality of the natural cycle is perhaps to look too narrowly. Similarly, the folk of Little Hintock can be said to exist somewhere between Paganism and Christianity, retaining traces of their Pagan past even as they are predominantly Christian. One scene that nicely reveals the existing tension between the two modes of spirituality is the midsummer's eve ritual, a Pagan fertility ritual with its roots in the past, in which the young women of the community participate. Such rituals were carried out in Dorset, and Hardy conveniently locates Little Hintock near the area of the actual Cerne Giant, the hillside carving of a generously endowed man who was held responsible for births resulting from revels such as the one in which Grace participates. A local custom that attributes such "Beltane-gotten"[5] children to a carved image allows young women to experiment sexually without committing themselves to a serious relationship and, as such, disables the cultural appropriation of women's sexuality through the glorification of virginity and chastity. However, for many of the Little Hintock women, their participation in the ritual is mingled with both fear and a slight degree of embarrassment, as is immediately apparent when one compares, for example, the beautifully somber May-walking scene in *Tess of the D'Urbervilles* or the celebratory heath fires in *The Return of the Native*. The Little Hintock women treat the ceremony like a game; one is reminded of children who play outside after dark for the specific purpose of scaring themselves. Yet Hardy repeatedly in his novels uses the motif of a fear of the dark to indicate a separation from nature. Furthermore, the specific form that their fear takes is significant. One remarks that the ritual "is too much like having dealings with the evil one" (176), revealing the presence of a Christian consciousness that would associate sexual cavorting with anonymous partners with Satan. Therefore, when the clock strikes, the young women tear out of the field, claiming to be pursued by Satan with his hourglass, when what they actually encounter is a man carrying a hat and a topcoat. Their own consciousness of sin, of the existence of Satan, who is of course a Christian, not a Pagan, construct, has stripped the ritual of its power. The hourglass the women imagine they see is also significant. Time has caused the demise of the old perception; time and Christianity together have destroyed the Pagan way of being in the world. However, as Brooks shows, the ritual does prove effective in terms of "nature's larger purposes" (218) in that Fitzpiers and Suke Damson come together in the haystack in the sexual act, the one act that constantly serves to pull humans, regardless how civilized they may assume themselves to be, back to nature.

Other details in the novel allow glimpses into the consciousness of the Little Hintock folk concerning nature and their Pagan roots. Hardy tells of the bonzai walking sticks characteristic of the men of the region, describing them as "monstrosities of vegetation, brought to that pattern by the slow torture of an encircling woodbine during their growth" (84). The unambiguously negative language describes not only the formation of walking sticks, but the treatment of nature in general by a culture that perceives nature as existing only outside of itself; in essence, the human community cripples the natural—in the landscape but also inside itself. The bonzai sticks become the emblems of the "monstrosities" human culture perceives within itself. Another similar detail surfaces at Giles' Christmas party. The fortune-teller "told her tale unskilfully, for want of practice" (121); clearly, the folk have lost faith in the woman's abilities and no longer require her services, indicating their distance from Pagan ways, unlike the folk in *Under the Greenwood Tree* and *The Mayor of Casterbridge*, who seek out their local witch and weather-prophet. One final significant detail is Hardy's treatment of the business of the life-leases. After Marty's father's death results in Giles' losing his home, Hardy says the young man "marvelled, as many have done since, what could have induced his ancestors at Hintock, and other village people, to exchange their old copyholds for life-leases" (130). These leases, which figure in other Hardy novels as well, can be seen as indicative of the amount of time left for the old ways to hold sway; the past has been signed away through a process that, having been set into motion, can no longer be impeded. The villagers' forebears, in exchange for more modern homes, sold their own heritage, their birthright. The generation that exists within the fictional time frame of this novel is powerless to prevent time from playing its hand. As in other of Hardy's novels, here, once a modern consciousness exists, it is only a matter of time before the old consciousness is totally destroyed.

But in this winding down of Paganism and this acceptance of cultural values, does the image of the Goddess figure at all? In spite of all the critical and narrative attention focused on Grace, the nature goddess figure in this novel is clearly Marty South. As Geoffrey Thurley points out, she is "an archaic figure, timelessly dressed, completely unanchored in the historical period the novel is set in" (119). Her timelessness and her removal from history point to her mythic status, but the archaic sense to which Thurley refers calls attention to the novel's setting within the mythical time-historical time continuum. Marty, once a goddess perhaps, is now merely a poor woman, out of place in the world, with limited agency. Interestingly, Hardy's narrative invokes the memory of the goddess at the time of Marty's greatest powerlessness, the incident in which, after she is coerced into cutting her hair, she cannot bring herself to look into a mirror, just as "her own ancestral goddess" avoided looking into a pond after "the rape of her locks by Loke the Malicious" (51). The comparison endows the scene with mythic significance, which is further emphasized by Hardy's earlier description of a candle causing "a moving thorn-pattern of shade" (48) to appear on Marty's face. Marty's crown of thorns inscribes her as a sacrificial victim, a scapegoat, and linked with her ravaged locks, it identifies her with the figure of the witch, whose hair was often hacked off before she was burned at the stake. Marty functions then as a Pagan sacrifical lamb, as the essence of what is foresworn to enable the community of Little Hintock to participate in a modern consciousness.

However, while Marty no longer has the power of the Great Goddess to imbue the community with renewal, Hardy configures her so that she shares traits possessed by the other goddess figures in his works. Like Eustacia and at times Tess and Bathsheba, she lives a life of utter loneliness, of one set apart from the community. Hardy tells us that her facial expression was "developed by a life of solitude" (41), and, even in the scenes where Marty works with the men of Little Hintock, she does not share in their conversation. Her strength also parallels her with characters such as Eustacia, Tess, and Bathsheba. Hardy continually stresses her capability and endurance; in one scene, as she works with Giles, "though her outstretched hand was chill as a stone, and her cheeks blue, and her cold worse than ever, she would not complain" (95). Like Bathsheba, she calmly looks death in the face, bravely sleeping in the same room with her father's corpse. Her skills further distinguish her from the folk of Little Hintock. During barking season, Marty works more efficiently than any of the men, using a tool that again identifies her with the natural—a horse's leg bone. After Giles' death, Marty will travel with his cider press, doing his work, not requiring even Creedle's assistance. From the novel's first scene on, Marty is made to look outstanding and even perhaps otherworldly. The narrative stresses Marty's ability in making spars, a trade that requires years to perfect, and emphasizes that she taught herself the craft in two hours. The narrative emphasis on her extraordinary abilities marks her as essentially other in the community of Little Hintock.

The associations between Marty and nature are abundant. Hardy depicts her as Giles' natural counterpart, although he indicates that she possesses the greater attunement to the natural. She is the one, for example, who hears the saplings sigh as they are planted; Giles claims never to have noticed the sound. Like him, she reads nature like an almanac, noting once, "It will be fine to-morrow . . . for [the pheasants] are a-croupied down nearly at the end of the bough. If it were going to be stormy they'd squeeze close to the trunk" (99). After Giles' death, Hardy's rhetoric directly addresses the supernatural power the two possess:

> Marty South alone, of all the women in Hintock and *the world*, had approximated to Winterborne's level of intelligent intercourse with Nature. In that respect she had formed his true counterpart in the other sex, had lived as his counterpart, had subjoined her thoughts to his as a corollary.
>
> The casual glimpses which the *ordinary population* bestowed upon that wondrous world of sap and leaves called the Hintock woods had been with these two, Giles and Marty, a clear gaze. They had been possessed of *its finer mysteries* as of commonplace knowledge; *had been able to read its hieroglyphs as ordinary writing* . . . ; together they had, with the run of the years, mentally collected those remoter signs and symbols which seen in few were of runic obscurity, but altogether made an alphabet. The artifices of the seasons were seen by them *from the conjuror's own point of view*, and not from that of the spectator. (357–58; emphasis mine)

However, Marty is not only limited by poverty and circumstance, but also by the novel's narrative focus on Grace. On the one hand, the text invites the reader to see Marty and Felice in opposition, on the extreme ends of the spectrum, with Grace poised between them. Marty then functions as a representative of nature in its purest form, but living in a time when nature is appropriated by culture, blighted, no longer capable of giving life, muted by capitalism and industrialism. Felice, as her counterpart, figures as the almost stereotypical lady of culture, alienated from the landscape and the work force. Caught between the two possibilities for existence is the character of Grace, herself one of the folk, but educated by a well-meaning if shortsighted father to a level where she has the manners and the morals and possibly even the money to make the leap to the middle class, but only if she erases her identity and severs herself from her family and community. To elucidate further the dualism Grace encounters, Hardy presents two suitors, one of the folk and one of the middle class, and links the two men in question to Marty and Felice. Such a reading, which possesses the sort of architectural balance that Hardy so enjoyed, is valuable; however, in places the discourse of the text problematizes such a reading of the characters as it unravels the configuration of Marty and Felice in a binary opposition.

Hardy's novels consistently resist being read on only a literal level; *The Woodlanders* is no exception. The interplay of Marty, Grace, and Felice shimmers with the uncanny. Their lives are too interwoven, too reflective of each other, too touched with "coincidence," as earlier Hardy critics have pointed out, to read them simply as three characters who share experience and desire. Rather, we are presented with a series of events, told and retold, in double-take, as if two film images are simultaneously projected over each other. The dual-lens view of certain events that occur in Little Hintock results in a constant reiteration of tableau and motif, a point and counterpoint that problematizes a reading of these three characters as individual and self-contained. Rather, we experience their characters as fusing, melding together and then flowing apart again, ever overlapping. A few examples will illustrate this. At one point, Marty literally scrawls a message on the side of Giles' house in a scene that again partakes of the uncanny, the poetic. Later in the text, Felice's words act "like a handwriting on the wall" (212) to Fitzpiers. Hardy's choice of this particular simile to describe Felice's discourse serves to parallel Felice with Marty, yet the parallel serves no narrative function. Rather, it is as if the scene were repeated, or as if the same scene occurs in a different time frame with a different agent. Similarly, Grace and Fitzpiers' relationship is catapulted beyond friendship when the horse drawing Grace's carriage threatens to bolt. Later, Fitzpiers is provided with an opportunity to meet Felice after her carriage is involved in an accident. A third example, again one that is particularly poetic and nonliteral, occurs in the descriptions of Fitzpiers' initial meetings with both Grace and Felice. He first encounters Grace when he is semi-awakened from a nap to glimpse her in a mirror in what he assumes to be a vivid dream. Later, when he is called to treat Felice, as he enters her chamber for the first time, the text states, "While the scene and the moment were new to him and unanticipated, the sentiment and essence of the moment were indescribably familiar. What could be the cause of it? Probably a dream" (217). Fitzpiers' *déjà vu* experience, as well as the other such repetitions, create a visual "echo," the result of which is a fusion of identity of Marty, Felice, and Grace.

In disallowing a reading of the characters as separate and self-contained, the text challenges the binarism that posits Marty and Felice as polar opposites. Certain passages within the text also serve to unravel that opposition. One such passage occurs when Hardy describes Felice's home. In a reading that would posit Felice as the bearer of culture, her home should appear as a grand, imposing structure. Yet Hardy tells us "it stood in a hole" (88) and its walls were "coated with lichen of every shade, intensifying its luxuriance with its nearness to the ground till, below the plinth, it merged in moss" (88). He goes on to refer to Hintock House as "vegetable nature's own home" (89), a description that would seem to refer to Marty's home, given the polarities he has established in his configuring of these characters. Conversely, he presents a scene in which Grace, observing Marty through a window (a framing technique usually associated with Grace herself throughout the text), notes that "the girl was writing instead of chopping as usual" (273). The sentence itself calls attention to the atypical character of Marty's task, recalling Jane Gallop's discussion of women writing and social class in *Thinking Through the Body*: "There is a class of women who write and a class who serve those who write" (167). Clearly, Felice and Grace are aligned with the class of women who write, yet it is Marty who is imaged as writing. However, as the embodiment of nature within the text, Marty cannot write, since writing is not only an act "prohibited" a woman of her class but also an act that falls on the culture side of the binary opposition Hardy has established. What the scene does, then, is to deconstruct the binarism out of which the work grows at the same time as it blurs the parameters of the individual characters.

In the positing of Felice and Marty as polar opposites and then in the unraveling of that opposition, Grace comes to be the place between, the body upon which the nature/culture battle is fought. Not too surprisingly, the text focuses on her dual nature; Grace's annoying inability to act decisively stems from her existence in a space that is not a space. As the intersection of nature and culture, she is a point rather than a plane. An act—even speech—will posit her in one world or the other, but to be in one place denies her totality. Her background serves to emphasize her dual—and divided—nature. Her father is a woodsman, but one who has striven to "rise" socially and hence to distinguish himself, to separate himself, from the community. The woman he initially chooses to marry, who becomes Grace's biological mother, is described as the Victorian cultural ideal—she is delicate and passive, described by one of the folk as a "*child of a woman* . . . [who] would cry like rain if so be he [her husband] huffed her. Whenever she and her husband came to a puddle in their walks together he'd take her up *like a halfpenny doll* and put her over without dirting her a speck" (58; emphasis mine). The diminutives trivialize this frail woman, who dies shortly after giving birth to Grace in what one might cynically claim to be good Victorian fashion. Descended from such a pair of parents, Grace's bond with the natural might seem a puzzle; however, the second Mrs. Melbury allows for an explanation. Throughout the novel, in her quiet, understated way, Grace's stepmother functions as a kind of wicca (wise woman) to her husband. For example, when Mr. Melbury regrets his earlier decision to encourage Giles' courtship of Grace, she wisely says: "It is not altogether a sacrifice. He is in love with her, and he's honest and upright. If she encourages him, what can you wish for more?" (50). Mrs. Melbury's words not only are sensible, but they permit Grace agency as well, in that they assume the young woman's consent is essential to any courtship that occurs. Mrs. Melbury entered the household in a serving capacity after the death of Grace's biological mother; as one of the folk, this kindly stepmother provides Grace a link to both the folk and nature. Once again Hardy reveals the matriarchal bond to be the privileged one, and to relate to the older, nature-centered world.

However, little of the typical Hardy heroine is apparent in Grace. Even her appearance is "wrong"; the narrative voice describes her as the Victorian ideal, and then goes on to critique that image:

> [S]he was of a fair and clear complexion, rather pale than pink, slim in build. . . Her look expressed a tendency to wait for others' thoughts before uttering her own; possibly also to wait for others' deeds before her own doings. In her small, delicate mouth . . . there was a gentleness that might hinder sufficient self-assertion for her own good. (78)

What by Victorian standards would be considered Grace's most admirable qualities—her tractability, her deference to others, her lack of self-assertion—are the qualities the narrative voice sees as problematic. In speaking for the young woman's "own good," Hardy reveals again his understanding of the co-optation of women's power by a male culture that gains from making women believe that modesty, obedience, and self-sacrifice somehow define the feminine.

The cultural side of Grace is dominant when she enters the novel. Having just returned from school, she is alienated from nature and removed from the folk. She fails Hardy's litmus test of unity with the natural: she, who has grown up among apple trees, can no longer distinguish one variety of tree from another, to Giles' great dismay. Hardy focuses on what each sees during the drive through the woods to point out their differences and to indicate the side of the duality to which each is aligned:

> where [Giles] was seeing John-apples and farm-buildings she was beholding a much contrasting scene; a broad lawn in the fashionable suburb of a fast city, the evergreen leaves shining in the evening sun, amid which bounding girls, gracefully clad in artistic arrangements of blue, brown, red, and white, were playing at games with laughter and chat in all the pride of life. . . . Moreover they were girls—and this was a fact which Grace Melbury's delicate femininity could not lose sight of—whose parents Giles would have addressed with a deferential Sir or Madam. (72–73)

Hardy comments on the above scene: "She had *fallen* from the good old Hintock ways" (74; emphasis mine). The word "fallen" is significant here, since from a social point of view she has risen. The religious connotations of the word come into play here: in her foray into the world outside Little Hintock, a foray made for the purposes of gaining knowledge, Grace has lost her prelapsarian innocence, her ability to walk daily in the garden in the presence of the deity—significantly, not the God of the Old Testament, but rather the Goddess who is the earth itself, the trees whose names Grace can no longer recall. This is the Grace who can no longer dance the old dances because new steps have supplanted the old, who anticipates further social advancement through Felice Charmond, and who causes Giles to compare her face to "the face of Moses when he came down from the Mount" (97) after her visit to Felice. Giles' allusion to the transfiguration allows Hardy to indicate the new divinity at whose altar Grace worships—that of culture.

The vision of the fashionable suburb fades, however, as Grace begins to frequent the woods. Her "lips sucked in this native air of hers like milk" (116); the sacramental sign of Grace's re-admittance to nature's realm appears in the same paragraph when a fox walks by her "tamely as a domestic cat" (116). This scene is instrumental in advancing the plot of the novel; moments later, Grace, no longer exuding cultured airs, is treated rudely by a "gentleman" who mistakes her for a country girl, fortifying Mr. Melbury's determination that Grace make a good marriage. For the first time, Grace appears to question her role as an exchange commodity and admits her unease "at being the social hope of the family" (117), a role she has previously relished. In the argument with her ambitious father which follows, Grace comes as close as she ever will to articulating her own desires and her own sense of self. Her arguments are predicated upon beliefs antithetical to Victorian culture. For example, she labels her father's speaking of title-deeds as "vain," yet one might argue that a founding basis of patriarchal culture is land ownership—the idea that mother earth can be bought and sold, hierarchy being determined by who may own and who may not. Grace further grows distressed at her father's economic rhetoric when he discusses her marriage prospects and pleads, "Don't think of me like that . . . [a] mere chattel" (119), yet the function of women in culture has been precisely that—an exchange commodity among men—as Grace's experiences away from Little Hintock would have taught her.

When Fitzpiers first sees Grace, she is again poised between nature and culture, as her movements reveal. She "walked as delicately as if she had been bred in town and as firmly as if she had been bred in the country" (143), the firmness of her country side indicating the strength she is acquiring under nature's tutelage. Her response to her new suitor, who represents the cultural world that intrudes on Little Hintock, is appropriately one of both attraction and repulsion. Even as she cannot "resist the supplicatory mandate written in the face and manner of this man" (160), she is never completely comfortable with him, at times even becoming agitated and tearful by his presence. Hardy has constructed the narrative in such a way that nature's response to Fitzpiers' courtship of Grace indicates authorial attitude, pushing the reader to accept the privileged reading of their relationship. When Fitzpiers has begun scheming his courtship/seduction of Grace, two large birds in the act of mating fall out of a tree into the hot ashes of a dying fire. The otherworldly, prophetic traces of the incident are emphasized when the witch/goddess Marty remarks, "That's the end of what is called love" (173), speaking the end of Grace and Fitzpiers' passion for each other.

The duality within Grace is readily apparent in the midsummer's eve scene, when she participates in the Pagan fertility ritual/divination. Although she is eager to join the festivities, she becomes ill as a result of her nocturnal cavorting, revealing her disjunction from both nature and Paganism. That illness serves to lead her back to Fitzpiers, who is called in to attend to her medical needs. To her credit, Grace is less smitten with her new suitor than her father is; she is reluctant to answer the door when Fitzpiers first comes courting, and she remains very half-hearted about the relationship once it is established. That Grace is never deeply in love with Fitzpiers becomes clear. The narrative reveals that Fitzpiers' attraction for Grace results from her education, which has left her desirous of intellectual conversation and "a refined and cultured inner life" (196); neither Fitzpiers' physical self nor his social standing enters into Grace's decision.

Grace's problematic marriage to Fitzpiers provides the narrative voice opportunity to comment on the Victorian concept of marriage. In the final days before their marriage, Grace's recurring feelings of uneasiness stem from her sense that Fitzpiers seemed to "be her ruler rather than her equal, protector, and dear familiar friend" (196). Yet the traditional Christian marriage service, and certainly its Victorian interpretation, sees the bond not as one between equals or friends but rather as a hierarchal arrangement. The woman vows to "obey" a man who is perceived by society, as well as by law, to be her ruler and who assumes complete economic and social control over her. Later, after Grace learns of Fitzpiers' affair with Felice, the young wife's lack of anger stems from the fact that "her ante-nuptial regard for Fitzpiers had been rather of the quality of awe towards a superior being than of tender solicitude for a lover" (233). Grace's reaction touches upon the problem of marriage as it was defined in Victorian culture, a matter that repeatedly surfaces in Hardy's texts, most blatantly in *Jude the Obscure*. Fitzpiers cannot be both Grace's superior and her soul mate. To be the latter implies a shared relationship between equals. However, Victorian society assumed husbands to be their wives' superiors even as they professed to an ideal in which marriage is based on love between the partners; those expectations, however, are mutually exclusive, as Hardy here reveals. Grace's spiritual dilemma begins in earnest when, deserted by her husband, she recognizes the depth of her feelings for Giles and is torn between love and desire for her childhood companion and societal dictates which insist that married women, even deserted married women, are not free to love where they choose. Hardy's narrative clearly supports Grace's reunion with Giles, encouraging the reader to sanction it as well by indicating not merely nature's approval of the bond, but also nature's responsibility for causing it to occur. He claims that "Nature was bountiful" in providing a new lover for the rejected Grace, one who "had arisen out of the earth" (236) to court the young woman. As Grace encourages Giles to take up his suit again, regardless of appearances, Hardy comments that "[s]he abjured all fastidiousness now" (306). The narrative approval of Grace's behavior challenges the church's claim that marriages exist until death unravels them, sanctioning unions based on similarity of spirit and shared vision, oblivious to the authority of the state.

However, for all the vacillations through which the reader must follow Grace, in a sense, although she seemingly is the novel's protagonist, she does not exist as a character in her own right, but rather functions as the reification of the desire of the other characters. Repeatedly she is framed, imaged, in lighted windows, in doorways, in mirrors, observed by other characters, created by their gaze. Rarely does she act decisively; instead, she is characterized by her continual inability to act at all. She lacks agency. Even her central "choice" in the novel, whether to marry Fitzpiers or Giles, is not an act on her part. Initially, her father coerces her into avoiding Giles and accepting Fitzpiers as her suitor. Later, when Grace wishes to break the engagement, Mr. Melbury uses the argument of family pride and respectability to enable the marriage. Once Melbury discovers Fitzpiers' betrayal, he encourages Grace to seek out Giles once again to atone for his own guilty conscience. Although a strong case can be made for how Mr. Melbury, Fitzpiers, and Giles all constitute Grace by their desire, it is primarily Marty who determines Grace if Grace is read as the projection of Marty's desire in her own life.

Critical attention on the women characters in this novel has been heavily concentrated on Grace, which has meant that Marty has often been treated summarily. Yet in one sense Marty can be read as the character with the greatest agency. On the surface, she appears powerless, of course; she is poor, dispossessed, unloved, ugly, and unempowered. However, in terms of narrative, Marty both begins and ends the text and determines, in one way or another, all of the action that happens in the work. Her power stems from the fact that she alone, of the five main characters, is desired by no one, is never constituted by desire, is a free agent. Rather than being a part of the community, she is apart from community, working with the folk but remaining unconnected to any of them. Even though she lives for a while with an invalid father, she is yet another of Hardy's independent women who are bound to no authority figures. But what distinguishes Marty from those other women characters is her lack of connectedness to men. While Hardy's typical pattern involves developing a strong woman character who is courted by at least two men, themselves the replication of the nature/culture duality Hardy is interested in exploring, Marty is courted by no one. Here, the two suitors still appear, but it is Grace, not Marty, they desire. Marty herself is not the object of any character's desire and as such she is not created by anyone's gaze. She is invisible, free to move, to speak, to write, to desire; she is not acted upon, and therein lies her agency. But what is the nature of her desire? She acknowledges to herself her love for Giles, the man with whom she works, but never speaks of her desire to him. Nor does she ever indicate a sense that she believes a relationship with him is possible, even though such a relationship would be not only logical but likely assumed in the narrowly circumscribed community of Little Hintock. Even once Grace is married to Fitzpiers, leaving Giles free, Marty is no way pursues her beloved, not even by arranging to work with him. Rather she virtually disappears from the text. If we read Grace and Marty as aspects of the same characters, what this suggests is that while Marty may love Giles, she herself disables that love because of a greater desire—and that desire is not for a man but in a sense for a woman, for a body, a place to create a new self, to be someone else, to escape life in Little Hintock, to be someone who is not poor, dispossessed, unloved, ugly, and unempowered. In a sense, Grace becomes the object of Marty's desire. Grace is Marty in history, Marty removed from the mythology of an edenic past living out its final days once the apple has been eaten. In the sense that Marty is emblematic of nature, she, like nature, is static and has no story. Nature's story is always the same story, a cyclical enactment and reenactment of fertility and decay, fruition and death. In terms of the discourse here, Marty has no story: virtually nothing changes for her from the text's beginning to its end. If there is to be a story, a narrative, it must be enacted in the body of a character who has a history, who has fallen out of Eden, who is no cosmic deity but rather who is limited, human, fragmented—a speaking subject, bound to others by desire. That body is Grace Melbury's. In the scene in which Marty is introduced, the narrator engages in speculation about other possibilities for her had the "cast of the die" (41) been different. Grace is the shaping of that desire, a version of Marty to whom fate has granted an education and a possibility of escaping life in Little Hintock—Marty's wish fulfillment of her own life.

The troubling haircutting business that introduces the novel takes on a different meaning, then. Of course Marty's hair can be read as emblematic of the sexuality of the women of her social class, appropriated by the upper classes, who view sexuality as their privilege, while they enact severe cultural strictures on the behavior of lower-class women. However, an alternative reading suggests that in this scene Marty is projecting her desire—and her sexuality—onto another figure, an alter ego, an other. After Marty cuts her hair and sells it to Felice, we never sense any sexual desire emanating from her, even in the scenes in which she works closely with Giles, the man she loves. What is significant is when and how the hair transaction occurs. Seemingly, Marty cuts her hair once she learns that Giles is informally betrothed to Grace. However, in the same conversation, Marty also learns that Felice is seeking a companion. Marty's haircutting can thus be read as her attempt to project her desire onto Felice, not her desire for Giles, but her desire for a way out of Little Hintock. Significantly, the discourse of the transaction implicates the sexual act—the barber wishes to "snip off what you've got too much of" (42) and even threatens Marty in the guise of Felice, claiming, "The lady that wants it wants it badly. And, between you and me, you'd better let her have it. 'Twill be bad for you if you don't" (43). The desire here is projected onto Felice: it is she who wants the hair and she who, repeatedly throughout the text, is revealed to be the desiring woman, the woman who allows herself to experience desire and to act on it. But the discourse also figures Felice in the masculine position—she is the agent behind the rape of these locks, and she who will become threatening if Marty does not assent. Similarly, when Felice first meets Grace, the older woman acts in a manner that can only be described as seductive: "those long eyes . . . became longer, and her voice more languishing" (90). Hardy speaks of her as one of those women "who lingeringly smile their meanings to men rather than speak them" (90), even though Felice's conversation and her smiles are directed not at a man but at a woman. In casting Felice as the desiring male, she is seemingly given the agency of the phallus, but what is revealed is the locus of Marty's (and by extension, Grace's) desire: wealth, prestige, freedom of movement.

Given Hardy's architectural structuring of the novel, Felice must also on one level be read as the bearer of culture, the female counterpart to Fitzpiers, another disruption of the world of Little Hintock from the world beyond. The text continually emphasizes Felice's alienation from her surroundings. Until her late husband brought her to Hintock, she had never been in the country and she never adapts to life there. Like Grace when she returns from school, Felice cannot tell one kind of tree from another, even though she owns the trees and lives her fine life partly as a result of their economic worth, another of Hardy's indictments of the class system which survives by the exploitation of nature and her folk without any understanding of either. It is Felice who destroys the old houses in Little Hintock, the carriers of the past, the locus of memory, and hence the bearers of identity. As Jean Brooks points out, Felice and Fitzpiers function as "aliens [who] drive a destructive wedge between the kinship loyalties, sacred to the woodland code, that arose out of the mutual interdependence imaged in the world of nature" (223). Like Alec D'Urberville later, Felice is the very image of the new and the modern. If the scene in which D'Urberville appears in his sportly driving outfit pulls that novel out of its mythic setting, here the portrayal of Felice sensuously smoking a cigarette in the dim light of her boudoir functions similarly. The folk of Little Hintock read Felice accurately; she tells Fitzpiers, "My neighbours think I am an atheist . . . and when I speak disrespectfully of the weather or the crops they think I am a blasphemer" (220). The religious language is appropriate in a work in which a Pagan-Christian tension underlays the novel's discourse. Felice does blaspheme—against nature, and the old gods and goddesses that represented nature in human consciousness. When she dies, then—significantly, abroad, far removed from

Little Hintock—her body is never returned for burial; not being of the land, she can ultimately find no home in it. She who never "looked for the earth" can find no peaceful resting place in it in death.

However, Felice functions not merely as the bearer of culture in the work but as a projection of Marty's desire, as the agent who can act and therefore can move from the static world of Little Hintock to a historical world permitting of a story. However, Marty's desire to escape her situation through Felice is complicated by her desire for Giles, which is projected onto Grace, hence Grace's attraction/repulsion for Giles. Marty's love for Giles, enacted in the body of Grace, will trap her in Little Hintock, in her life of poverty; hence it is necessary that Giles be destroyed. His downfall occurs as a result of the fusion of the actions of the three women characters who are themselves fusions of one character. Virtually simultaneously, Marty mocks Giles, Grace rejects him, and Felice has his house pulled down. Leaving aside the obvious Freudian reading of the destruction of the house-as-self, a reading that would fuse the Grace and Felice characters, the scene provides the cause of the illness that will destroy Giles. But Marty is in some sense the primary agent of this action as Felice again acts out Marty's desire. Felice comes to own both Marty's and Giles' houses after the death of John South, Marty's father. While the text explains the life-leases amply, on another level Felice functions as South's heir, as the daughter, again merging the identities of Felice and Marty. Felice does not pull down Marty's house, but does destroy the man who threatens Marty's desire.

For Marty's desire to fulfill itself, Grace must make a "good marriage" and the only appropriate bridegroom is Fitzpiers. Marty, both loving Giles and wanting to escape from him, both fosters and thwarts the romance as she vacillates emotionally. She scrawls a mocking message on Giles' house to deter him from pursuing Grace, but she also positions herself in Grace's path on the night of the midsummer revels to coerce Grace into Giles' arms. In the first example, Marty, seemingly the woman for whom the act of writing is prohibited, uses the act of writing, the act that tropes her fusion with the other women, to foster her desire. But her vacillation plays itself out through Grace's body so it becomes Grace who must choose between the two suitors, neither of whom she desires for herself, desire having been situated in the body of Felice. Grace here functions as a puppet with Marty as puppeteer: when Marty's love for Giles is dominant, Grace is drawn to him and to what he represents, the simple life of Little Hintock. When Marty's desire for escape predominates, Grace is drawn to Fitzpiers, her ticket away from her birthplace. As her wedding to Fitzpiers approaches, Grace becomes more and more reluctant and less and less able to act—or to feel. She is alarmed at her lack of passion, aware of "what an attenuation this cold pride was of the dream of her youth, in which she had pictured herself walking in state toward the altar, flushed by the purple light and bloom of her own passion, without a single misgiving as to the sealing of the bond" (202–3). But as Grace figures as the body enacting Marty's desire, she cannot feel passion, since Felice is the locus of desire within the text, identity having been fragmented by the selling of the self through the exchange of hair.

After the marriage, Grace's crisis intensifies. Grace's affirmation of her bond with the local working people—she claims to her husband, "[M]y blood is no better than theirs" (209)—triggers Fitzpiers' anxiety about the propriety of having married out of his own social class, causing him to distance himself from his new wife, who experiences alienation from both her husband and the community. At this time, she is drawn to Giles once again, and Marty is absent from the narrative, in a sense extrinsic to it, living through the body of Grace. During this time, Grace encounters Felice in the woods, and her onetime friend and idol is now unrecognizable to her; Hardy tells us Grace "stood like a wild animal on first confronting a mirror or other puzzling product of civilization" (266). The images are significant here. Grace is compared to a wild animal because she is attempting to reject culture, her only way of being in the world, but what she sees in looking at Felice is herself, a self she does not know. In a prelapsarian state, identity would be unified and no other self could exist. But the plentitude of apples in Little Hintock suggests that many of those apples have been eaten, that the fall into disunity has occurred. Grace, as the body upon which the battle is fought, does not recognize her own being because she has little, if any, sense of her self and the self that does exist is fragmented—part wild animal, part society lady. The "puzzling product of civilization" she observes is the culmination of Marty's desire, the place it exists. What follows elucidates this point. Wandering off into the wildest part of the woods, for the first time since childhood, when, untainted by the knowledge her education outside of Little Hintock has given her, Grace was completely safe and certain in the woods, she becomes hopelessly lost and immediately rediscovers Felice, equally lost and frightened. In their fear, they cling to each other for warmth and survival, their identification with each other restored and Grace's vision of what she must become—as the body of Marty's desire—once more clarified. Significantly, however, their encounter is once again sexually colored. As they cling together, "each one's body . . . alternately heaved against that of her companion" (271); however it is Felice who "embraced Grace more and more tightly" (271) and Felice whose breaths "grow deeper and more spasmodic, as though uncontrollable feelings were germinating" (271). Any sexuality revealed in the text is situated in the body of Felice, the site of desire. But the desire for the body of another, for escape from self, is complicated and threatened by Marty/Grace's love for Giles.

Faced with the knowledge of her husband's affairs, Grace appears truly noble—and truly unconventional—for the first time in the novel. In her refusal to condemn either Felice or Suke for her sexual involvement with Fitzpiers, Grace reveals her understanding of the triviality of such sexual indulgence and the absurdity of the convention that would allow her to berate and scorn the other women. Recognizing the great love that both women feel for her husband, Grace feels not jealousy but rather pity for these objects of her husband's selfishness. As Boumelha points out, "through [Grace], that contemporary sexual ideology which would polarize virtue and vice into wife and mistress is tested and discredited" (108). However, while Grace may have abandoned some notions of Victorian propriety, she cannot completely unlearn what she has learned. Therefore, even as she appears to lead a life in nature, she experiences mediation from such a life. The woodcutting scenes leave her feeling "acute regret" (265) because "she had estranged herself from them; craving, even to its defects and inconveniences, that homely sylvan life of her father" (265).

Frustrated in her efforts to be legally free of Fitzpiers, Grace must choose between abandoning convention to become the mistress of the man she loves or abandoning that man. Hardy's theological rhetoric appears again as Grace contemplates action; she wishes "to put off the old Eve" (315), a phrase that problematizes Hardy's discourse in that one must invert the traditional categories to which it refers. The allusion is clearly to a portion of the baptismal liturgy, which speaks of putting off the old Adam to put on Christ. In its original context, the old Adam refers to the sin-ridden man, the one doomed live in a physical body that must die and decay; the Christian alternative is Christ, who allows for the eternal life of the soul and an escape from the terrors of carnality. However, Hardy subverts the intention of the Christian reading in that in putting off the old Eve, Grace would abandon her cultural self, she who has been co-opted by the Christian patriarchy, to return to her Pagan, physical self, to enjoy illicit love in the flesh with Giles. However, Grace is not able to make the giant step necessary to flaunt Victorian convention. Instead, she attempts the middle ground, choosing the form of the unconventional (moving into Giles' cabin in the woods), while she coerces the man's removal to the woods, carefully misinterpreting all the signs of his ill health—"the heat of his palm, and its shakiness" (333)—in "romantic" terms, thinking, "He has been walking fast in order to get here quickly" (333). For Grace, having "risen above her raising," Giles alive can never completely be the object of her love. Although she never questions his goodness or his worth, she is continually, to her own frustration, offended by his crudeness, by the forms of his outward behavior. Even when she teases him into kissing her passionately, it is she who breaks away from the embrace and bursts into tears, seemingly concerned about whether it is permissible to love him. Her timing, however, suggests some resistance to his physical being, to the idea of being sexual with him (particularly since her embrace with Felice in the woods lasts much longer and is much more passionate). Only once Giles is dead, removed from the physicality that houses the crudeness, can Grace love him wholeheartedly. Dead, he is apotheosized as the nature god, the longed for but unapproachable object of desire. Even as he is near death, as Grace sets out through the dark woods for a doctor, she does not grieve or despair but rather finds that the "spirit of Winterborne seemed to keep her company and banish all sense of darkness from her mind" (342).

Once Giles, the tie to Little Hintock, is dead, Felice can also pass from the narrative, since Grace will now occupy her narrative space. Again Marty functions as the agent of the action, and again specifically the agent of death, since it is her letter to Fitzpiers that causes the lover's quarrel that leaves Felice alone to be preyed upon by her jealous ex-lover. Also, with Felice, who has functioned as the body of desire, erased, Grace begins to take on her own sexuality as well. She begins by informing Fitzpiers, quite proudly, that she and Giles were lovers, which forces him to acknowledge her as a sexual being, as a body capable of feeling desire as well as being desired. Marty, to enable Fitzpiers' return to his wife and the furtherance of her own desire to escape Little Hintock through Grace's body, tells him the truth, but Grace's words continue to indicate her claiming of her own sexuality. Fitzpiers understands that while the words are not literally true, they do speak the truth of Grace's desire, and it is that knowledge, more than Marty's truth-speaking, that rekindles his interest in his wife. Hardy writes, "It will probably not appear a surprising statement . . . that the man whom Grace's matrimonial fidelity could not keep faithful was stung into passionate throbs of interest concerning her by the avowal of the contrary" (359). What Fitzpiers responds to is Grace's newfound sense of her own sexuality, her being able to speak her desire.

For a short while after Giles' death, the characters of Marty and Grace, although existing narratively as separate characters (compared with the section of the novel in which only one of the characters appears but functions as both characters), live as friends sharing experiences, their focus continually on the grave of Giles Winterborne. While their seemingly stable existence as separate characters, not fusing into each other in the uncanny, would seem to indicate that some state of balance has been achieved, that the cultural, in the guise of Felice, has been banished, the emblem of what unites them—the grave—suggests the only place where such an equilibrium can occur. The character of Grace has joined Marty in the realm of the mythic, in time out of time, in a remove from history, in stasis. Their lives, were they to play them out, would have no story, no action. For that to occur, Grace, as the body on which desire is enacted, must reenter the narrative, history, by leaving with Fitzpiers. When he reenters the narrative to win back his wife, significantly, one of his best courtship strategies is to quote Shakespeare to her. The world beyond Little Hintock, the world of Grace's education, tugs at her again. Shortly after this scene, the narrative voice refers to Grace as "Mrs. Fitzpiers," her identity as the doctor's wife reestablished. Grace begins retreating from the woods into the house, spending more and more time reading, first literature, and then her prayerbook, specifically, the marriage service, which leaves her "appalled at her recent off-handedness" (380). Christianity becomes Grace's path away from nature, Giles, and the Pagan world he has represented. When Grace chooses to reunite with Fitzpiers, her father points out that she went out to gather parsley one evening and never returned. Her movement from the natural to the cultural is encapsulated in that evening's journey. Jean Brooks claims that the reunion of husband and wife represents the "gradual reassertion of life" and specifically speaks of Grace's sexual reawakening (232). I disagree; Grace may indeed be claiming her own sexuality, but she is doing so with a man who will ensconce her solidly within Victorian culture, which will at once co-opt and repress that sexuality. Furthermore, as Penny Boumelha points out, after Grace leaves Little Hintock, authorial consciousness shifts away from her (112). Such a shift occurs as well in *Tess of the D'Urbervilles* after Tess has gone to live with Alec in the fashionable boarding house. In that instance, the narrative distance removes the reader from the presence of the deity, but here, since Grace has never functioned as the Goddess, it simply alienates the reader from her—she is falling out of the world of Little Hintock into a historical world to which, given the parameters of the text, the reader has no access. However, the scenes of Tess' and Grace's alienation are different in one significant way. Both women are living in elegant hotels after their removal from the landscape. However, whereas Tess looks noticeably out of place in her sophisticated surroundings, Grace has come home. Hardy writes that she "appeared descending round the bend of the staircase, looking as if she lived there" (388). In the narrative rupture that removes the reader from Grace's consciousness, a fragmentation from self is suggested, but that remove, that disunity, is necessary if there is to be a story, a text. The prelapsarian unity that figures so nostalgically in Hardy's work does not allow for language, for text to emerge. For a speaking subject to occur, that unity must be ruptured.

The novel ends with Marty taking on Giles' role, traveling with his cider press, which suggests a possibility of renewal for her. However, her gaze remains focused on Giles' grave, and her final words indicate that she has achieved her desire: "Now, my own, own love . . . you are mine, and only mine" (393). Marty now possesses Giles in the only way she could ever possess him, since his desire is no longer able to constitute her being or shape her existence. As a fragmented self, she now shares his grave, permanently a part of the world out of time, while she has left that world through desire, in the body of Grace. However, Marty herself has moved very little throughout the course of the novel: the stasis that informs her has limited her movement from the coffin-stool by which she sits at the novel's beginning to the grave on which she stands at its end, in other words, she has proceeded from death to burial. Where Marty has arrived is the place outside desire (death), but that is in a sense where she began as well, since she never acknowledged her desire in the body. If Marty functions as a kind of harbinger of death in the novel (iconically tied to the coffin-stool, miraculously appearing at the time of Giles' death, etc.), it is because her inability to fuse desire and body can lead only to death.

What is suggested by Marty's fragmentation of self and the exorcising of her desire is significant in terms of Hardy's vision of an edenic world. The novel cannot envision any possibility of renewal for the world of Little Hintock. Tied as that agrarian world is to a mythic consciousness, to a unity that does not permit of speech or individual consciousness, movement itself is impossible, and death is where all texts that attempt to delineate such a world must begin and end. For there to be a narrative, Grace must abandon myth for history, must align herself, even though the alignment will be fraught with difficulties—with sexuality, with desire. She must be both subject and object, gazer and gazed upon, and she must exist in community, interrelating with others. While Hardy attempts to inform his works with a nature/culture duality, the duality cannot maintain itself because for language and text to exist, there is always culture already. The fragmented self is inevitable then; Marty's existence requires Grace's body. Neither woman is an integrated self. Any concept of Eden that culture is capable of representing will evolve out of culture's postlapsarian consciousness, and, as the myth suggests, a return to the garden—even through the agency of the imagination—is impossible. The angel with the two-edged sword, the blade of disruption, of fragmentation, will see to that.

While this novel, like many other Hardy novels, focuses on the situation of the women characters in the work, two male characters demand critical attention. In a pattern already familiar in Hardy's works, the narrative presents two suitors who here function as polar opposites of each other. Fitzpiers is textually constituted from the beginning as the "wrong" choice. Very rarely has Hardy so consistently portrayed a character as so unlikable. Even more unusual, Fitzpiers is one of very few despicable male characters in Hardy who is not tied to the church in some way. In Fitzpiers, Hardy has created yet another satanic figure (which of course places the character solidly within the Christian tradition), who in this case is less Mephistophelian than Faustian. Fitzpiers' acts—his medical experiments (arranging to purchase Grammer Oliver's brains, for example), his signalling with magic lanterns from his window at night—align him with the legendary figure who contracts with the devil to gain power. And Fitzpiers is revealed as having a kind of demonic power, which specifically manifests itself in his relationships with Grace and Felice. When Grace first meets Fitzpiers, even though the awkwardness of the scene prompts the young woman to return home quickly, she finds she is unable to "resist the supplicatory mandate written in the face and manner of this man" (160). She wishes to leave, "but the compelling power of Fitzpiers' atmosphere still [holds] her there" (162). Similarly, Felice feels that "her soul was being slowly invaded . . . that she was losing judgment and dignity" (262) after she gets involved with Fitzpiers. She tells Grace that she "*cannot* give him up until he chooses to give [her] up" (272). Her reason, on the most superficial level of the narrative, is that she and Fitzpiers have had sexual intercourse, but such reasoning indicates a hole in the seam of the narrative. Having sex with a man does not enslave a woman to him—unless the man possesses powers, as Fitzpiers does. His power reveals itself in other ways as well. He uncannily intuits that Grace has seen Suke leaving his home and constructs an elaborate lie about his morning's activity, which results in Grace's reinstating her engagement with him.

Fitzpiers in many ways fits Hardy's pattern of the suitor from the outside world who, as the bearer of culture, contributes to the destruction of the female protagonist. In many ways, he parallels Damon Wildeve and Alec D'Urberville, who function similarly in their interactions with Eustacia and Tess. Hardy reveals Fitzpiers to be descended from an old family, which distances him from the folk and establishes a hierarchical relationship with them. However, Fitzpiers does not live in his ancestral home, but rather rents a modern house, an apt symbol for his modern alienated state.[6] The appearance of his house, and specifically its gardens, which are completely regular and patterned, unlike flora in its natural state, also indicates his removal from the folk and from nature. His flirtation with philosophy aligns him with the cultural academic tradition and establishes the basis of the narrative disapproval of him. In his courtship of Grace, he is aware that "if any other young lady had appeared instead of the one who did appear, I should have felt just the same interest in her" (147), a sentiment that appalls Giles, who loves Grace and only Grace and therefore cannot consider substituting another woman in her place in his heart.

Fitzpiers' alienation from nature provides one of the novel's few glimmers of humor. Repeatedly, Fitzpiers' inability to handle horses is treated as comedy: he is uncomfortable riding, he falls off horses, he falls asleep on horses. But humor aside, Hardy's development of Fitzpiers' character emphasizes the implications of a life apart from nature and discloses the source of Fitzpiers' and, by extension, modern humankind's unhappiness. In speaking of a particularly wet and gloomy day, Hardy points out that the folk of Little Hintock, attuned to the natural, can find the seasonal variations, the subtle changes in weather, a source of fascination and wonder and, as a result, do not suffer from the worldweariness that plagues Fitzpiers. However, Hardy adds, "[T]hese were features of a world not familiar to Fitzpiers, and . . . he felt unutterably dreary" (155). As Jacobus points out, Fitzpiers' rootlessness is partly caused by the absence of memory ("Tree," 132). The separation from his own past alienates Fitzpiers from himself. In having removed himself from his ancestral lands and his family, Fitzpiers represents the modern man who exists as fragmented and fractured, not bound to the earth and ultimately not bound to any other person as well.

Fitzpiers' modern, cultural mind set further reveals itself in the doctor's obsession with social stratification. Initially very scornful of the idea of marrying and settling in Hintock, he experiences profound discomfort contemplating his future once he meets Grace. His early attraction to her stems in part from the haughtiness he senses in her—he is pleased to think that she may share his sense of social hierarchy. His embarrassment at what he perceives as marrying beneath him results in his demanding a small wedding, to avoid attention. He dares to tell Grace, "It will be far better if nobody there [Budmouth] knows much of where you come from, nor anything about your parents" (195). After he and his bride return from their honeymoon, he remarks proudly, "I feel as if I belonged to a different species from the people who are working in that yard" (209), and he virtually forbids Grace from interacting socially with those he considers inferior. However, for all the narrative disapproval of this man and his pretension, he is nonetheless acting in accord with the Victorian concept of class ranking and in a sense is simply the product of cultural conditioning.

Fitzpiers' fundamental lack of respect for women is also condoned—and even encouraged—by his society, although Hardy magnifies his misogyny so as to make him offensive to virtually all readers, regardless of sexual values and assumptions about gender. For example, once Fitzpiers learns that Grace's family is not as socially prominent as he had assumed, he would have "played with her as a toy" (154)—in other words, seduced and abandoned her—had he not been dependent upon the community for his medical practice. He willingly takes advantage of Suke's mistaking him for her fiance in order to have sex with her, and keeps her as his mistress even after he becomes engaged to Grace. Regarding the night of the midsummer revels, when the affair with Suke is initiated, Thurley claims that Fitzpiers is at this time more natural to the woods than Giles, since the former is sexually involved and the latter is not (113). Thurley overlooks the nature of

Fitzpiers' sexuality; it is predatory rather than celebratory, cultural rather than natural.

As Fitzpiers' wedding to Grace approaches, he "kept himself continually near her, dominating any rebellious impulse, and shaping her will into passive concurrence with all his desires" (200). From a patriarchal viewpoint, Fitzpiers' actions, particularly insofar as "training" his future wife is concerned, are not inappropriate; however, the obvious sense of superiority those actions indicate on his part, while sanctioned by Victorian society, render him contemptible within the world view of the novel. Grace's ultimate choice of him as a life partner, however, indicates her acceptance of the cultural suppression of the feminine and her own sense of her own inferiority.

Giles is, of course, Fitzpiers' polar opposite within the text; if there is a sacrificial victim in the work, it is not the expected female protagonist but rather Giles. Hardy refers to Giles as a "fruit-god" and a "wood-god" (305), presenting him as nature incarnate:

> He looked and smelt like Autumn's very brother, his face being sunburnt to wheat-colour, his eyes blue as corn-flowers, his sleeves and leggings dyed with fruit-stains, his hands clammy with the sweet juice of apples, his hat sprinkled with pips, and everywhere about him that atmosphere of cider which at its first return each season has such an indescribable fascination for those who have been born and bred among the orchards. (235)

As Thurley claims:

> The genius with the trees stands revealed for what he is—a satyr, a creature of ancient lineage, part of Nature, and in contact with deeper springs of knowledge than Grace's finishing school or Fitzpiers' demonic dabbling could claim awareness of. Giles is a pagan, a Dionysian worshipper of the earth and the seasons, associated profoundly with growth and fruitage. (119)

Giles' divinity reveals itself through his work as well: "He had a marvellous power of making trees grow. . . . [T]here was a sort of sympathy between himself and the fir, oak, or beech that he was operating on; so that the roots took hold of the soil in a few days" (93-94). His fingers "were endowed with a gentle conjuror's touch" (94). As Jean Brooks claims, "The deeper meaning that accumulates into myth and the factual, sensuous descriptions of Giles at his seasonal work are inseparable" (223-24). Even as he is dying, his spirit accompanies Grace in the woods and "banish[es] all sense of darkness from her mind" (342). After his death: "The whole wood seemed to be a house of death, pervaded by loss to its uttermost length and breadth. Winterborne was gone, and the copses seemed to show the want of him" (353). Grace, understanding to some degree what Giles represented, claims, "I almost worship him" (371), a statement borne out by her and Marty's ritualistic visits to his grave. Giles, as the nature god, is a fitting object of their devotion.

Giles is further differentiated from Fitzpiers in his attitudes toward both women and social class. Giles routinely does "women's work" in his own house, unlike Fitzpiers, who has a rural couple provide for his needs. Although Giles keeps what might nominally be called a "servant," Creedle and Giles share in their labors and are closely bonded; as Creedle's grief at Giles' death reveals, the two are virtually family. Grace's attraction to Felice and what the older woman represents distresses Giles because he understands that Grace's social pretensions will not allow her to be fulfilled or content as his wife—and her fulfillment and contentment matter to him, as they do not matter to Fitzpiers. Giles himself is unimpressed by class distinction. When, for example, Mr. Melbury frets that, upon returning from school, Grace will find her former home rustic and scorn her family and friends, Giles replies simply, "Not scorn us" (63). He is not ashamed of his position in society, and he will not let Grace create that shame in him. When, for example, she begins name-dropping authors with whom she is familiar, Giles, with no sense of embarrassment, chides, "Suppose you talk over my head a little longer, Miss Grace Melbury" (98). The threat to the social order implicit in Giles' obliviousness to social status becomes apparent in the scene in which he refuses to back up the lumber wagon, forcing Felice to make way for him. Uncowed as he is by her name and position, speaking a logic that cannot be gainsaid (his load was heavier than hers and would be far more difficult to back up), his revolution against what Felice represents must be undermined if hierarchy is to prevail. Hence Felice has his house torn down, effectively disabling any further rebellion.

Although religion plays a far less significant role in this novel than it does in many of the other works, Hardy makes a point of revealing Giles' disinterest in Christianity at the same time that he emphasizes Giles' goodness and spirituality. The text reveals that "he had never gone near a church latterly, and had been sometimes seen on Sundays with unblacked boots, lying on his elbow under a tree, with a cynical gaze" (202). He keeps a prayerbook mainly to whet his knife upon. However, Hardy affirms, "He was not an outwardly religious man; but he was pure and perfect in his heart" (350). These passages, along with the aforementioned references to Giles as a "wood-god" and a "fruit-god," suggest Giles' spirituality does not ground itself in Christianity but rather in Paganism.

Just as Tess and Eustacia are destroyed by their contact, specifically through their romantic/sexual relationships, with a way of life alien to their natures, so Giles is undone through his association with the Marty-Grace-Felice triad, through their drive for culture, their need for articulation, and their desire to escape the limitations of a pastoral world outside of history. While Giles himself is to some degree co-opted by the cultural world, he also cannot negotiate that world. His passivity in dealing with the life-leases, for example, could be read as a self-destructive impulse, but it also bespeaks his lack of comprehension of a world in which ownership of property is a viable option, in which forethought is required. As "Autumn's very brother," Giles is present only to the situation at hand, whether it be planting, felling, or pressing. When his work involves interaction with the natural cycle of the land, Giles is tremendously capable; it is only in the social sphere that he grows inept and bumbling, for example, when he attempts to host a Christmas party. The event he chooses to celebrate—the birth of Christ—is the same event that prefigures his own demise. The mythic world has collapsed into history, allowing no place for such a divinity as Giles. Some critics read Giles' death as a continuation of the cycle of nature. Jean Brooks claims, "Giles' gentle slide toward death mirrors the absorption of all human, animal and vegetable purposes into the whitey-brown of the earth" (228). While such a reading is recuperative, it does not address what is crucial here: the impact of Giles' death upon the community. Penny Boumelha points out how, by the end of the novel, the natural cycle is no longer operative, adding, "The community of *The Woodlanders* is not merely depleted by the loss of Giles, but radically devitalized" (101). Although the death of the vegetation god is an integral part of Pagan thought, that god is inevitably reborn with the new crops the following year. However, the community Hardy portrays possesses no vitalizing myth that allows Giles' death to be interpreted as a part of a continuing cycle. He will not be reborn with the spring; the natural cycle itself will of course continue, but human perception of the significance of its own relationship to that cycle is destroyed. Life becomes perceived as linear, death as finality; the myth of a prelapsarian unity with nature which allowed for a different perception has collapsed.

Essentially, of course, Hardy's fiction ends as it inevitably must, since the fall it replicates is a prior condition, having always already occurred. The community, by its definition, partakes of the cultural; any consciousness it possesses of an edenic state is a contaminated one, and no text, no language, can access a world of pure nature, untainted by culture, because such a world does not admit of the human. Once the human is achieved, the cultural exists. Hardy's fictions can only approximate a world untouched by those particular Victorian values that he disliked. One such Victorian value was the attitude toward human sexuality. In novel after novel, we encounter a narrative voice that associates the human processes of experiencing both love and desire, either together or separately, with the natural processes of plant and animal life. Such is the case here, where Grace and Giles' love for each other is sanctioned, even though Grace has contracted herself to another man. However, for all the narrative sanction of the naturalness of the human sexual drive, particularly in his women characters, Hardy is far more comfortable attaching that drive to the male characters he particularly wishes the reader to dislike than to his heroic male characters. Hence Wildeve, Troy, Alec D'Urberville, and here Fitzpiers, are sexually driven, admittedly in a predatory fashion, using sexuality as a way of gaining power over, rather than as giving pleasure to, another person. Giles, on the other hand, is not a strongly sexual character; Hardy speaks of his "freedom from the grosser passions, his scrupulous delicacy" (341). Therefore, the one quality of nature that guarantees the eternal return of life—the drive to the sexual—is sorely vitiated in the character who is otherwise nature's embodiment within the text. A case can be made that even Giles, hidden away in Little Hintock as he is, has been co-opted by Victorian values. When, for example, the possibility of Grace's obtaining a divorce arises, Giles is joyous, but his joy is tempered by a cultural sense of guilt. When Grace all but begs him to kiss her, he sees the act as "wrong," as "social sin" (318). That same social scrupulousness drives him out into the rain, and ultimately to his death, refusing even to enter the cabin once Grace has overcome her own sense of impropriety. Frank Giordano claims that "his fidelity to the social proprieties demonstrates . . . the perversion of natural sexual impulses by the artificial codes of courtship and marriage" ("Martyrdom," 77). However, at issue may be Hardy's own inability to perceive of a strong male sexual drive that is not exploitative or predatory.

The novel ends, as do most of the Wessex novels, with the triumph of a new perception and system of values and the demise of a mythic, Pagan sensibility and way of life. Giles, doomed to linearity, will not resurrect with the spring; Grace has ruptured the world of Little Hintock and escaped into a world that allows her a story, a history. Marty, fractured and dissociated, remains behind, weak, unattractive, childless, emotionally crippled, and grieving. Little Hintock is even grimmer at the end of the novel than it was at the beginning.

NOTES

1. Gregor speaks of the novel as a "story about a world already completed" (*Great Web*, 169).

2. The ghosts of the Two Brothers are referred to several times in the work, always very matter-of-factly.

3. Gregor suggests that the inability of the folk "to energize, or even engage, [Hardy's] imagination is symptomatic of the changes that have taken place in his fictional world" (165).

4. The Burning Times is the Wiccan name for what is otherwise known as the witch trials or the persecution of witches that occurred in Europe during the sixteenth and seventeenth centuries.

5. The term is another Wiccan one, addressing children conceived during the maypole revels on May-eve. Such children were regarded as sacred to the Goddess, and no shame came to the mothers who bore them. The same is true in earlier culture of the children born to the women who celebrated the Goddess in her temples in the act that contemporary culture calls ritual prostitution. Such children were called "Virgin-born" and were seen as children of the gods.

6. As I have already indicated, the folk of Little Hintock, who also live in rented houses, or houses that will be lost to them through the life-leases, are similarly fragmented.

5

Tess of the D'Urbervilles: And Nature Became Flesh, and Dwelt Among Us

For many readers, Hardy's crowning achievement is his creation of Tess Durbeyfield, who has become one of the most memorable women characters in all of literature. Something about her haunts the imagination; she is at once child and woman, strong and fragile, masterful and timid. In her, myth and history fuse. We are presented, on the one hand, with a very tangible English cottage girl and, on the other, with a goddess figure of immense stature. She exists in time while she remains timeless.

The novel itself is equally haunting and moving. Michael Millgate assesses it accurately when he says it "resonates with allusions to larger, more universal patterns which lie beyond its own world" (269). J. Hillis Miller is like-minded, claiming, "The idea of a present which is a repetition or reincarnation of the past recurs through the novel" (102). But while Miller interprets this repetition primarily on the personal level—as it is played out in the lives of Tess and her family, it also functions archetypically. Ultimately, the novel returns to the great myth which informs both *Far From the Madding Crowd* and *The Return of the Native*, the Ashtaroth-Yahweh struggle which for Hardy results in a world forever severed from primordial innocence, joy, and hope, a world blighted by consciousness.

Reading the character of Tess in mythic terms takes no great leap of the imagination. Even critics who do not deal primarily with the mythic implications of the novel will make claims such as Katharine Rogers does when she refers to Tess as the "least human" (250) of the Hardy women characters. From her introduction in the novel at the Pagan Mayday fertility ritual, where she is set apart from the other young women by her red hair ribbon, Tess functions as one differentiated and marked, as one whose experience and consciousness are essentially different from those of her would-be peers, as one whose life is fated to enact a story already narrated and concluded. Read mythically, she becomes emblematic of the Great Goddess, the informing spirit of a Pagan consciousness.

Hardy emphasizes her mythic (i.e., nonhistorical, nonhuman) nature by endowing Tess with qualities that culture, particularly Victorian culture, claimed were alien to a woman's nature. One such quality is her queenly pride, which reveals itself first at the very beginning of the novel, when she attacks her friends who ridicule her drunken father. After the unfortunate incident involving Prince, when Tess is coerced by her parents to "claim kin," it is her pride that causes her to hesitate. When, in her encounter with Alec, he insists she use the surname "Durbeyfield," rather than "D'Urberville," the name he has appropriated, Tess responds with dignity, "I wish for no better, sir" (67). Pregnant with his baby, she not only refuses to marry him but will not even inform him of her condition, even though he has assured her that he will provide for her financially in such circumstances. "Any woman would have done it but you" (110), says her mother, who apparently recognizes her daughter's extraordinary nature. Once Tess has borne the child, she goes to work in the fields "with dignity, and had looked people calmly in the face at times, even when holding the baby in her arms" (120). It is this same pride that serves to sever her from Angel Clare once he learns of Tess' involvement with Alec. When her young husband rejects her, the text emphasizes that had Tess "been artful, had she made a scene, fainted, wept hysterically, in that lonely lane, notwithstanding the fury of fastidiousness with which he was possessed, he would probably not have withstood her" (278). That Tess' pride—dignity, if we will—is often read as a flaw in her character, especially in this scene, reveals the double standard that characterizes a patriarchal culture. What is seen as unnatural, and therefore reprehensible, in Tess would be admired in a man; similarly, the behavior expected of Tess (fainting, weeping hysterically) would be considered irrational and weak in a man. The cultural construction of womanhood, which places limitations on women's behavior, is challenged by Hardy's characterization of this extraordinary woman.

In addition to her pride, Tess, like Bathsheba and Eustacia before her, possesses a strength—both physically and psychologically—that distinguishes her, especially in a culture that defined woman as essentially weak. Several times throughout the novel, Hardy portrays Tess' inner strength as compelling an otherwise uncaring person to respond to her strongly and sympathetically, even against his or her will. One such instance occurs after Tess has baptized her dying baby herself, taking onto herself the authority of the minister of God. Yet, when she informs the parson of what she has done, her strength of character impresses him so tremendously that he assures her *against his reason* that her action is acceptable. The narrative voice reveals satisfaction as it states, "The man and the ecclesiastic fought within him, and the victory fell to the man" (124). Similarly, Tess' physical presence is so strong that one glance at her completely unravels Alec. Even as he is preaching a sermon, he is so shaken by seeing Tess that he is stricken dumb until she averts her gaze from him, and, even then, he lapses into confusion and becomes incoherent. It is this same power, inexplicable and even terrifying, that leads Alec to insist that Tess swear never to tempt him. Finally, it is this power, a power not permitted women in history, that leads Tess to her mythic death, since it is what allows her to avenge herself in a very unambiguous way on Alec by killing him. History wins, in a sense; women with a power such as Tess' are denied presence in the world. Only myth can contain them.

A third quality denied women, specifically in Hardy's time, that Tess possesses, setting her apart from the historical, and therefore the human, is her sexuality. Repeatedly, Hardy describes Tess in sexual terms. We are told she reveals "a luxuriance of aspect, a fulness of growth" (66); that she has been "stirred" (110) by Alec; that the germination that occurs in the spring "moved her, as it moved the wild animals" (127). Textual evidence reveals that the Tess of the early versions of the novel was even more blatantly sexual than the final one; Hardy was forced to bowdlerize his manuscript to make it more acceptable to a Victorian public.[1] Critics have, of course, noted Tess' sexual nature. Dorothy Van Ghent, for example, sees Tess as doomed by a "violent potency, that of sexual instinct" (81). However, Van Ghent's rhetoric is problematic in that it implicitly suggests Tess is somehow at fault for her sexual instinct. I would suggest rather that Tess is doomed by a culture that cannot accept the sexual. Tess, as an incarnation of nature, must be sexual. Hardy recognizes that sexuality is not a minor aspect of, nor a perversion within, human nature; rather, it is the life-force, that which is crucial to the existence of human nature. For this reason, Hardy was very reluctant to compromise Tess' sexuality. The earlier versions of the text portray her sexual initiation unambiguously as a seduction, unlike the final version which has led some critics to believe Tess was raped. Laird shows how the passage about Tess' "sobbing" in the Chase does not occur until the 1892 edition of the novel. However, even as the novel now stands, what is described of the actual sexual act does not lend support to the idea of rape. That Tess' response may be somewhat unconscious, given that she is asleep when Alec accosts her, only serves to emphasize how deeply a part of her nature her sexuality is. Awake, the voices of her education would have prompted her to resist; asleep, it is her body that responds first, and responds willingly. Hardy's locating the scene in a "primeval" wood, in the absence of what he calls Tess' guardian angel, is not mere whimsy on his part. A guardian angel, a Christian concept, is inappropriate in a Pagan primeval wood, while the sexual act is not; nor is Tess' abundant sexuality out of place in such a setting. To emphasize that sexuality, Hardy indicates that the sexual encounter between Tess and Alec recurs.[2] A few weeks after the initial seduction, as Tess prepares to return home, Alec says, "You don't give me your mouth and kiss me back. You never willingly do that" (107). His use of the word "never" implies that he has more than two experiences to draw on, and that while she may not willingly give her mouth, she does willingly give the rest of herself to him. Hardy also insists on the purely sexual nature of Tess' relationship with Alec. Lest any reader think Tess has responded out of love and later grew to dislike Alec, he writes, "She had never wholly cared for him, she did not at all care for him now" (110).

Once settled at Talbothays Dairy, Tess again experiences a strong sexual attraction, this time for Angel Clare. Her passion is shared by the three women with whom she lives. Hardy writes, "The air of the sleeping-chamber seemed to palpitate with the hopeless passion of the girls. They writhed feverishly under the oppressiveness of an emotion thrust on them by cruel Nature's law" (174). These women, who as unschooled dairymaids function within the text as Hardy's representation of the human community in nature, apart from culture, all would readily engage in sex with Angel given the slightest opportunity; Hardy delicately writes that "Angel Clare had the honour of all the dairymaids in his keeping" (168). Their response to him is primal and natural, differentiated from a societally dictated rule which sets conditions upon sexual attraction. As Philip Weinstein points out, in the world Hardy portrays here, "Sexual identity appears . . . as an ultimate ground of amoral meaning, lying beneath the relative and collapsible ones of moral assertion (139). As Tess and Angel fall in love, Hardy's rhetoric associates their feeling for each other with the natural processes of the landscape and points to the inevitability of both: "Amid the oozing fatness and warm ferments of the Var Vale, at a season when the rush of juices could almost be heard below the hiss of fertilization, it was impossible that the most fanciful love should not grow passionate" (176). When, then, Angel first approaches Tess sexually, as she is milking the cow, she responds "with unreflecting inevitableness" (178) to his embrace. Her response does not grow out of cultural conditioning, but rather is the response of birds, of animals, of all of nature.

Once the two begin articulating their love for each other, Angel immediately begins to pressure Tess to marry him; however, the text reveals that Tess would prefer to be Angel's lover rather than his wife.[3] Given her understanding of and to some degree acceptance of Victorian social mores, part of her feeling may of course be attributed to the guilt she has been made to feel for her past actions. However, as Anne Mickelson points out, Tess "refuses to accept the loss of virginity as meaning she has no value" (75). Tess, because of her sexual nature, can see a sexual relationship, especially a loving sexual relationship, as an end in itself. She does not require a formal vow to endorse what she feels, nor does she view courtship as a prelude to another stage in her relationship with Angel. Her view is more radical than it initially may seem to be. It subverts the patriarchal assumption that women, and subsequently (and more importantly) their children, become the possession of men, and once that assumption (what some have called fictions of paternity) is shaken, the patriarchy is threatened.

Tess's response to her own sexuality is important; she does not see herself as a victim of her sexuality—does not, as Tony Tanner suggests, "all but helplessly [submit] to the momentums of nature in which, by her very constitution, she is necessarily involved" (224). To see Tess in such terms is to separate Tess from her sexual nature, but that cannot be done. Her sexual nature *is* her nature; it is not something that possesses her, some alien presence that determines her actions and denies her agency. Nor is it something she can, or would care to, relinquish. When, for example, Angel, distraught at her wedding night confession, begs her to tell him that her story about her past affair and the child she has borne is a lie, she refuses, even though Angel "would willingly have taken a lie from her lips, knowing it to be one, and have made of it, by some sort of sophistry, a valid denial" (263). Similarly, in the bitter days after the confession, Tess' only advance toward reconciliation is a sexual one: she tilts her head to receive Angel's kiss, a gesture he declines to act upon. Words, the medium of culture, are not a viable alternative for Tess; she can act only according to her nature, and for that she is rebuffed.

After Angel rejects her, her sexual drives lead Tess back to Alec. In writing to her husband, Tess says: "I am . . . worried, pressed to do what I will not do. It cannot be that I shall yield one inch, yet I am in terror as to what an accident might lead to, and I, so defenseless on account of my first error" (360). Later, after she is living with Alec, she tells Angel, "[Alec] has won me back to him" (401). Given that Tess never liked Alec's personality to begin with and that nothing in the text suggests her earlier opinion of him has changed, one must assume that Tess has been attracted back to Alec by his sexuality.

Tess' identification with nature in all its guises gives a new dimension to her affinity with the land and with animals. As he did in his portrayal of Eustacia in *The Return of the Native*, Hardy usually presents Tess in the out-of-doors; she is consistently so strongly identified with the earth that the atmosphere and the elements reflect her moods. When, for example, Tess sorrowfully reflects upon the "blighted star" she is living on, the wind sympathizes, becoming the "sigh of some immense sad soul" (56). In her first real encounter with Angel Clare, Tess becomes a piece of the "uncultivated" garden she is walking through, "gathering cuckoo-spittle on her skirts, cracking snails that were underfoot, staining her hands with thistle-milk and slug-slime, and rubbing off upon her naked arms sticky blights which, though snow-white on the apple-tree trunks made madder stains on her skin" (108). Later, when she begins to feel passionate for Angel, the days become sultry and hot, "an effort on the part of Nature to match the state of hearts at Talbothays Dairy" (176). After Angel rejects her, Tess' despair is echoed in the bleak landscape of Flintcomb Ash and in the atypically bitter winter that paralyses the area. The "correspondence of event and season" (80) that Miller sees as thematically important to the novel becomes apparent.

Tess' affinity with nature reveals itself in her knowledge of nature as well. Nature is not merely a setting for Tess; it is her work, her livelihood. Even as a fairly young girl, Tess is proficient at haymaking, harvesting, milking, and butter-milking. Throughout the novel, she is revealed as at home with the land and its animals, "physically and mentally suited" (156) for her tasks. Her attitude toward her work reveals itself best during the harvest, when she holds the sheaf of corn "in an embrace like that of a lover" (117). As the bearer of nature within the novel, she is, understandably, most fully realized when she is in a natural setting. She also takes comfort in the natural. It is the awareness that "the trees were just as green as before; the birds sang and the sun shone as clearly now as ever" (119) that rouses her to start a new life at Talbothays Dairy. The day she finally leaves her home for a new life, "the stir of germination was almost audible in the buds; it moved her, as it moved the wild animals, and made her passionate to go" (127). Her contention to Angel that she is never afraid outside is given credence when she spends an entire night in a pile of leaves after an encounter with some boorish men; in spite of weird noises and strange animals, Hardy tells us "she had no fear" (302). Finally, it is nature that continually reminds Tess that she has done nothing immoral, that the shame she sometimes feels is "based on nothing more tangible than a sense of condemnation under an arbitrary law of society which had no foundation in Nature" (303).

The role nature plays in *Tess of the D'Urbervilles* transcends Romantic concepts of the natural. In speaking of the novel's "thematic concept of Nature as norm," Laird suggests Hardy is reminding his readers "that natural phenomena were once objects of veneration" (90). Hardy does this by creating a world in which to some degree they still are. In this novel, he most clearly treats the worship of nature as a religion in its own right, claiming that "a saner religion had never prevailed under the sky" (115). The sane religion he affirms is Paganism and Tess functions as its deity, its goddess. However, Paganism, rooted as it is in nature, celebrates deity as both female and male, as goddess and god. While in this text no nature god of the Gabriel Oak mode appears, the male deity appears as the sun, which consistently figures in significant ways in Tess' life, recalling the brother-sister deities who become consorts in many non-Christian religions.[4] The sun cheers a disheartened Tess on her first morning at Tantridge, and she celebrates the sun's presence (albeit using the words of a Christian psalter) as she strikes out for a new life at Talbothays Dairy. When she sacrifices herself at Stonehenge, she is awakened by a ray of the rising sun, a consummation that results in her self-sacrifice. That Tess' actual death occurs on a July morning may not be accidental. The Pagan celebration of Lughnasa, a harvest festival in which the cutting of the grain is referred to metaphorically as the sacrifice of the Corn King, occurs in late July or early August. The cyclical nature of life is affirmed in the ritual through the seeds retained for next year's planting; it is understood that while the god has died (even as the sun begins waning, moving toward the dark of the year), the goddess (the earth) is pregnant with his son. Read in the context of this myth, Tess' death becomes terrifying, since she who is the bearer of life, the keeper of the seed, the goddess, herself is lost to the world and with her goes the possibility of renewal. G. Glen Wickens, in his reading of Tess in terms of the Demeter-Persephone myth, claims, "When Tess is hanged at Wintoncester, there are no pagan or Christian gods left to witness her death" (104). The sun does witness her death, but the consummation at Stonehenge that would have allowed for the birth of the new sun/son with the new crop is rendered ineffectual through the loss of Tess. With the death of the nature goddess, the sun is no longer a deity but simply a mass of burning gases.

The brilliance of Hardy's novel lies in the double articulation of Tess as both worshiper of nature and nature goddess. Her name, a form of Theresa, which, Marken writes, is Greek for "to glean" or "to reap" (320), emphasizes her dual role within the novel. On the one hand, she is Tess the dairymaid, who through her tasks—milking the cows and harvesting the corn—functions as nature's loving worshiper. On the other hand, she is the goddess who sacrifices herself, the wheat which is gleaned. Angel becomes aware of her divine nature in their early mornings together at the dairy. In the time of transition from night to day, a liminal time that, as such, is mythically and mystically charged, Tess exhibits "a dignified largeness both of disposition and physique, an almost regnant power" (157). Hardy goes on to add, "Then it would grow lighter, and her features would become simply feminine; they had changed from those of a divinity who could confer bliss to those of a being who craved it" (158). It is her presence that makes the dairy a paradise for Angel and for the reader as well. Hardy keeps the narrative focus on Tess, making the other characters circle around her. It is her beauty that beautifies the dairy, her life that animates it, her spirit that infuses it. After the wedding, when Tess and Angel return to Talbothays, "the gold of the summer picture was . . . grey, the colours mean, the rich soil mud, and the river cold" (271). When Tess despairs, the landscape echoes her despair; just as Ceres' grief for her daughter in the underworld turns the world cold and bleak, so Tess' grief at Angel's desertion unleashes a wild and terrible winter on the land. But for all her despair, Tess does not consider leaving the land, even though the narrative reveals that, with her "intelligence, energy, health, and willingness in any sphere of life" (299), she would readily have found employment in a city. However, given the narrative fusion of Tess with the landscape, neither she nor the reader can conceive of such a move. The story of Tess takes place out of time and out of history—there are no cities to turn to within the mythic framework of the novel. When Tess finally does leave the land, mythic time and space are destroyed and the fall into history occurs.

Hardy is not subtle in his treatment of Tess' bond with a Pagan past. He might even be accused of excess in revealing her to be descended from Sir *Pagan* D'Urberville. Tess herself is introduced in the novel at a May Dance, a fertility ritual, as Van Ghent points out (80), carrying a peeled willow wand, a symbol of fertility, according to Langdon Elsbree (609). It is the women, the narrative stresses, who keep the Pagan customs such as the May-walking alive; all the men's clubs have abandoned the practice. The specific link between women and Paganism is established early in the text. As Tess sings a hymn to creation, Hardy points out that, although the words are Christian, the spirit behind them is far older, emphasizing that women, particularly those women who routinely work out-of-doors in nature, have not lapsed from the Pagan ways typical of humankind in an earlier period. Women, the text suggests, have more to gain in retaining their Pagan heritage since it empowers them and allows for the articulation of their sexuality, which Christianity adamantly strives to co-opt and repress. In its emphasis on virginity and chastity (certainly central themes of Hardy's novel), Christianity attempts to control the sexual behavior of women and to divide women against themselves. The narrative voice here consistently positions itself against the Christian values, reading women's sexuality from a Pagan perspective. As Weinstein points out in a discussion of the passage in which flies become trapped in the gauze skirts of the church-bound dairymaids, "A writer who can see these flies—and elsewhere it is pollen, peat, lichen, algae, scrub plants, caterpillars, and moths—is not likely to take virginity of any sort seriously" (119). Hence Joan Durbeyfield consistently advises her daughter to be circumspect in what details of her past she reveals to her intended husband. Joan, a wise woman of the folk, refuses to put men on any sort of pedestal; rather, she accepts a natural "conspiracy" among wise women, understanding that men have no right to make claims on women's sexual behavior. Joan understands that men accept the new patriarchal system because of the power they gain by it, but that women must subvert it if they are to claim their own empowerment. And for Joan, that empowerment involves the very natural act of sex. She sees Tess' affair with Alec as a natural, almost inevitable, act and never upbraids her daughter for bearing his child. Interestingly, some critics, such as Laird, consider her "amoral" (145), presumably because her system of morality is grounded in an older, naturalistic, specifically Pagan world view, which threatens the patriarchy by refusing to give assent to it.

Throughout the novel, Hardy aligns Paganism with matriarchy by emphasizing Tess' bond with Joan. Jack Durbeyfield, like most fathers in Hardy, is not only ineffectual but never functions as any sort of an authority figure to Tess.[5] Even in begetting Tess, his influence is limited. Although Tess bears the D'Urberville likeness, it is from Joan that she inherits her prettiness. It is also from Joan, her conjuring mother who keeps her copy of the *Compleat Fortune-Teller* in the outhouse because she so strongly believes in its power, that Tess inherits her link with Pagan ways. Significantly, Joan's family derived from the area near Stonehenge, where Tess returns to end her mythic journey. However, Hardy portrays Tess' earthly home in Marlott as sharing in Stonehenge's mythic time and space as well, particularly in that the people who live there cling to their beliefs in the witches and fairies that once haunted the locale.

Tess' matriarchal bond reveals itself most clearly when, anguishing over whether she should marry Angel, she seeks out her mother as "the only person in the world who had any shadow of right to control her action" (220–21). From a patriarchal perspective, that right belongs first to her father and second to her affianced lover, but Tess allows neither man a claim over her actions. But Tess' mother is not the only mother figure in the text. When her own mother cannot physically be with her, Tess finds a spiritual mother in the old woman who serves her tea after her unsuccessful journey to find Angel's parents. Not accidentally, the old woman is the only villager Tess encounters; all the rest have gone to hear the now-Christian Alec preach. The woman's appearance in the deserted village at a time when Tess has just abandoned her search for Christian parents lends a fairy-tale quality to the incident; that a fairy godmother magically appear at the moment of Tess' need suggests the power of the matriarchal bond.

While Hardy cannot construct Tess as a full-blown Pagan character, he does his best to distance her from Christianity. When she encounters the fanatical sign painter who, for all his "cut and paste" theology, does paint biblical passages on any available space, she exclaims, "Pooh—I don't believe God said such things!" (109). Her incredulity reveals both her unfamiliarity with scripture as well as her sense that Christian theology is flawed. That she does not go to church often is clear. When her baby dies, she cannot seek out the parish parson, having never met him and not knowing his name. At Talbothays, when she does go, the text indicates that she is motivated more by the opportunity to wear her black shoes, white stockings, and prettiest dress than to participate in worship; when Angel asks her opinion of the parish clergyman, she admits her inability to understand his message. Finally, in murdering Alec, an act which to Angel suggests a lack of "moral sense" (408), Tess reveals a moral sense at odds with Christianity, one older, more primitive, more Pagan. Marie Louise von Franz speaks of a "feminine justice" that exists in antithesis to the male law upon which contemporary society's moral code is founded. She identifies this "feminine justice" with "revenge and punishment" and ultimately labels it "the revengefulness of nature" (33). Since Tess here functions as the embodiment of nature, her revenge upon Alec is a literal enactment of this "revengefulness of nature."

Tess' life and death can be read as a Pagan inversion of the life and death of Christ. Hardy has deliberately drawn parallels between the two, beginning with the cock's crowing on the day of her marriage. By joining herself with Angel, Tess is betraying her essence, is compromising herself to culture. Later that day, when Angel and Tess wash their hands in the same basin, Pontius Pilate's handwashing comes to mind. Tess, in response to Angel's query, "Which are my fingers and which are yours?" claims, "They are all yours" (245), renouncing her right to self and to her own sexuality, making it easy for Angel to feel absolved of any guilt for the destruction he wreaks upon her. Later, Hardy interjects more echoes of Christ's life when Tess, Joan, and the Durbeyfield children can find no room in the inn when they travel to their spiritual homeland. Like Christ, Tess has her night of agony and her descent into the hell of life with Alec in a fashionable boarding house, completely removed from the natural world, which is her essence. Significantly, after this point, Tess no longer functions as the focalizer for the scenes, and the narrator voice no longer accesses her thoughts and emotions; as a result, the reader is distanced from Tess. The deity has withdrawn itself, and the human is no longer privy to her thoughts and feelings. The sacred has retreated, has become the stuff of legend, of the "word," but is no longer immediately available. Finally, like Christ, Tess endures a sacrificial death; this "sun-goddess incarnate"(152), as Kozicki calls her, is captured at Stonehenge, a Pagan site which, significantly, feels familiar to her. She is sleeping on an altar when the authorities come for her. "It is as it should be" (418), she says, recognizing that she is "playing the role of pagan, sacrificial victim-hero (Kozicki, 151), dying for the sins that have been committed against nature. But through the narrative distance, and through the diminishment revealed by the narrative after Tess' death, the reader understands that this ritual will not be repeated. As was the case with the deaths of Eustacia and Giles in the earlier novels, with Tess' death the cycle of nature is ruptured and flattens into a linear telos. The old Pagan world view has been defeated by a new Christian way of perceiving.

In Tess' life, that defeat results from the combination of her relationships with two men belonging to the new order: Alec the rake and Angel the saint. Guerard speaks of Tess' destruction as occurring first because of Alec's relentlessly seeking his own pleasure but then also because of Angel's "prudery" (80). From a feminist perspective, what is significant is Hardy's continual development of parallels which indicate how, as Mickelson puts it, Angel and Alec "are one and the same man. Their concept of woman reflects society's view of her and the myths constructed about women" (118). That society, it is necessary to remember, is informed by Christianity and characterized by patriarchy.

Alec, Tess' first lover, is frequently regarded as another of Hardy's Satan figures. The text frequently portrays him surrounded by smoke from his cigar; at night, the cigar's glowing tip is often the first sign of his presence. Allen Brick points out the satanic allusions involved in Alec's feeding strawberries to the innocent Tess (118). However, what is significant in Hardy's portrayal of Alec is the fact that this Satan repents to become, temporarily, an evangelical preacher, an incident of plot that Laird, for one, cannot accept, claiming, "the motivation for Alec's unexpected reappearance in the story as an evangelical preacher is inadequate" (140). In considering the entire structure of the novel, however, Alec's conversion functions to establish a parallel between Alec and Angel, who does a similar about-face. At the beginning of the novel, in spite of his protestations to the contrary, Angel is a product of the church. Even as he informs his father of his decision not to become a minister, he admits to loving the church "as one loves a parent" (143). In his courtship of Tess, he continually alludes to the Bible, referring to Tess as Eve or as Rachel. Even then, however, this "angel" is possessed of evil. Van Ghent speaks of him as "diabolic . . . in his prudery" (49), and Guerard claims he "contaminates the green innocence of Talbothays" (22). After Angel's marriage and wedding night disillusionment, though, Angel becomes the character in the text who is rhetorically identified with Satan. For example, his laugh is "as unnatural and ghastly as a laugh in hell" (255), and his form appears "black, sinister, and forbidding" (257), paralleling Alec's later description as a "man in black" (338). Hardy further identifies Angel with Satan, specifically with Milton's Satan, by depicting him "fiendishly" whispering heterodox ideas to the eminently righteous Mercy Chant, as well as by having him proposition Tess' friend Izz, an incident that Laird reports as occurring only in later versions of the text (151), suggesting Hardy's deliberate attempt to emphasize both Angel's conversion and the identification of the two lovers. From Tess' perspective, both men are equally destructive; from a Pagan world view, Christian saint and Christian devil are products of the same system of thought, one that is antithetical to all that Tess is—female, Pagan, and identified with nature.

Alec and Angel (one suspects Hardy chose the names of these characters to call attention to their similarities) are alike in other ways as well. Both accept in its totality the patriarchal dictum that women are somehow at fault, tainted, for being sexual beings. After his miraculous conversion, Alec calls Tess a temptress and a witch, forgetting how he all but coerced her into their sexual encounter. His rhetoric is significant here, since the Christian notion of witches is inextricably woven into the concept of sexuality. Barbara Ehrenreich and Deirdre English claim, "In the eyes of the Church, all the witches' power was ultimately derived from her [sic] sexuality" (11). They go on to point out how in the eyes of the Christian church, witches were all identified as women, since "The Church associated women with sex, and all pleasure in sex was condemned, because it could only come from the devil. . . . Lust in either man or wife, then, was blamed on the female" (11). The seemingly diabolical Alec echoes mainstream Christian rhetoric in his accusations against Tess, displacing his desire onto her. Angel thinks along similar lines. He is all too ready to overlook his own sexual activities while he damns Tess for hers.

Both men function within the novel as heralds of the future while Tess is a vestige of the past. Hardy's description of Alec when he arrives to take Tess to her ancestral home is almost comically inappropriate in that it is such a caricature of the modern man-about-town; Hardy presents a man "of three-or-four-and-twenty, with a cigar between his teeth; wearing a dandy cap, drab jacket, breeches of the same hue, white neckcloth, stick-up collar, and brown driving gloves" (76). Everything about him bespeaks the new; even his lack of a true family history suggests that he is not rooted in the past. Angel's modernism is more philosophical than sartorial. Like Clym Yeobright, Angel anticipates a time when education will have solved the world's problems. He has accepted his culture's faith in progress, along with the assumption that the old ways are benighted and ineffectual.

Angel and Alec further share the assumption that they are entitled to the power to determine Tess' actions and being; neither man seeks her out as a loving, equal partner. Alec reveals his feelings of superiority initially on the ride in the Chase, when he exclaims, "[W]hat am I, to be repulsed so by a mere chit like you?" (98). Clearly he assumes a cultural right, by virtue of class and gender, to possess Tess' body. Later, after he has proposed to Tess, he reveals his motive to be not love but a desire for power when he states: "I was your master once! I will be your master again" (355). Angel's desire for mastery has less to do with Tess' body, but it nevertheless parallels Alec's attitude. Even before she has agreed to marry him, he is already presuming to order her to change her last name to D'Urberville. Once she agrees to the match, he tells her he will carry her off "as [his] property" (239); his language reveals his sense of the power dynamics at work in their relationship. Even after what may be seen as his night journey in the wilds of South America, what ultimately brings him back to Tess is the memory of her obedience and docility—how she "had hung upon his words as if they were a god's" (364). A product of Victorian culture, Angel cannot conceive of a relationship of equality with a woman; in his mind, his gender determines his superiority.

Hardy fuses Angel and Alec yet again when he rhetorically identifies them as figures of death insofar as Tess is concerned. Early on, Tess views Alec as "dust and ashes" (110), death images which are later echoed when he rises from a tomb in the dark cathedral. Similarly, Angel's affection causes Tess to flinch "like a plant in too burning a sun" (199); instead of jumping off a sarcophagus, he places Tess on one as he sleepwalks, dreaming she is dead. When he returns from South America, he looks like a skeleton, a figure of death, as he seeks out Tess. Together, both men do of course bring Tess to her death. Neither by himself possesses the power, but at the point where the two intersect, where both make claims upon her at once, the power of the patriarchy becomes greater than Tess' power, and she is destroyed.

Angel remains, however, a far more complex character than the almost stereotypically villainous Alec; his problems are more far-reaching. Like Clym

Yeobright before him, Angel is almost completely devoid of sexuality. Early in the novel, the dairymaids tell Tess that he is "too much taken up wi' his own thoughts to notice girls" (141), hardly a typical—or natural—state for a healthy young man. Later we see his obsession with purity, far beyond what even his religion demands. When his father reads aloud from Proverbs on the qualities of a good wife, even that biblical text makes no mention of sexual innocence. The narrative suggests that Angel's sexual problems, while they may cohere in his religious training, do not stem simply from the Christian church's teachings. Hardy claims, "Some might risk the odd paradox that with more animalism he would have been the nobler man" (269), a line that Laird points out Hardy added in later editions of the text, obviously to emphasize Angel's neuroticism. Jean Brooks accurately speaks of Angel's "repressed sexual guilt and fear of the powers of life" (248), qualities that become evident initially when, unlike Tess, Angel cannot view their lovemaking as an end in itself, but rather only as a prelude to marriage. He lacks what Hardy calls a "healthy thought of a passion as an end" (203); for Angel, passion results in distress rather than in pleasure, a distress that can only be alleviated by channeling the passion into prescribed forms, such as marriage. However, the thought of marriage triggers anxiety in Angel as well, since the ritual will coerce sexual activity. Hence, when Tess and Angel announce their plans to marry, Angel will allow for no celebration to mark the event. Repeatedly in Hardy's novels, the inability to celebrate a wedding joyously indicates an unhealthy attitude toward sexuality. Angel's sexual dis-ease informs his bringing the giant bough of mistletoe (significantly, a Pagan symbol) to their bridal chamber. Like Sue Bridehead with her Pagan statues, which initially attract but then intimidate her, Angel presumes he desires a sexual relationship with Tess, but after confronting her sexuality, he is terrified and repulsed. That Hardy intended to emphasize Angel's vitiated sexuality becomes clear from the development of the character through the different versions of the text. Laird shows how Angel is construed as less and less physical, less and less sensual, in each succeeding edition of the novel (136). Penny Boumelha argues convincingly that Angel and Liza-Lu appear diminished at the end of the book because of their "expulsion from sexuality, and not by the loss of a pre-sexual innocence" (126). Angel never fully accepts his own sexuality, his physicality, even after his night journey in the "underworld." It remains a threatening force, something alien, that he attempts to control, causing him to become what Hardy calls a "slave to custom and conventionality" (290).

Angel's problem stems in part from his excessive reliance on his intellect and consequently his obliviousness to his instincts. In Jungian terms, an undeveloped anima prohibits his functioning as a healthy whole. In the Hardy canon, characters who respond intellectually rather than intuitively almost always are presented as problematic characters, both in terms of their own neuroses and for their destructiveness to others; such is clearly the case with Angel. Hardy emphasizes Angel's one-sided nature throughout the novel; for example, the text reveals that, like Sue Bridehead, Angel looks to Greece, to the seat of Western *thought*, as the ideal civilization. When Tess is first becoming acquainted with Angel, she regards him "as an intelligence rather than as a man" (153). Hardy's language is significant; Angel is all intelligence. He has suppressed his intuition to the point of rendering it dysfunctional, as is repeatedly revealed during his courtship of Tess, when her extreme agitation and distress at his frequent proposals of marriage, even as she continually avows her love for him, go unnoticed by him. Therefore, when he cannot deal with Tess' confession, the text claims that he "was becoming ill with thinking, eaten out with thinking, withered by thinking" (268). Hardy's recurring fascination with the decayed condition he believes characterizes modern man is apparent here, as well as its cause. Had Angel been capable of responding intuitively to Tess, as he does in his sleep, when he reveals his love for her, the couple could have been spared their agony. However, Angel does not merely ignore his intuition; he is hostile to it. Tess never reveals to Angel what he has done in his sleep, aware that "it would anger him, grieve him, stultify him, to know that he had instinctively manifested a fondness of her of which his common-sense did not approve; that his inclination had compromised his dignity when *reason slept*" (276; emphasis mine). Similarly, he chides himself for having married Tess in spite of her noble lineage rather than having "stoically abandoned her, in fidelity to his principles" (285). Angel, the product of his patriarchal society, suppresses all that is female, even the female within (the anima). On the mythic level, he represents Logos, the Word, the embodiment of the intellect, removed as far as is possible from the physical and the sensual.

Angel's link with the cultural is evident in his classism as well. Although he lives among the folk and intends to undertake farming as a profession, he is set apart from the rest of the Talbothays folk both literally, in that he has his own quarters and his own table in the dining room, and figuratively, in that he will be a gentleman-farmer, an overseer. For all his amiability, he believes himself essentially superior to the folk, not only in outward trappings (money and social position, which are obvious), but in substance as well. When he falls in love with Tess, he not only wants to elevate her to his social position, but he also insists on her inherent difference from the other dairymaids, claiming, "Our tremulous lives are so different from theirs" (211). He intends to delay Tess' introduction to his parents until he is able to educate her in what is culturally acceptable, particularly insofar as speech and manners are concerned, because the Tess he has fallen in love with will prove an embarrassment to him otherwise. When he lashes out at her in anger after her confession, he imagines his greatest insult to be his labeling her an "unapprehending peasant woman, who [has] never been initiated into the proportions of social things" (258). Clearly, Angel does not truly question, but only endorses, his culture's assumption of the superiority of class, never recognizing the arbitrary nature of that hierarchy.

The root of Angel's damaged psyche lies in his separation from nature. Superficially, Angel has rejected the values of culture—and of his parents—in his attempt to discover/recover the natural. Once removed from society and living at the dairy, he abandons his stereotypical assessment of the dairy folk as lacking in dignity, coming to truly enjoy his interactions with them. At this point, he "became wonderfully free from the chronic melancholy which is taking hold of the civilized races with the decline of belief in a beneficent Power" (146). At the dairy, Angel begins discovering a new deity, one worshiped by the "uncivilized" races, and consequently begins to shed his modern angst. He surprises himself by seeing "something new in life and humanity" (146), at the same time that he makes "close acquaintance with the phenomena which he had before known but darkly—the seasons in their moods, morning and evening, night and noon, winds in their different tempers, trees, waters, and mists, shades and silence, and the voices of inanimate things" (146). The simultaneity of Angel's new vision of humanity and his familiarity with nature is not accidental. The novels as a whole emphasize Hardy's belief that familiarity with nature is necessary for balance, wholeness, and joy in life. Without it, these works suggest, one's view grows skewed, allowing for the malaise that Hardy characterizes as endemic to modern civilization.

Once Angel achieves comfort in his life at the dairy and begins to experience nature directly, he finds it difficult to return to his parents' home, which feels "distinctly foreign" to him. Hardy writes that Angel's parents' Christian beliefs, particularly regarding heaven and hell, "were as foreign to his own as if they had been the dreams of people on another planet" (187); Angel has been changed because he has "seen only Life, felt only the great passionate pulse of existence, unwarped, uncontorted, untrammeled by those creeds which futilely attempt to check what wisdom would be content to regulate" (187). Here, Hardy focuses the nature/culture opposition that informs the novel specifically on the tension between Paganism and Christianity. Like Angel, Hardy apparently believes that orthodox beliefs are "[unreal] amid beliefs essentially naturalistic" (193). Hardy's metaphor in describing Angel's return to the dairy from his parents' home is telling; coming back to Talbothays is "like throwing off splints and bandages" (197). Only by returning to the natural—and therefore to the Pagan—can psychological and spiritual healing mend the bruises and wounds inflicted by culture, and specifically by Christianity. Therefore, later, after Angel experiences despair at Tess' confession, it becomes necessary for him to travel still further away from what the text encodes as culture—to South America, where he begins to come to terms with the arbitrariness of his culture's values.

As James Hazen points out, when Angel comes to Talbothays, "he enters a new moral world" (788), one that he finds very attractive. Nevertheless, Angel cannot embrace the new system entirely, because his ties with Victorian culture, with its repressive attitudes toward human sexuality, cause him to resist what nature would teach about sexuality. So, for example, Angel tells his mother he desires a wife who is as "pure and virtuous" as Mercy Chant, but who also "understands the duties of farm life" (192), never comprehending the mutual exclusivity of the categories he defines. The sort of purity and virtue Angel values in Mercy, that is, sexual purity, virginity, is achieved only as a result of cultural indoctrination. Since virginity serves no function in the natural world, it is not valued by the Pagan community in the way, for example, that fertility, that which enables the planet to flourish, is revered. Angel claims to want a "mate from unconstrained Nature" (202) and in fact marries such a woman, without grasping the significance of his words. Unconstrained nature is first and foremost sexual in the most primal way possible. Tess, as nature's embodiment, is equally sexual, but Angel fears and is repulsed by sexuality. While he believes he seeks out the natural, in actuality he would limit and constrain nature. How little his sojourn at Talbothays Dairy has taught him becomes clear when, after Tess' confession, Angel imagines he sees a "seal of maidenhood" (263) on Tess. To imagine that a virgin would physically look different from a woman who has experienced sexual intercourse is utter nonsense, but precisely the sort of nonsense that a culture that both fears sexuality and oppresses women perpetrates. Similarly, Angel accepts the cultural notion that because Alec has been Tess' first lover, he is her "husband in Nature"(268). Had Angel truly had his eyes open at the dairy, he would have seen that in nature there are no "husbands," only mates. For all his months at the dairy, Angel remains estranged from nature, unable to comprehend it, never losing his affinity with the cultural half of Hardy's equation.[6]

Unable to deal with sexuality, the rest of what he has learned at the dairy unravels; Angel essentially becomes a Christ figure and as such Tess' mythic antagonist. Even at the dairy, that role is hinted at; he plays a harp, as popular consciousness suggests all angels do, and he lives in a loft—on high. Tess also lives in a loft, suggesting her divinity as well, and setting up the archetypal conflict in which the two deities must engage. The first time Angel leaves the dairy, it is to return to his father who is, significantly, a minister, a man of God, and here, in mythic terms, God the Father himself. The bond between father and son is emphasized in the text, which states that "Angel often felt that he was nearer to his father . . . than was either of his brethren" (196). Returning to the dairy, Angel moves from the spiritual realm to the physical; significantly, he must *descend* topographically to do so; once he arrives on the physical plane, he enters a sensory world of "the languid perfume of the summer fruits, the mists, the hay, the flowers" (196). Angel's association with Christ is suggested again in a conversation with Tess after her murder of Alec. When Tess questions whether the lovers will be reunited after death, Hardy writes, "Like a greater than himself, to the critical question at the critical time he did not answer" (417). At the end of the novel, Angel is alive, the values he represents permanently established in the world, while Tess, in being destroyed by society's mandate, takes from the world a sense of the physicality and sexuality essential to a unified concept of nature. Angel walks off with Liza-Lu, the spiritualized Tess, the Tess minus sexuality. His final act is to pray with his new mate, a gesture that Daniel Schwarz sees as indicating a "need to embrace the kind of formalism that sentences Tess to death" (31). Angel embraces that formalism because archetypically he is its essence. Tess' death establishes the dominance of Christianity in Wessex and marks the death of Paganism and, with it, the end of humankind's understanding of its own interconnectedness with nature.

The vestiges of Paganism evident in the book exist precisely because the folk have lived their lives bonded with nature. In speaking of the folk, Van Ghent writes, "[They] are the earth's pseudopodia, another fauna; and because they are so deeply rooted in the elemental life of the earth—like a sensitive animal extension of the earth itself—they share the authority of the natural" (86). This link with the natural is repeatedly evident in their response to the world around them. At Talbothays, for example, when the butter will not come during the churning, the obvious solution is to seek out a conjurer. As Charlotte Bonica concisely explains, "At the heart of the country people's paganism is the tendency to see congruence between events and situations in their own lives, and phenomena in the natural world" (851). As a result of seeing such connections, the folk evolve a set of values based on the processes that occur in the natural world, values that to Victorian, patriarchal consciousness, removed as it is from such connectedness, look immoral. This contrast in values is most clearly evident in the response of the folk to Tess' status as an unmarried mother. Although Tess herself feels she is the object of shame, the folk are neither scandalized nor outraged at Tess—they pity her because they understand that her life will be more difficult because of the child, but they assume Tess' actions in conceiving the child are natural and understandable. Of Tess' despair, one calmly retorts, "'[T]is wonderful what a body can get used to o' that sort in time!" (118), not condemning but realistically aware that Tess will love and cherish her child whether or not she has married its father. Similarly, when Angel asks Izz to go to Brazil with him, he points out that her act will condemn her in the eyes of society. Izz's response, "I don't mind that; no woman do when it comes to agony-point" (294), reveals not, as some would claim, a lapse of moral values, but simply *different* values. For Izz, as for many of the folk, love does not require sanctification by marriage, and a couple may choose to be lovers regardless of what society may say. Significantly, though, Izz's rhetoric reveals her understanding that women in particular deny patriarchal notions of morality. The women of the folk, through their daily interactions with the natural world, would understand not only that such a system of morality is unfounded in nature but also that women suffer more from it than men do. Again, women in Wessex preserve the link with the Pagan past because Paganism empowers them.

But the folk cannot withstand the effects of contact with the historical world beyond their mythic realm, and as a result the Pagan past is dying. As Bonica explains, "[B]ecause [the folk's] culture is circumscribed by the encroachment of civilization, their paganism is powerless" (851). Within the novel, two systems of values, two different worlds, are portrayed, and as Andrew Enstice explains, "The damage is done when the different worlds are unthinkingly mixed" (*Landscapes*, 144). However, Hardy creates a fictional world that cannot stay uncontaminated by culture. Even though Marlott appears set apart, existing out of time in its Paganism, separated by a ridge from the historical world, where, for example, May-walking no longer occurs, vestiges of the new—and of the Christian—have penetrated the geographical barrier as well as the psychological one. The world of pure nature cannot exist; it is always already constituted by culture, as is evident in the very first scene in the novel, when Parson Tringham, another of Hardy's destructive Christian clergymen, broaches the issue of John Durbeyfield's lineage. Significantly, Tringham is a late addition to the text; in earlier versions of the work, Tess already knows of her ancestry (Jacobus, "Tess," 81). Hardy's emendation of the text serves to implicate Christianity for the destruction that ensues. Furthermore, as Enstice points out, the attitude that privileges some family backgrounds over others inheres in the imported new culture (*Landscapes*, 144), the patriarchy. The presence of Christian values in Marlott also is apparent in the fanatical sign painter, another later addition to the text (Laird, 151), presumably to drive home the point about the destructive effects of Christianity. Just as the painter spoils the beauty of the lush landscape by defacing fences and sides of buildings, so his message warps the people of the region, making them turn ugly, too. So even within Marlott, there are those who gossip about Tess when she returns from Tantridge pregnant, those who have accepted the Christian, cultural notion that under certain circumstances it is shameful to be fruitful. The Clare family, while they do not live in Marlott, can be read in these terms as well; they represent the historical world that will destroy/has already destroyed the mythic one. Angel's brothers are, beyond a doubt, despicable, more evidence of Hardy's locating destructive qualities within Christian clergymen.[7] Enstice claims they are "Hardy's revenge on the moral conformity, arrogance, and certainty of the Church of England" (*Landscapes*, 609), and Hardy's mocking contempt for them is unmistakable:

> They were both somewhat short-sighted, and when it was the custom to wear a single eyeglass and string they wore a single eyeglass and string; when it was the custom to wear a double glass they wore a double glass; when it was the custom to wear spectacles they wore spectacles straight-way, all without reference to the particular variety of defect in their own vision. When Wordsworth was enthroned they carried pocket copies; and when Shelley was belittled they allowed him to grow dusty on their shelves. When Correggio's Holy Families were admired, they admired Correggio's Holy Families; when he was decried in favour of Velasquez, they sedulously followed suit without any personal objection. (187)

However, the two function as more than simply comic relief. In one scene, they, together with Mercy Chant, the co-opted woman who embodies the patriarchal definition of virtuous womanhood, steal Tess' boots. Their act is paradigmatic of patriarchal culture's treatment of women: it binds their feet, restricts their movement, makes progress difficult, keeps them barefoot.

Initially, however, Angel's parents do not appear as unlikable as the brothers, and in one sense they are not. For the most part, they are kind, generous people whose devotion to others makes life much more bearable for those with whom they come into contact. But they remain firmly established in the Christian patriarchal world, espousing its destructive values and, as such, cause as much harm, if not more, than their sons do. The elder Clare's devotion to St. Paul, the most antifeminist and the most intellectual of the apostles, linked with his hatred of St. James, who is regarded as anti-intellectual and egalitarian, reveals his distance from a Pagan system that values intuition over intellect and that disables gender as a determinant of hierarchy. And while the text asserts that the Clares would have gladly taken in the impoverished Tess, it also points out that what they would have responded to in the young woman was her modesty and despair. A woman who fits Victorian notions of femininity—helpless, passive, modest—would be welcome in their home; a fierce, strong, sexual woman would not. Such a mind set, which forces women into a male-determined concept of gender identity, is very destructive, all the more so because it disguises itself as loving kindness.

Hardy's comprehension of the link between the destruction of the old ways of life, and with it, the destruction of the land, and the Christian patriarchy becomes apparent in his depiction of the diabolical threshing machine, run by the sinister man from the north (where, according to medieval lore, the devil lived), of whom Hardy writes: "He was in the agricultural world, but not of it. He served fire and smoke; these denizens of the fields served vegetation, weather, frost, and sun" (248–49). The biblical allusion ("in the . . . world, but not of it"), together with the satanic images, would appear to suggest that the engineer is severed from Christianity, but, as with Alec D'Urberville, what develops instead is a fusion of the demonic and the Christian. The threshing machine, for all its devilishness, is also described as a "Jacob's ladder" (357), a medium for achieving the Christian heaven. Yet, significantly, the harvester destroys the land, while it breaks the spirit of the folk. However, the manifestation of the Christian within a device as mechanical as the harvester has an integrity of its own. As Mircea Eliade points out:

> Western science can be called the immediate heir of Judaeo-Christianity. It was the prophets, the apostles, and their successors the missionaries who convinced the Western world that a rock (which certain people have considered to be sacred) was only a rock, that the planets and the stars were only cosmic *objects*—that is to say, that they were not (and could not be) either gods or angels or demons. (128)

Christianity privileges the spiritual over the physical, which comes to be devalued and desacralized. The implications of this attitude become apparent in the two harvest scenes in the novel, which comment on something more far-reaching than, although inherently linked to, the industrialization of England. Not only is the work actually more grueling with the machine (although undoubtedly the profits are greater for the landowner), but also the attitude of the people has changed. The Pagan sense of joy and harmony that pervades the first harvest scene is lacking in the second. Life has become the proverbial "vale of tears"; Tess' body—her physicality—is jarred and bounced until her senses are completely numbed and she is totally oblivious to the physical world around her. What the sign painter could not accomplish, the threshing machine could.

However, Tess can be said to enable her own destruction in the sense that she has been co-opted by culture. From early in the novel, she gives her assent to the values of the patriarchy, of the culture alien to her Pagan Marlott. However, she does not choose to be co-opted; the forces of the patriarchy bear down upon her with the speed and force of the modern mail cart which impales Prince, her horse, pulling his old-fashioned wagon. Although Tess has been reared in Pagan Marlott, she has been educated to a degree in the National School, which has resulted in more than her simply being able to speak two languages—folk dialect as well as culturally sanctioned "proper" English—although the division in her speech metaphorically reflects the result of the education overall. As Enstice points out, "two opposing elements struggle for dominance within her: the laws of nature and the laws of Victorian morality" (*Landscapes*, 130). Her contamination by the latter affects her perception, so that, for example, on her return to Marlott after she has been Alec's lover, she sees her beautiful village "now half-veiled in mist" (104). Having accepted to a degree culture's assessment of a seduced woman as fallen, she can no longer see her home, the site of the old values, clearly. Brooks claims that Tess' "consciousness isolates her" (241) from the natural world. The problem is one of perception. Hardy addresses this relativity, when, in discussing Tess' despair over her "fatherless" child, he emphasizes that, removed from a societal context, Tess would have delighted in her child's existence, adding, "Most of [her] misery had been generated by her conventional aspect, and not by her innate sensations" (120). When her child grows ill, Tess moves even closer to embracing the values and the religion of the patriarchy. She becomes frantic to the point that she undertakes the baptism of her baby to prevent his damnation to the Christian hell that up until now she has not accepted as plausible, and even makes a cross for his grave. Rosemarie Morgan accurately assesses the scene as "subverting . . . church ritual and dogma" (102). She claims, "The concept of a sin-laden Tess and a sin-laden Sorrow is clearly risible in [Hardy's] eyes. Irony and skepticism point to his scorn of a cultural ideology that fosters, under the mantle of Christianity, both the myth of the fallen woman's guilt and the guilt of unbaptized innocents" (102). Nevertheless, while Hardy may be laughing bitterly, Tess is not; her anguish over the future of her dying baby is real and indicates the degree to which she has accepted Christianity's harsh doctrine. However, she remains capable of believing in the eventuality of her own renewal with the seasons and in the possibility of rediscovering joy. Only after she enters into a love relationship with Angel Clare, mythically her opposite, her enemy, and her destroyer, does she lose sense of who and what she is. Hardy's discourse makes it clear that Tess turns this Angel, this Christ, into her god. She, who is the essence of the natural and the physical, has "hardly a touch of earth in her love for Clare" (221); he becomes "the breath and life of [her] being" (223). As she anguishes over whether or not to marry him, she wishes for a counsellor, even as she rejects her previous counsellor, her mother, having turned her back on the matriarchal bond. Van Ghent sees her as "incapacitated . . . by her moral idealism" (89). I would suggest rather that she has accepted a moral system that is antithetical to everything she embodies, as well as violative of Hardy's perception of what permits the human to thrive. Tess' only true crime is abandoning her sense of self, allowing herself to become an object Angel can manipulate, but one cannot blame her for occupying the only space culture has permitted women to fill. She is so inculcated with patriarchal definitions of the status of women that "it pleased her to think [Angel] was regarding her as his absolute possession, to dispose of as he should choose" (273). Her lack of her own self-worth leads her to the point where she even offers to be Angel's servant. Her identity is so determined by Angel that when he deserts her, she is virtually destroyed. She goes so far as to make herself ugly, dressing in old clothes and clipping off her eyebrows in a desperately self-destructive act. She begins to be ashamed of her sexuality, her essence, and wishes men would not look at her. The text reveals that she felt that "in inhabiting the fleshly tabernacle with which Nature had endowed her she was somehow doing wrong" (334); that she has arrived at such a perception indicates her complete inculcation with the teachings of the Christian patriarchy about physicality and sexuality, specifically insofar as those qualities bear upon women.

In her despair, Tess abandons even nature. As Brick points out, "The price that Tess is forced to pay for her rebirth [by Angel's love] is the loss of her intimate relationship with nature" (123). She poignantly writes to Angel, "The daylight has nothing to show me, since you are not here, and I don't like to see the rooks and starlings in the fields" (360). If anything, nature terrifies her; she imagines witches and fairies behind hedges and trees. Her separation from nature—paralleled by Christ's descent into hell—takes her to the fashionable apartment where she wears elegantly embroidered dressing gowns. She is no longer Tess the dairymaid; she no longer functions as the embodiment of nature—she has lost her self, her identity. Only when she stabs Alec, when she again accepts the values of the folk culture rather than of the patriarchy, can she, as Van Ghent says, return to "the fold of nature and instinct" (209). Only then will the sun return to accept her sacrifice.

The novel's brilliance lies in its depiction of the fall into the historical, which is essentially Tess' story. The archetype dictates her fate. Just as the Great Goddess is now regarded by most of the Western world as a mythic figure, while Christ is considered real in some sense, so Tess' existence in the novel occurs in prehistory, in mythic time and space. But modern culture, science, religion, destroy the mythic, just as Tess and her world are destroyed by the many guises of the historical—the things that "actually exist": science, Christianity, the patriarchy. After her fall into the historical, living in a modern hotel in a modern city, where nature is not allowed to intrude except in very controlled ways, Tess temporarily returns to the mythic world (reminiscent of the short time Christ lives on earth after the resurrection) for her mysterious, dreamlike honeymoon with Angel Clare. But Angel is a part of history. Whether or not he loves Tess, she cannot exist for him. Mythic time and historical time can only overlap for brief moments. In the end, the historical invades the mythic, seizes it, carries it off, and kills it, while a waving black flag marks the execution of Tess the dairymaid.

NOTES

1. Both Mary Jacobus in "Tess: The Making of a Pure Woman," in *Tearing the Veil: Essays on Femininity,* and J. T. Laird in *The Shaping of "Tess of the D'Urbervilles"* give ample support for this point.

2. Laird reveals that in the earlier versions of the text this point is also made more clearly; there Hardy stresses the time that had elapsed between the seduction and Tess' departure for her home, a time when she is presumably living with Alec.

3. Mary Jacobus cites textual evidence that in earlier versions of the novel Tess

expressed a desire to live with Angel rather than marry him.

4. The brother-sister archetype is not lost within the Judeo-Christian tradition, appearing in such forms as Abraham and Sarah, Moses and Miriam, and Jesus and the Virgin Mary. The medieval Marian hymns are the best example of the recurrence of the myth, since they often articulate the Jesus-Mary relationship as one of siblings (since both are children of the same father), but with blatantly erotic overtones.

5. Marjorie Garson also addresses fathers in Hardy, claiming, "Mothers tend to be redundant, fathers deficient, in Hardy's fiction: while mother-figures proliferate, fathers tend to be lacking" (55). Speaking specifically of Jack Durbeyfield, Laird points out how the character becomes more and more contemptible as Hardy reworked the novel. Clearly, Hardy intended us to view Durbeyfield as weak and despicable.

6. Alec exists at a similar remove from nature, as Hardy reveals by having him get lost in the Chase. Hardy is fond of having the male characters he dislikes get lost in nature, an appropriate metaphor for their entire state of being.

7. Only one brother actually makes his living as a clergyman, but the other has been trained to the work as well, and simply comes at it from the other side, teaching those who will become clergymen. Hardy's rhetoric treats the two as virtually interchangeable in their smugness and their hypocrisy, and, appropriately, most readers can never remember which one is Cuthbert and which one is Felix.

6

Jude the Obscure: There Was Darkness Over All the Land

Jude the Obscure is possibly the grimmest English canonical novel of the nineteenth century. Hardy's tale of young Jude Fawley—naive, idealistic, but ultimately likeable and sympathetic—haunts readers, who grieve over the futility and hopelessness of the young man's journey through life. Yet in structure, the novel is remarkably similar to several others of the Wessex novels. A central protagonist is conflicted between two lovers, one of whom is sexual but ultimately uses sexuality as a means of power, the other of whom is loftily idealistic but finally even more destructive than the blatantly sexual one. The protagonist is torn between the two and perishes. Eustacia and Tess fit the pattern precisely, while Bathsheba and Grace present variations on the theme. At first glance, the only significant difference in *Jude the Obscure* is the gender of the protagonist; Jude is male and the lovers who together undo him are both women. However, that difference is, in a more thorough analysis, less significant than the tonal difference that distinguishes this work from Hardy's earlier novels. The narrative voice here is bitter and despairing. The edenic world that informed the earlier novels—even that as grim as *The Woodlanders*—is absent. The waning spirituality that threatened destruction in those works has flickered out. The universe—and specifically, the earth and all its inhabitants—is no longer perceived as sacred. The mystical glimpses into the other world which the other novels offered have disappeared. The modern world has been achieved; the past is no longer within grasp and the bitterness evident in the narrative voice suggests that likely it never was.

Critics have, of course, discussed this tonal shift at length. Mary Jacobus points out how the world of *Jude the Obscure* "is more social and less natural than the world of any of the earlier novels" and cites Jude's nonagricultural profession and urban life as exemplifying that change ("Sue," 206). In discussing the few rural scenes that Hardy portrays, Enstice claims "there is no sense of beauty in Man's partnership with Nature" (*Landscapes*, 158). Thurley more bluntly states, "Nature has gone, now people just fight it out" (183). Enstice, however, locates the shift internally rather than externally, claiming, "The landscapes are the same; only our perception has altered" (*Landscapes*, 180). His point is significant. The narrative consciousness of the novel remains very closely aligned with the consciousness of Jude, who usually functions as the narrative's focalizer. The alienated, spiritually empty world view the novel posits is Jude's world view. Readers are provided with no alternative consciousness, no other mode of seeing to offset Jude's grim vision and thereby to provide a critique of it. Like the characters within the novel, readers are locked into a modern consciousness that is despairing and destructive of spirit. The perceptions of nature as sacred held by characters such as Gabriel, Tess, and Giles allowed readers access to Hardy's mythical world; here, like Jude and Sue, readers are confined within the limitations of their skepticism.

The novel explores the implications of life lived divorced from the strength that nature can lend. As Anne Mickelson points out, "Society completely triumphs over nature in the book, and the triumph of society for Hardy leads to the throttling of man-woman's natural instincts" (124). She goes on: "Most important to this book is the underlying assumption that people divorced from nature . . . will have certain psychic disorders—disorders which will lead to a split personality"(125). One need only reflect upon the turmoil that defines Jude and Sue's relationship to understand that what occurs here is very different from the problems that plague the lovers in the other novels, for example, Angel Clare's inability to deal with Tess' sexuality. Mickelson's perceptions provide an access to the doomed Jude's angst-ridden consciousness.

Marygreen, the site of the novel's beginning, is the sort of typically Hardyean village that recurs throughout his novels; in it, the old and the new coexist, hinting at the simultaneity of two modes of consciousness. However, as Enstice points out, Hardy describes the buildings of the town in purely functional terms, suggesting that they are devoid of spirituality; by implication, Marygreen appears debased (*Landscapes*, 157–58). However, the spirituality, or the absence thereof, of a place is determined by the perception of the viewer, and here the focalizing gaze, which is most often Jude's, does not recognize the spiritual as existing within the natural. In its outward form, the day-to-day life of the residents of Marygreen resembles that of the Weatherbury folk; however, the residents of Marygreen, and particularly Jude, view their home through modern eyes—in Jude's case, eyes that are focused on the spires and towers of Christminster. Such a vision privileges the urban over the rural and the new over the old; hence these folk view their home as insignificant, as extrinsic to their being, as unrelated to the processes of identity formation. Modern consciousness, which alienates "self" from "other," typifies this novel. In Marygreen, then, more and more of the old houses have been pulled down,[1] and, significantly, a "tall new building of modern Gothic design" (31) serves as the local church. Christianity, it would seem, is alive and well in Marygreen, which through this description of the new church building becomes linked with the razing of the old and the substitution of the new. Marygreen initially appears to be contrasted to the town in which Sue and Jude first live together, Shaston, where "beer was more plentiful than water, and . . . there were more wanton women than honest wives and maids" (221). However, both places resemble each other as they resemble the other many towns in which Sue and Jude, together or separately, reside. No place stands out as possessing a unique character. The towns are neither Christian nor Pagan, but rather, like most of the landscape of the novel, are defined by the absence of the sacred and by a singular dullness. Modern vision has stripped the world of charm and magic, rendering all equally empty and bleak.

The folk do not function here as a lively, bawdy chorus against which the actions of the protagonists unfold. No sense of strong community exists in this novel. Marlene Springer points out how here the rustics usually appear "as naïve buffoons, or as merely curious, often insensitive commentators—not as the wise counsellors of the earlier novels" (153). However, individual rustic characters occasionally glimmer with the sort of consciousness that resulted in the vitality and life-affirming humor of the Egdon or Weatherbury folk. Most often, the *Jude* folk share with their earlier peers a distrust of education and a scorn for the civilized. When, for example, the boy Jude questions his elders about Christminster, which functions in the book as the epitome of civilization—religion and academia's highest achievement—he is told that "We've never had anything to do with folk in Christminster" (37). One adds, "I always saw there was more to be learned outside a book than in" (140), an attitude that recalls the Egdon folk upon learning that Clym intends to create a school for them. One other of the rustics explains that scholars study

> [o]n'y foreign tongues used in the days of the Tower of Babel, when no two families spoke alike. They read that sort of thing as fast as a night-hawk will whir. . . . And though it do take . . . five years to turn a lirruping hobble-de-hoy chap into a solemn preaching man with no corrupt passions, they'll do it . . . and turn un out wi' a long face, and a long black coat and waistcoat, and a religious collar and hat . . . so that *his own mother wouldn't know un.* (44; emphasis mine)

The distrust of religion that characterized the Egdon folk resurfaces here, along with the unconscious awareness that Christianity is destroying/has destroyed Pagan ways, severing the natural bond between mother and son for a new unity between Father and son. For these folk, Christminster is a dead place—"auld crumbling buildings, half church, half almshouse, and not much going on at that" (132)—a view Hardy affirms through his choice of the name Sarcophagus College and his claim that the colleges as a group "had put on the look of family vaults above ground" (103). Dale Kramer comments that Hardy typically creates situations in which characters draw their strength from their association with nature. Here, he points out, Sue and Jude are estranged from nature; however, he emphasizes that nature continues to exist, whether or not characters accept what it has to offer. In their desire to enter contemporary society, to rise socially, Sue and Jude break with nature, not it with them (158 and 160). Kramer's comment informs Jude's constant movement within the text, his inability to establish roots anywhere. Unlike Giles, who lives his entire life in Hintock, or Gabriel Oak, who moves only when his circumstances demand it, Jude roams the countryside restlessly, never at home, unable to achieve the stasis of a life attuned to the natural, exhibiting rather the dull frenzy of the modern, alienated soul.

For the most part, however, the folk do not figure at all in this work, because they are not significant to Jude; his inability to find them meaningful results in their absence from the text. They are beneath notice. The one or two who enter the text remain for the most part nameless and anonymous; no eccentric Grandfer Cantle or pathetic Joseph Poorgrass appears here. The narrative perspective (Jude's perspective) forces the reader to share its modern viewpoint, which perceives the folk as an indistinguishable blob of humanity, insignificant since they lack any social status. One of the few exceptions is Dr. Vilbert, who is portrayed as a quack and a fraud. As Enstice points out, his power has been stripped by a modern belief in science, unlike, for example, the witch in *Under the Greenwood Tree* or the weather-prophet in *The Mayor of Casterbridge* (*Landscapes,* 173). However, it is further significant that it is the narrative voice that accords Vilbert no respect; the folk believe in his remedies and seek him out, as is evidenced by his economic survival. However, readers are influenced by the focalizing voice to perceive him from a modern perspective, which would claim that, lacking a formal education, he cannot possibly be an effective healer.

However, Vilbert's countryside rambles receive less attention than do the lives of the working classes of Christminster and the various small towns in which Jude lives. With the shift away from the rural and the rustic comes a parallel shift away from the Pagan rituals and references that inform the other novels, another indication of the modern state of consciousness that pervades *Jude the Obscure.* Jude's world contains no heath fires, no May-walkings, no midsummer revels, no book-and-key divinations; the world is a desacralized place. Outside of one reference to a weather god (113), no mention is made of deities other than the Christian and the classical Greek and Roman ones. The Celtic goddesses and gods have totally disappeared; the pale Galilean's conquest is complete. Like Angel Clare and Clym Yeobright, Jude, for all his seeming rebellion against Christianity after Sue's return to Phillotson, remains solidly within the Christian tradition. Unlike his earlier counterparts, however, Jude is not implicitly descended from solid Christian stock. Aunt Drusilla's recurring warnings about marriage may perhaps hint at a Pagan past: "The Fawleys were not made for wedlock; it never seemed to sit well upon us. There's sommat in our blood that won't take kindly to the notion of being bound to do what we do readily enough if not bound" (91). However, if the earlier Fawleys were Pagan, Jude has more than compensated, becoming the embodiment of modern consciousness and beliefs.

The only representatives of the earlier consciousness presented in any depth are Aunt Drusilla and the Widow Edlin. Drusilla in some ways has been co-opted by culture and has become a fairly staunch Evangelical. However, she retains a sense of pride and a desire for freedom that Victorian society would have deemed inappropriate to one of her gender and social class. When, for example, Jude's sympathy for the birds is not appreciated by Farmer Troutham, who severely beats the boy and sends him home, Drusilla defends Jude even though she could have used the money he earned: "Farmer Troutham is not so much better than myself, come to that. . . . His father was my father's journeyman, anyhow, and I must have been a fool to let 'ee go to work for 'n, which I shouldn't ha' done but to keep 'ee out of mischty" (37). Hardy also leaves it ambiguous whether Drusilla's opposition to marriage stems from an abhorrence of sexuality, as does Sue's, or from her awareness of the Fawley personality and her own desire for personal freedom. That she has more sexual intuitions than Sue is certain, however. She tells the younger woman, concerning Phillotson, "there be certain men here and there that no woman of any niceness can stomach. I should have said he was one" (210).

If Drusilla's attitude about sexuality remains vague, the Widow Edlin's views on the subject are perfectly clear: she has no inhibitions regarding the sexual side of marriage. She is a testimony to the healthy, vital Paganism that informs the other novels. Unable to understand Jude and Sue's opposition to marriage, since they so clearly love each other, she reveals that her own marriage was a celebration of sexuality that lasted a week. However, the young couple's unmarried state poses no moral problem for her. As Kramer says, "Mrs. Edlin opposes Gillingham's ideas of social decorum by her forthright acceptance of individuality: she has no moral or social objection to Sue and Jude's not marrying" (157). Her ability to focus on the individual and to judge accordingly, rather than to assume one dictate must control all action, sets her apart from a modern consciousness. Furthermore, she is rooted in nature enough to understand that, church and state notwithstanding, Sue and Jude's relationship is valid and justifiable; furthermore, she attempts to convince Sue that the legal status of Sue and Jude's relationship concerns no one else. However, Victorian society claims the right to make their relationship its concern. The Widow Edlin, though, is not daunted by societal expectations. She pleads with Phillotson to call off his marriage to Sue, unconcerned that he views her behavior as inappropriate. True to the pattern of the folk of the other novels, she "was never much for religion nor against it" (386). Nevertheless, she doesn't hesitate to mock the words of the marriage ceremony, saying, "God hath jined indeed!" (389), aware that no priestly blessing or divine sanction can make the marriage between Sue and Phillotson anything other than an abomination.

However, the Widow Edlin is old, and few of the young possess either her spirit or her sensibilities. Hardy's pessimism about what the future holds, a pessimism he has explored in other works, comes to a head in the figure of Little Father Time, who, significantly, does not survive the novel himself. The physician who is called to witness the murder/suicide sees Jude and Arabella's son as typifying the wave of the future, as one of many who "seem to see all [life's] terrors before they are old enough to have the staying power to resist them" (327) and hence who no longer cherish life. The "staying power to resist" in the earlier works has come from an intimate knowledge of nature, from an awareness of the unity of all of life, a knowledge which is lacking here. None of the main characters exists in any close relationship with nature; as a result, the sense of nature these characters express is sentimental, shaped by a society that itself is on no intimate footing with nature. When they are confronted by the inexplicable, having no understanding of the complexity of nature, they label nature cruel and vicious; hence they repeatedly state, "Nature's law [is] mutual butchery" (244).

   Initially, Arabella would seem to be the exception. However, Arabella is no Tess or Eustacia. Virtually her only natural attribute is her sexuality; however, she exploits that quality, seeking not pleasure but respectability in the form of marriage and social status, whether or not she feels love for the man. Hardy succinctly assesses her character when he describes her as possessing an "instinct toward artificiality" (79), an attribute that sets her in antithesis to the natural realm. Arabella is a scheming woman who wants nothing more than to rise socially and who has learned all the artifices associated with women in society to allow her to do so, down to her fake dimple and her artificial hair.[2] The duplicity in her appearance mirrors that in her character—she is constantly conniving, from her first date with Jude, when she reveals to her girlfriends every word he spoke to her, not in celebration of her attraction to him, but to procure their help to snare him.

   One might, of course, wish to argue, as Elizabeth Hardwick has done, that "Arabella is the bad side of the ignorance and pain of the country" (71), that she represents the brutality of nature, the uncaring, wanton, random action of natural processes. In those terms, Jude's response to her might approximate his response to nature. He is attracted to her/its sexuality at the same time that he is repulsed by her/its cruelty. Certainly the graphic pig-killing scene could be read as embodying the viciousness of the natural world, and most modern readers, I would guess, sympathize completely with Jude as he commiserates over the sufferings of the poor animal. Arabella maintains her matter-of-fact attitude almost to the end, caring only that the pig bleed long enough for the meat to sell for a high price. Similarly, while Arabella's conduct at Jude's death can be read as calloused and cruel, many critics have commented on the unsentimental survivalist instincts she reveals. Such critics, if considering Arabella as the embodiment of nature, would see her actions as reflected in nature when a breathtakingly serene, beautiful day follows a night of complete destruction by storm.

   A closer look at Arabella's nastiness, however, reveals its origins to be cultural. Just as she has learned her artificial beauty secrets in society, so has she assimilated society's values and viciousness. As Enstice shows, Arabella "is a symbol of the hypocrisies and self-interest of society" (*Landscapes*, 174). For example, she lies about a pregnancy to trick an unsuspecting Jude into marrying her. Admittedly, she feels a powerful sexual attraction to Jude, but obviously her feelings stop at loving him or her conscience would not permit her to act on her lie. She shows no regard for his feelings or his dreams. The fault, however, lies equally with a society that grants an unmarried woman no status. Arabella acts in self-defense, as she must in a sexist, patriarchal society, but the cost of her acting is her soul. Her defense, that "Every woman has a right to do such as that. The risk is hers" (88), is morally indefensible, but it reveals her understanding of the powerlessness of women in Victorian society and her own drive for survival. Similarly, Arabella's cold-blooded pig-butchering seems less vicious when she explains, "Poor folks must live" (86). Her additional comment, "What's God got to do with such a messy job as a pigkilling, I should like to know!" (86) indicates her unconscious awareness of the sentimentality of much of Christianity, which at times fosters the impression that prayer can eliminate all the ugliness of life. Were the society Jude and Arabella live in less classist, were poverty not tolerated, were the pain of animals taken seriously, such vicious acts would be less necessary and women like Arabella would not need to sacrifice their morality for survival.

Arabella's enculturation reveals itself also in what Enstice calls her "adherence to accepted social forms" (*Landscapes*, 174). Her obsession with marriage is one example. However, Arabella accepts not only the institution of marriage in general but also the Victorian definition of that institution—when it is convenient for her to do so. When, for example, she discusses Sue and Phillotson's first marriage with the religious schoolmaster, she says:

> But you shouldn't have let her [escape]. That's the only way with these fanciful women that chaw high—innocent or guilty. She'd have come round in time. We all do! Custom does it! it's all the same in the end! . . .You were too quick about her. *I* shouldn't have let her go! I should have kept her chained on—her spirit for kicking would have been broke soon enough! There's nothing like bondage and a stone-deaf taskmaster for taming us women. Besides, you've got the laws on your side. Moses knew. . . . 'Then shall the man be guiltless; but the woman shall bear her iniquity.' (232)

In what is essentially her defense of wife-beating, Arabella is revealing the level to which she has absorbed culture's messages, even to the point where she can cite scripture to condone violence against her own gender. Admittedly, in mindlessly parroting societal dicta of this sort, she does not for a moment consider that such practices should apply to her—one need only imagine the consequences if any man tried to chain up Arabella. However, her words reveal her to be a post-Darwinian survivor who will turn on her own gender to achieve her ends. Arabella survives; any sense of morality or ethical behavior does not.

The world of *Jude the Obscure* is in many ways a world of callousness and brutality, a social nightmare in which any sense of community or love for one's neighbor is all but absent. However, Hardy repeatedly locates the cruelty and the source of trauma solidly within the human community. By contrast, for example, in *Far From the Madding Crowd,* the natural world is in several instances the source of human pain: Gabriel Oak's dog, having tasted fresh meat, runs amok and destroys a flock of sheep; lightning causes a raging fire which threatens the hayricks which are the source of food for the winter. Here, however, Hardy, unlike the characters within the work, is disinclined to blame nature for human suffering. One good example is when the youthful Jude, tired from clacking away the birds that are feeding in the field he has been hired to guard, begins to feel sorrow that some of nature's creatures must go hungry. His reading of the scene is naive, however. All of his clamor would not result in one starved bird, as any farmer would attest to. Were he to actually observe the birds, he would notice that when they fly up, they merely alight somewhere else in the field. Jude's grief is a result of his alienation from nature and his assuming he is more effective at his task than is actually the

case. Similarly, when Jude mercifully kills the trapped rabbit that cried out in the
night, he overlooks the fact that the trap was set by a human hand—an animal would
typically have torn the rabbit apart quickly and eaten it at once. Repeatedly, Hardy's
narrative shields nature from the charges that Sue and Jude hurl at it. What they fail
to see is that the "mutual butchery" they bemoan grows out of human consciousness,
specifically human consciousness removed from nature.

The separation of the human from the natural manifests itself here in that no
character functions as the embodiment of nature; in other words, no vegetation god
or goddess exists in this novel. Hardy's initial description of Arabella recalls in
some ways his earlier goddess figures, but the narrative voice always qualifies those
descriptions to deflate any sense of divinity. When, for example, Arabella is
described as a "fine dark-eyed girl" (59), the sentence continues, "not exactly
handsome, but capable of passing as such at a little distance, despite some
coarseness of skin and fibre" (59). The text praises her "round and prominent
bosom, full lips, perfect teeth, and the rich complexion of a Cochin hen's egg" (59),
but qualifies the description with the words "She was a complete and substantial
female animal—no more, no less" (59), hardly a derogatory sentence, but one that
leaves Arabella appearing somewhat less that human, and certainly far from divine,
in a way that Tess, Eustacia, and Bathsheba are spared. Hardy's rhetoric suggests
he sympathizes with Arabella's plight, with her need to be strong to survive, but he
does not admire her.

Of Arabella's strength there is no question; in this respect she is the equal, if not
the superior, of the other Hardy women. Resembling Eustacia perhaps more than
any of the others, Arabella is "a little bit thick in the flitch" (402), a far cry from the
diminutive Sue. When she speculates that she could kill the pig herself, the reader
does not for a moment doubt her words. The scene that recurs in Hardy novel after
Hardy novel, that of a woman physically supporting a man weaker than herself,
appears here as well, when Arabella helps carry the drunken Jude to his room. Her
strength extends to her demeanor as well. Arabella does not mince words, nor does
she play coy or demure, for the most part. She is straightforward—even vulgar—in
her honesty. Her strength makes psychological sense given the life her poverty has
forced her to lead. However, Hardy does not depict her as possessing any sort of
uncanny, otherworldly power beyond that which derives from the sort of life she has
been forced to live. While she may have an unsettling habit of turning up in Jude's
life at inopportune moments, only once is such an encounter narrated to suggest she
is a malevolent force rather than a desperate, passionate woman. Sue and Jude's
blissful "honeymoon" ends after the agriculture show at which they encounter the
jealous Arabella, whom Jacobus discusses as the serpent in Eden spying on an
unfallen Adam and Eve ("Sue," 317). The text claims the young couple felt "as if
the visit had brought some evil influence to bear on them" (318). However, apart
from this scene, Arabella's mean-spiritedness and duplicity are a function of her
social position and psychological makeup rather than of demonic wickedness.

A significant portion of Arabella's psychological makeup is predicated upon her
sexuality, which is abundant. Jude's initial reaction to her typifies what other men

feel as well; her body sends out "the unvoiced call of woman to man" (60), and Jude is unable to resist that call, nor does she wish him to do so. In one of the few comic scenes in the novel, Arabella does her best to seduce the innocent Jude on a hillside—to no avail. No other Hardy woman is as blatantly sexual as Arabella when she falls on her back under a leafy tree and pulls Jude down to her—on the pretext of looking at a pretty caterpillar. While Arabella's motive is to trap Jude into marriage, she desires him sexually as well. Her meaning is unambiguous when she tells her friend Anny, "He's the sort of man I long for. I shall go mad if I can't give myself to him altogether" (69). After her return from Australia, when she reencounters Jude in the Christminster public house, it is she who boldly suggests they spend the night in Aldbrickham—for purely sexual reasons. After their one-night stand in Aldbrickham, Arabella is perfectly comfortable getting on with her life without Jude, oblivious to any sense of impropriety or any obligation to him. Later, after her other husband dies and Arabella has taken up religion, it is her sexual urge (specifically her sexual feelings for Jude) that cause her to abandon her newfound faith. She says, "After all that's said about the comforts of this religion, I wish I had Jude back again!" (335) To a woman as sexual as Arabella, the comforts of religion do not compare with the comforts of a man in bed.

Interestingly, whatever real wisdom or insight into the human condition (other than her knowledge of sheer survival) Arabella possesses comes through her sexuality. When she first visits Sue and Jude in Aldbrickham, she immediately intuits from Sue's manner that the couple have not consummated their relationship. The next day, when Sue claims she and Jude are lovers, which in the most literal sense of the word has been true only for a few hours, Arabella understands that Sue is acting out of jealousy, saying, "I expect my visit last night helped it on" (288). Similarly, Hardy gives Arabella the last word in the novel, her comment about Sue's rejection of Jude, which the narrative structure invests with authority: "She may swear that [she's found peace] on her knees to the holy cross upon her necklace till she's hoarse, but it won't be true. . . . She's never found peace since she left his arms, and never will again till she's as he is now" (428). Arabella possesses a profound understanding of the significance of the sexual to the human totality; however, she lacks any concept of the role of love.[3] In Hardy, love repeatedly is associated with selflessness, with a privileging of the beloved over the self. It is what Gabriel feels for Bathsheba, Tess for Angel, and Giles for Grace. In Arabella's case, however, her sexual desires, along with her desire for respectability, lead her to overlook Jude's dreams, allowing her to imperviously trap him into a marriage with her. Her actions at his deathbed reveal an equal callousness. Even though she has married the man twice, she will not give up one evening of pleasure to stay with him as he dies. Arabella acts alternately out of lust and a will to survive, and as a result appears less than human, devoid of the spirituality that would allow her to achieve wholeness.

Hardy emphasizes Arabella's bond with the artificial and the cultural by developing virtually no associations between her and nature. While she is adept at pig-raising (and pig-killing) and gardening, the narrative points out early in the text that Arabella considers her life in the country to be temporary and her marriage to Jude an economic exchange that will allow her to acquire new frocks and hats once she can intimidate him to the point that he forgoes his dreams of an education. To further emphasize her alienation from nature, in his descriptions of Arabella Hardy does not compare her to animals, as he usually does with his women characters. Arabella is never identified with cats, snakes, deer, birds, and so on, as are Tess, Eustacia, and, significantly, Sue. In only one instance is such an association suggested—the scene in which she supposedly attempts to hatch an egg by carrying it in her bosom. However, for all her platitudes about her act—claiming, "I suppose it is natural for a woman to want to bring live things into the world" (75)—she merely uses the egg as a seduction ploy and abandons it once she has aroused Jude. She uses pregnancy in the same way, again claiming to be bringing something live into the world when she knows very well that she is not.[4] Of course one might wish to view Arabella, as one may view Eustacia, as the dark side of the goddess, as nature in its destructive rather than its creative mode. However, Hardy renders Eustacia virtually one with the landscape, which all but forces a mythic reading of the work. Arabella, on the other hand, never resonates with the mythic. She is not rooted in the landscape, but migrates even to Australia and back, and her natural milieu strikes the reader as being not her father's pig farm but a Christminster public house. Although she bears a child, Hardy has structured the novel so that we never see her involved with the boy in any way; in essence, he disallows a reading of Arabella as a mother. One may make the case that Hardy is uncomfortable with mothers. Very few of the women in his works bear children, and when, like Sue, they do, Hardy usually averts his narrative gaze from them in the act of caring for their children. However, in the cases of Tess and Sue, Hardy at least allows for the expression of love for the children. Not so with Arabella. Little Father Time's death does not affect her deeply, because she is incapable of deeply feeling for anyone. Spiritually, she is dead.

Hardy emphasizes Arabella's spiritual emptiness by severing her character from the Paganism that imbues his earlier characters with life and mythic power. Arabella is neither Pagan nor Christian. Although she experiences a temporary conversion to Evangelicalism after the death of her husband, her religious posturing is reminiscent of Alec D'Urberville's similar about-face and her hasty backsliding comes as no surprise. In terms of religion, Arabella is, like Sue, completely modern; she possesses no sense of the sacred. Her claiming of her sexuality prefigures a twentieth-century attitude much more than it harks back to an idealized, mythical, holistic sense of the sacredness of the sexual act. If Arabella is an archetype of anything, it is of the kind of modern woman who grabs what pleasure she can while remaining emotionally uncommitted, constantly struggling to survive in a spiritually devoid world. Arabella is not caught between two worlds, but fully inhabits a barren, modern world.

That modern world similarly contains Sue, who remains, in most ways, Arabella's complete antithesis. Whereas Arabella's most obvious characteristic is her sexuality, Sue's is her intellect. The two women reveal the fragmentation of body and soul that typifies patriarchal thought. However, the two women do share their spiritual emptiness. The embodiment of intellect, Sue exists in no other dimension. Just as it is possible to read Marty, Felice, and Grace as aspects of one character, so Sue and Arabella can be seen as two sides of one person—a brilliant, highly sexed woman who lacks spirituality and who perceives herself as fragmented, not a unified whole. Although Sue frustrates the reader, as she frustrates Jude, with the lengths to which she will go to avoid sexual contact, she remains a far more appealing character than Arabella (although amazingly some critics prefer Arabella). However, it is impossible to read Sue as emotionally healthy or balanced within herself, and her internal fractures are what make her so annoying. Dealing with Sue as a character is very similar to dealing with a neurotic person outside of fictions and texts—it can quickly drive one to distraction.

Sue's psychological problems reveal themselves also in her alienation from community. Her usual pattern is to bond intellectually with one man at a time, but to steer clear of women friends and allies. Hardy typically focuses the narrative gaze on his women characters as they interact with men, but in most of the other novels, he at least hints of close friendships between women. Bathsheba and her lady's maid, Liddy, while seemingly in a hierarchical relationship that would disallow affection, are portrayed on several occasions as mutually nurturing each other, sharing confidences, laughter, work, and grief. Tess' bonds with Izz and Marion are amply demonstrated, and the glimpses of Tess' early life in Marlott reveal close friendships with several other girls. Grace befriends Marty but also recalls fondly her time at school because of the friendships she had formed there; when she claims to have run away to visit one of her friends, the scene does not seem implausible, as does the scene in which Sue is recovering in the home of a strategically unnamed, undescribed school friend. Only Eustacia shares Sue's stoic isolation, but Eustacia remains far more a representation of nature embodied than an actual woman; her removal from society serves to enhance her status as Persephone, as a dark goddess. Sue, lacking mythic grandeur, walking the streets of Christminster and Aldbrickham, teaching children under Phillotson's tutelage, and selling cakes on the streets, becomes Hardy's representation of an emotionally crippled Victorian woman. Her lack of connectedness with other women reveals a hatred of her own gender and her own self.

Hardy makes it clear from the text that he intends Sue to be perceived not as a timeless figure from myth, but rather as a modern woman very much caught up in the time in which she lives. Sue has no tolerance for the old, as she demonstrates when, preferring to sit in the train station rather than the cathedral, she exclaims, "The Cathedral has had its day!" (153). Similarly, she shows no interest, not even an academic one, in ruins, and she disregards the Bible, not because it is patriarchal, but simply because it is old. However, while the Bible does not especially interest her, she does know it quite well, and particularly enjoys the Song of Solomon, which she reads as a celebration of human, sexual love, mocking the attempts of prudish church fathers to interpret the text in exclusively spiritual terms. Tradition, in terms of either scholarship or the social structure, is insignificant to her. Jude's assessment of her as "an urban miss" (159) is accurate; Sue could only exist as the product of an industrialized society, separated from the natural, with the leisure time to pursue thought for its own sake. One could argue that, just as Tess and Eustacia embodied the landscapes of which they were a part, so Sue is the embodiment of her modern, urban world, that she is Hardy's bearer of culture within the text. She has read far more extensively than Jude and is familiar with art and music, the determiners of "culture." For a while, significantly, she is a teacher, spreading the culture she represents; by contrast, neither Eustacia nor Bathsheba would consider becoming teachers. Since Hardy on several occasions uses characters' professions as a way of commenting on their systems of value (e.g., Troy as a soldier, Wildeve as an engineer), Sue's choice of a profession is significant in that it reveals her desire to inculcate children with the values and culture of Victorian society. Sue's challenges to society are intellectual; she dislikes the stifling prudishness of Victorian England, but she is very comfortable with the scholars and philosophers of the time who equally reject nonacademic Victorian thought, and with them she looks to the future as a time of enlightenment. Given that she essentially never steps far outside the parameters of culture, her conversion to a severe form of Christianity is understandable, since such forms of religion are inherent in Western culture.

Surprisingly, however, Sue possesses the dark hair and eyes of Hardy's mythic women, although her resemblance to them ends there. Physically, except for her hair color, Sue typifies the Victorian ideal in her petite and delicate build. Hardy writes that she is "light and slight, of the type dubbed elegant. . . . There was nothing statuesque in her; all was nervous motion. She was mobile, living, yet a painter might not have called her handsome or beautiful" (109). Nonetheless, her attractiveness is affirmed repeatedly throughout the novel. Jude becomes obsessed with her simply from seeing her photograph, and Phillotson quickly becomes enamored of her, well before he knows her as a person.

As befits such an ethereal creature, Sue is not possessed of great strength, either physical or psychological. Images of her as frail and at times cowering appear throughout the novel. Interestingly, however, Hardy indicates a far different past for Sue than such frailty would suggest. As a child, she was a capable tomboy, able to compete with boys as a peer. Even when she first appears in the novel, she possesses a vibrant energy, if not actual strength (although she is strong enough to drag the drunken Jude into her house). Her handwriting is "bold, womanly" (181). The first indication of Sue's attenuation comes, significantly, when she is virtually imprisoned in the teacher training school. When Jude first encounters her there, he notes that "[a]ll her bounding manner was gone; her curves of motion had become subdued lines" (151). The second severe vitiation of Sue's energy comes with her first marriage to Phillotson. From then on, until the end of the novel, Sue's strength continues to fade, sapped by encounters with a culture hostile to strong women. Mary Jacobus sees Sue's decline as indicating the young woman's gradual alienation from herself ("Sue," 307). Penny Boumelha suggests that the sapping of her strength is somewhat necessary, growing out of her recognition that she is "not transcendent of time, place, and material circumstance" (149). Some of her circumstance, however, is societally mandated rather than inherent in the human condition. Sue's movement from tomboy to madwoman/martyr is psychologically explanatory given her brilliance but also her acceptance of her culture's encoded messages about the status of women.

Those messages result in Sue's warped sexuality. By far Hardy's most complex female character, Sue cannot be dismissed as merely frigid. Her aforementioned joyous reading of the Song of Solomon is only one indication that she intellectually understands the place of the sexual within the human whole. However, her revulsion toward her own involvement in the sexual is a further example of Sue's enculturation. As the bearer of culture, Sue is the logical extension of its sexual ethos. As a girl, Sue possessed no prudishness and enjoyed scandalizing Aunt Drusilla by baring her legs and then taunting the shocked older woman. The result was predictable—Sue was beaten, repeatedly, according to Drusilla. It should not be surprising, then, that Sue began to associate bodies—and any pleasure derived from them, whether the pleasure be as simple as wading barelegged in cool water on a hot day—with wickedness.[5] Similarly, while at the teacher's training college, Sue is forced to dress "in a nunlike simplicity of costume" (156) which is intended to conceal sexual attractiveness. Again, society reinforces the concept of sexuality as unwholesome and sinful. Sue, unlike the earlier Hardy women, spends most of her time in culture rather than in nature and hence is presented with little opportunity to observe the sexual in nature. As a result, her sense of the sexual act as distasteful should come as no surprise; she has never seen the sexual celebrated and affirmed.

In Sue's early interactions with her undergraduate and with Jude, she at times appears oblivious of the possibility of sexual interaction between men and women. Sue's intellectual brilliance makes contemporary readers question her literal ignorance of the sexual act and suspect her of levels of deep repression; however, Sue is a young woman, younger than her dazzling mind would suggest, and her response to the sexual is typical of a young Victorian woman. Fraser Harrison, in his discussion of Victorian sexuality, writes:

> Although the Victorian man could only contemplate sex through a fog of guilt and anxiety, he could nevertheless define and identify the act of copulation in his mind—it was a realizable concept—before he had achieved any actual experience. For the majority of women, however, copulation, if not the entire sexual function, remained either a non-existent concept or a nebulous target for unresolved, uninformed speculation, until the moment of the wedding night. (52)

Harrison goes on to discuss the situation of Marie Stopes, an educated woman, specifically a zoologist and a botanist, who in 1911 married a man and for six months had no knowledge that her marriage had not been consummated (50–51). If as late as 1911 a woman educated in the biological sciences has no knowledge of the sexual act, it is possible that Sue is equally oblivious of it. When Sue's first companion asks her to come to London to live with him, Sue assumes their relationship will be nonsexual. Blake suggests that Sue deals with society by making herself nonsexual: "She removes the sexual barrier by as much as possible removing the sexual element from the relationship. This she does by repressing sexual invitation in herself" (710). However, Blake's statement suggests agency on Sue's part, whereas it is likelier that Sue's repression simply happens as a result of her inculturation into a society incapable of dealing with sexuality. When she marries Phillotson, she does not seem to understand that sexual intimacy with the man will inevitably follow. However, even after the two are technically lovers, Sue does not appear sexually knowing, but rather appears perpetually virginal, "unaltered," to use Jude's word. The alteration that does occur leaves her weaker and more subdued, the result of finding the act of sex with her husband "a torture" (232–33). In her attempts to rationalize her behavior, she reveals her level of societal inculcation. She tells Jude, "And it is said that what a woman shrinks from—in the early days of marriage—she shakes down to with comfortable indifference in half-a-dozen years" (233). Sue's words and her subsequent behavior suggest Sue understands well the role society expects her to play, that of the "angel in the house." Harrison speaks of the myth of the self-sacrificing woman who is celebrated as "the quintessence of femininity" (42) as "the most deceptive and pernicious" (42) means of co-opting women's power, specifically because women themselves accepted the myth and perpetuated it through their own writings. Sue believes the act of sex is something to which she must submit; to engage in it becomes an act of self-sacrifice. Nowhere has she heard—as Tess, Bathsheba, and Arabella heard through their interaction with the folk—that sexuality is an avenue to pleasure, that women can actually physically desire their lovers. However, Sue cannot be labeled unnatural for lacking an understanding of that to which she has never been exposed; rather, a society that fosters aberrant notions such as those Sue expresses is the site of the unnatural.[6] But Sue's complexity lies in the fact that she accepts her culture's values at the same time that she critiques them. In addition, she is amazingly free-spirited, what no angel in the house may be. So she does not wait around for six years to get used to sex with Phillotson, but jumps out the bedroom window to avoid it.

But switching lovers and households does not allow Sue to shift deeply ingrained attitudes. Once she is with Jude, whom she deeply loves, she cannot simply become sexually uninhibited. However, Sue is once again a product of her age in her lack of sexual response. Harrison cites women's self-hatred as one of the effects of Victorian culture's obsession with virginity. Having had to severely repress sexual desire during adolescence and specifically during courtship periods, women could not simply abandon that repression once social restrictions on their sexual behavior were removed. Rather, he points out, women felt assaulted by their husbands' sexual advances and ashamed of their own physicality, coming to loathe all that was sexual, including themselves (35). Sue's sense of the degradation involved in the act of sex leads to her expectation that Jude be physically faithful to her even though she will not become his lover. Once again, Sue is fulfilling the myth of the angel in the house, one of whose functions is to be "the moral savior of her baser mate" (Harrison, 42). Her demands on Jude are her way of saving him from what Victorian society regarded as vice. She tells Jude, "I think I would much rather go on living always as lovers, as we are living now, and only meeting by day" (278).

Only from Victorian society could Sue acquire the idea that lovers meet only by day. Similarly, when Sue attacks Arabella for being a "low-passioned woman" (283), she is again acting out of a cultural context—and in fact when the novel was published, a good deal of England echoed that attack.

Sue and Jude do become lovers, of course, but Sue never becomes completely comfortable with the sexual act—nor with its consequences. When, for example, Arabella encounters Sue and comments on her pregnancy, Sue begins to cry. To Arabella's comment, "[W]hat is there to cry about? Some folks would be proud enough!" (331), Sue weakly retorts that she is not ashamed, although clearly she is. Again, one must consider Victorian attitudes concerning pregnancy—a woman went into "confinement" because it was not proper for her to be seen in public in her "condition"—to discover the source of Sue's shame. Poverty has forced Sue to sell her cakes publically even though she is pregnant, but Sue, always sensitive, accepts society's judgment of the inappropriateness of her actions. Once again, the body is a source of shame rather than of pleasure.

For all her acculturation, though, Sue is not totally sexless. As Blake says, Sue "knows that sexual repression means loss as well as gain" (716). She tells Jude, when discussing her experience with the undergraduate, that "better women" would not have refused his sexual offer, grasping, it seems, at least intellectually, that her squeamishness is unnatural, for all that society says. But that intellect is ironically what ultimately prevents her from accepting the sexual. As Robert Heilman claims, "Her deficiency in sex, whatever its precise psychological nature . . . is a logical correlative of her enthroning of critical intellect" ("Hardy's," 222). Boumelha agrees, claiming, "[Sue] must learn that sexuality lies to a large degree outside the control of rationality, will, choice" (144). Jacobus sees Sue's sexual reluctance differently, however, ignoring the idea that Sue may be frigid or neurotic, focusing rather on Sue's desire to affirm her *self* and to make choices as an individual not attached to a man ("Sue," 311-12). Sue does, of course, feel passion for Jude—the clasped hands after the Good Friday song, the kiss at the train, are evidence of it. Sue's words at her final separation from Jude suggest she has more than simply tolerated his lovemaking. She refuses one last sexual encounter because it would "tempt [her] back" (374), and later she admits she still loves Jude "grossly" (413). Even in Sue, the natural breaks through, if only weakly and occasionally.

Given Sue's repression of her natural sexuality, psychology would suggest it must reveal itself in some other form. In Sue's case, I would suggest it takes the form of sadomasochism. The early beatings would certainly fit the pattern, but throughout Sue's adult life we see leanings in that direction as well.[7] On the one hand, she enjoys torturing the three men in her life by withholding sex, but then equally enjoys her own sense of pain at viewing their pain. She feels "a terrible remorse . . . for [her] cruelty" (168) when the first man dies, but starts the same pattern again with Jude. Similarly, right before her marriage to Phillotson, even though she knows Jude loves her passionately—and that she loves him, too—she walks through the ceremony with her cousin, admitting, "I like to do things like this" (192). Jude intuits what she means by her ambiguous "this"; he understands that she is willfully hurting him, and also herself, by her actions. The text claims, "she would go on inflicting such pains again and again, and grieving for the sufferer again and again" (194).

Even after she becomes sexually active, the pattern continues. She tortures Phillotson by preferring to sleep in a closet with spiders rather than in bed with him, but then feels remorse for her cruelty to such a kind man. Interestingly, she first admits her sexual feelings for Jude after the incident involving the Good Friday hymn, saying that "playing morbid Good Friday tunes . . . make[s] one feel what one shouldn't!" (225). It does not seem probable that Good Friday hymns serve as an aphrodisiac for many people, but considering the sorrow and renunciation that mark the holiday, it becomes understandable that, given Sue's inclinations toward the sadomasochistic, she would be powerfully aroused by the emotions associated with Christ's passion. That same day she speaks of her "aberrant passions" (226), suggesting that she may be intelligent enough to understand that her sexual psychology is somewhat skewed.

After the tragedy with the children, Sue's sadomasochism resolves itself into full-blown masochism. Initially, Sue's self-torture does not take a sexual form; she speaks of physical pain, saying, "I cannot humiliate myself too much. I should like to prick myself all over with pins and bleed out the badness that's in me!" (365). However, she quickly discovers a much more effective way to torture herself—she forces herself to do the one act she considers the most repulsive in the world—to have sex with Phillotson, an act she calls her "penance"; she says she "will drink [her] cup to the dregs!" (414). Her masochism, itself the product of a culture alienated from nature, along with her ready acceptance of the values of that culture, have led to a moment that Sue shared with many of her Victorian sisters, when the joy of sexuality is reduced to duty, humiliation, and punishment. To make her humiliation greater, Sue confesses to her meeting with Jude and then formally begs Phillotson to admit her to his bedroom. The scene appropriately recalls images from sadomasochistic pornography, in which the victim's humiliation is increased by forcing her to beg to be punished. Quaking with terror and almost unable to keep herself from crying out or flinching, Sue, like a good Victorian woman, performs her marital duty. It is impossible to label this act lovemaking, yet any more enthusiasm on Sue's part would have branded her as lewd in the eyes of many Victorians. Although it is impossible to read this scene as other than utterly disgusting and abhorrent, at least one contemporary critic defends Sue's action as moral, a reading that is impossible to comprehend. Hyman claims, "Thus, although seemingly conventional, Sue's return to Phillotson is, for her, an act of honesty and courage, a movement forward. Although she has lost her belief in freedom and happiness, she is still striving for something worthy and admirable" (173). Such a reading completely overlooks both the intensely personal nature of the sexual act and the patriarchal assumption of women's bodies and women's sexuality for purposes of its own—in fact, Hyman's reading grows out of and perpetuates such thought. Jacobus' reading of the scene is much more enlightened, claiming that Sue "offers up her body on the altar of conventional morality, as she has earlier offered up her mind to a repressive form of Christianity" ("Sue," 322). Jacobus recognizes the cultural—specifically sexist—implications of Sue's act, seeing it as "the subjection of the female to a covertly sadistic sexual code which demands the total surrender of her consciousness, individuality, and specialness" ("Sue," 322).

Given Sue's antipathy toward the natural, especially as it manifests itself in the sexual, one would not expect to see Sue described in imagery that recalls the natural world. Nevertheless, Hardy bonds Sue more closely to that natural world than he does Arabella, although neither woman functions as a goddess figure. Hardy presents Sue's happiest moments as occurring in nature. In her idyllic night in the country with Jude, Sue claims she wants to escape from "all laws except gravitation and germination" (158). That Sue can speak comfortably about "germination" while she is surrounded by the natural suggests that were she to continue to live among the folk, she would eventually come to a greater acceptance of her own sexuality. However, Sue's time is spent in towns and in and out of schools and colleges, which mediates her relationship with nature. Sue's perceptions of nature are revealed in the scene at the Agricultural Show, where she is completely enamored of the roses that have been bred and cultivated, that are essentially a cultural version of the natural. These roses are, I think, the key to understanding Sue's character. Sue celebrates what she perceives as the natural, without understanding that the elegant roses are a far remove from the wild roses that grow in the hedgerows of fields. Her understanding of nature is determined by culture, her own experience of nature being so limited. Even her night journey through water to get to Jude does not amount to a significant rebirth for her—the cultural is too strong in her. As a child, she had strong intuitions that guided her—she seemed "to see things in the air" (131). Those intuitions, for the most part, abandon the adult Sue, who relies overmuch on the intellect and who reveals a deep distrust of the irrational. Therefore, although Sue thinks she understands the natural, she admits that her understanding may be limited. Even so, she feels that "Fate has given us this stab in the back for being such fools as to take Nature at her word!" (358). Living at a remove from the natural, Sue does not grasp that nature, too, has a bitter side to it, that loss and pain are a part of all existence. Bathsheba and Tess experience despair without sharing Sue's terrible disillusionment because the two rural women have seen the cycle of nature, have seen the crops destroyed and the animals slaughtered. Sue perceives her bond with Jude, their "perfect union—[their] two-in-oneness . . . stained with blood" (357), not comprehending that blood—and death—are inevitable to the human, natural condition. Sue, like many moderns, cannot reconcile the idea of nature's butchery with nature's joy. Having been raised in a sentimental Christian tradition, Sue has ignored the brutality that is intrinsic to nature; her vision is fragmented, as she is. She wishes to co-opt nature for her own ends. As Ian Gregor points out, in discussing the aforementioned roses, "Like Miriam in *Sons and Lovers*, [Sue] can encounter the sensual world only when she can impose herself upon it, when it cannot make reciprocal demands, but is simply there to feed the contemplative soul" ("A Series," 241). Furthermore, as Dale Kramer points out, Sue "has no sense of the unity of lives, and gains no strength from associations"

(159). The lack of unity to which he refers results from her distance from the natural and, in Hardy's schema, is endemic to the modern mindset.

For all that, however, Hardy has structured his narrative to depict nature responding to Sue's plight in a way that it never does for Arabella. On the morning of Sue's second wedding to Phillotson, the "fanatic prostitution," as Jude aptly calls it, when she sacrifices herself "on the altar of what she was pleased to call her principles" (388), nature unleashes a terrific rainstorm and creates such a fog that the couple can scarcely find the church. The talk of "self-sacrifice" recalls Tess at Stonehenge; then nature beamed its approval and acceptance of the sacrifice. Here nature appears inclined to disrupt the proceedings, acting out Sue's own unspoken desires. Similarly, on the night when Sue forces herself to Phillotson's bed, a fearful wind and rain storm hits the village. Hardy's narrative strategy privileges Sue as a character. Since nature identifies with her, the reader understands her to have authorial blessing, to be the character with whom to sympathize rather than despise.

And Sue is likable, for all her frigidity and emotional instability, in a way that Arabella is not. She is typically direct, honest, and straightforward. Until her encounters with Phillotson and the training school, she is characterized by an appealing energy and a vitality quite unusual for a Hardy woman character; the text claims that "she was so vibrant that everything she did seemed to have its source in feeling" (122). Her intelligence is not of the sterile, pedantic sort; she attracts with her brilliance and draws not only Jude and Phillotson but also the reader to her. She can usually see through the arbitrariness of convention, and she keeps a perspective on the world. Reader sympathy for her is intensified during her virtual imprisonment in the teacher training school, where her personal freedom is so severely limited. In fact, Sue's strong desire for independence is one of her most appealing characteristics. That quality, along with her brilliant mind, causes her to see the world and its injustices clearly, as she reveals in her sarcasm regarding the marriage ceremony: "[M]y bridegroom chooses me of his own will and pleasure; but I don't choose him. Somebody *gives* me to him, like a she-ass or she-goat, or any other domestic animal. Bless your exalted views of woman, O Churchman!" (190). Sue here functions as a spokeswoman for Hardy's own views; her (and his) hesitations concerning marriage are reasonable and certainly understandable to today's readers, if they were not so to Hardy's Victorian audience. Hardy has Sue continue to discuss the ludicrousness of attempting to legislate emotion. "Domestic laws should be made according to temperament" (243), she says, a view inconsistent with a patriarchal notion of law, which mandates a fixed rule for all society, regardless of individual circumstance, but very in tune with feminine justice, which views each case separately. Sue's revulsion at the idea that one has "contracted to cherish . . . under a Government stamp" (278), as well as at the unfeeling, legalistic language of the civil ceremony, reveals both her fineness of mind and her sensitivity of spirit. Her comment that "in a proper state of society, the father of a woman's child will be as much a private matter of hers as the cut of her under-linen" (260) indicates both her understanding of the historical basis for marriage (not love or spiritual union, but a means of verifying paternity) and her refusal to be co-opted by society's sentimental gloss of the institution, which attempts to make a woman believe her entire reason for existence is to someday be a bride. All in all, Sue is a likable young woman, who, until she becomes distraught by grief, knows that "we shall . . . be dead in a few years" (243) and therefore does not intend to spend those years slavishly following every societal injunction, especially when reason would dictate otherwise.

But while Sue is as personable as most of the Hardy women (and more so than some), she differs significantly from most of them in her lack of spirituality—most specifically in her dissociation from the Pagan. Ironically, Sue is the only one of the Hardy women who openly calls herself a Pagan at the same time that she is the least Pagan of the women characters. Her Paganism, such as it is, is all intellectual and cultural; it never lives for her. Paganism is rooted in the cycle of the seasons, in a profound understanding of nature as it impacts all that exists, including humankind. Sue's knowledge is all academic; she is removed from the natural world and cannot comprehend its mysteries, either in the land or in herself. Sue is attracted to what she identifies as Hellenism, which remains a scholarly avenue of access to knowledge. One need only contrast Sue's very self-conscious adoration of her Pagan statues, in language that is not her own but borrowed from contemporary literature, filtered through her intellect, with Tess' May-walking or the Egdon folk's jumping over their heath fires to understand the distinction between Hellenism and Paganism. For the folk of Hardy's novels, rituals are not self-conscious events nor do they require mediation by culture (i.e., Swinburne's poetry). Sue's experience with the statues of Venus and Apollo becomes the paradigm for her interaction with what she considers the Pagan; although initially she is attracted to what they represent, once she has bought them, "they seemed so very large . . . and so very naked" (114). Sue has obtained her understanding of what Venus and Apollo represent through her reading and hence through her intellect. But before those deities were written about, used as symbol and allegory, and turned into metaphor, they existed as life-forces that were spontaneously worshiped. At one time, those deities bespoke the reality of Paganism, the celebration of the natural and the sexual, but that time has long since past. When Sue confronts a fleeting glimpse of their former glory, significantly through their nakedness, she is terrified. One might claim that while Sue has nothing to do with Paganism, she is an appropriate embodiment of Hellenism. She talks about sexuality, but her own sexuality is virtually inaccessible to her. She talks about nature's laws, but uses scholarly sources to support her opinions. Hardy even describes her in terms that recall sculpture and statuary from time to time; she is compared to a figure on a Grecian frieze as she emerges from the river, and the text emphasizes her pallor, her alabaster-like appearance. By contrast, Tess and Bathsheba are solid, vital women, tanned by the sun, completely at home in a field or amid a flock. The distinction between Sue as statue, as a dead reminder of a living, or once-living, presence, and Tess and Bathsheba as embodiments of the Great Goddess enacting the seasonal changes in their own lives, points out the distinction between Paganism and Hellenism. Essentially, Hellenism is dead Paganism, is the statue of the living reality that once existed, is the rhetoric that replaces true ritual. Sue's true attraction is to culture. She claims, "I fancy we have had enough of Jerusalem" (126), so she shifts her gaze to "Athens, Rome, Alexandria" (126), cities virtually overdetermined as signifiers of the cultural.

To understand Sue it is necessary to begin with her intellect. Jude comments, "she was a woman whose intellect was to mine like a star to a benzoline lamp: who saw all *my* superstitions as cobwebs that she could brush away with a word" (419). Sue's brilliance is not balanced by spirituality. The fact that Sue has no "superstitions" indicates that she has no access to a spiritual world, since superstitions become the means to experiencing nonrational reality, what some would call the supernatural. Sue, eminently rational, does not allow the validity of any reality that is nonrational. Early on, she speaks of Christminster as "a place full of fetishists and ghost-seers!" (171). What she is scorning is not Christianity, but all religions, including Paganism, since all demand of their followers an acceptance of some level of reality beyond the simply material. Although Sue is hostile to Christianity through most of the novel, what she opposes is not merely its patriarchal de-sacralization of the world, which Hardy himself dislikes, but also its demand for faith. She continually condescends to Jude, not simply because he believes in the message of Christianity, but because he believes at all. Hardy writes, "[H]er cousin interested her, as one might be interested in a man puzzling out his way along a labyrinth from which one had one's self escaped" (157). The labyrinth does not appear to be Christianity per se but rather faith. When Jude asks Sue to pray with him, understandably she declines to share in his meditation, but she does not avail herself of the opportunity to approach what she calls her own "patron-saints," Apollo and Venus, through her own meditation. In fact, her referring to those deities as such is merely a rhetorical act; to Sue, they remain intellectual constructs, not living representatives of what she believes. When, therefore, she must deal with a grief that is rationally inexplicable, she has nowhere to turn but back to the Christianity of her culture, a religion she knows well in spite of her seeming rejection of it.[8] At that point, given Christianity's doctrine concerning both idolatry and adultery, it is understandable that Sue virtually goes mad with a sense of guilt for what she has come to perceive as sin.

For all her intellectualism, Sue ignores what she herself preaches to Jude, that "intellect at Christminster is new wine in old bottles" (170). While Sue at times grasps the inherent link between culture and Christianity, she at times lets the knowledge of that bond slip, assuming instead that the two forces are somehow in a dichotomous relationship with each other. While, for example, she refuses to read the Christian authors, she instead reads the scandalous Boccaccio, Sterne, Defoe, Smollett, Fielding, and Shakespeare, among others, forgetting that those writers themselves grew out of a Christian culture which exerted a tremendous influence over them. Sue never removes herself from a cultural, academic tradition and therefore never understands that one approaches Paganism not through the word, through literature or texts, but through ritual and through silence, the silence of nature, the silence so known to Eustacia on Egdon Heath. Sue fills the silence of nature with culture, with the word, and eventually, with the Word, and as a result never touches the essence of Paganism. Similarly, while Sue considers herself a rebel for having male friends, she is oblivious to the many ways in which her interactions with those friends are informed by her culture's attitudes toward sexuality and gender. As I have shown, her sense of her own sexuality is conventionally Victorian/Christian. Similarly, her fanatic claim to "try to learn to love [Phillotson] by obeying him" (286), while it sounds demented from a twentieth-century standpoint,[9] is fairly traditional Victorian reasoning. When Sue shreds the pretty nightgown she had bought to please Jude, she indicates her thorough understanding and acceptance of Christian and Victorian views of sin, sex, guilt, and the position of women. Jude assesses her accurately when he speaks of "her enslavement to forms" (419); for all her seeming defiance, Sue remains essentially conventional. She simply substitutes the enslavement to one culturally accepted form (the scholarly) for another (the religious), without grasping the systemic identity of the forms.

Although Jude is locked into some of the same patterns of thought as Sue, for the most part he is portrayed more sympathetically. Interestingly, his function in the novel resembles that of the major female protagonists of the earlier works; it is he who is caught between two world views, two mind sets, in a way that neither Sue nor Arabella is. In a sense, one can read Jude as the "female" character of the work in that he exhibits the qualities usually considered characteristic of woman, and, significantly, of victim: he is the powerless one acted upon by forces outside his control. In Anne Mickelson's discussion of Jude, the terms she uses to describe his character are ones that stereotypically would be seen as gender-linked, as signifiying woman. She speaks of his "feelings of insignificance, passivity, and masochism" (135), his "inhibitions about asserting himself and being able to say no" (136). As a child, Jude is portrayed as an extraordinarily gentle boy who cannot stand to see or cause pain. Given his rural upbringing, his sympathy for the birds is especially unusual, since typically rural boys hunt birds. Similarly, Jude is totally devastated by the pig-killing. In this gentleness, Jude takes on a characteristic that is culturally assigned to the feminine. Other "feminine" traits manifest themselves as well. For example, he makes decisions based on emotion rather than through the intellect, which Hardy claims "is often the case with young men" (96), but which culture associates with the feminine. Furthermore, he is the one character who has a kind of sixth sense—several times in the novel he experiences visions, usually of the scholars at Christminster. Again, intuitions and sixth senses are most typically associated with the feminine.

But it is in his lack of agency that Jude seems most stereotypically female. At no time in the novel is Jude in control of his own destiny, or even of his own situation. In an ironic reversal, Jude is always in the power of some woman—first Drusilla, then Arabella and Sue, together and separately. Admittedly as a poor man in a patriarchal culture, Jude is understandably a victim of the dominant culture's attitudes, and he most certainly is powerless in his attempted interaction with the Oxford dons and with the various self-proclaimed enforcers of so-called morality in the various small towns in which he lives. But his helplessness in dealing with women of his own social class, with his own wife, in the case of Arabella, sets him apart from other male victims of classism who at least assume patriarchal authority within the home. Jude has assumed what can be called a feminine personality. He cannot make demands, show anger, make decisions; furthermore, he is continually apologizing, deferring to someone else's agency, being acted upon rather than acting. As a boy, Jude is under Drusilla's complete control. In his marriage to Arabella, she makes the decisions and wields the power. In yet another ironic reversal, given Victorian ideas about women's sexual "innocence," it is she who seduces him and she who repeatedly initiates their sexual activity. The result is that Jude's sexuality is appropriated in the way that the sexuality of women is usually appropriated in patriarchal culture—one need only consider Tess by way of example. When women desire Jude, he is expected to perform; when they do not desire him, he is expected to be chaste; when he attempts to speak of his own desires, he is chidden for his "gross" nature. He simply cannot win. When he confronts Arabella with the knowledge of the horrible deception that leads to their marriage, she is unapologetic and refuses to rise to the level of his concern, thereby erasing the validity of his outrage. Similarly, Jude tolerates Sue's constantly shifting the day of their marriage and her endless sexual ambivalence, this in a society in which men were empowered as the sexual aggressors and which assumed that once a man had "possessed" a woman, he had complete control over her.[10] When Arabella decides she wants Jude back, he finds himself drunk in her bed. Virtually the only decision he makes in the novel is to commit suicide, but he is not forceful enough to make the ice break. He refers to himself as a victim, a term that culturally is synonymous with the feminine. In speaking of marriage, he insists that the institution is as destructive to a man as it is to a woman, referring to the man as "the other victim" (306). However, marriage in Victorian society was in fact far worse for the woman than for the man, since legally the man possessed control not only of the woman's body—no concept of marital rape existed, since a man's choice of when and how to engage sexually with his wife was seen as his right—but also of any material goods or money that she brought to the marriage. However, Jude consistently identifies with the woman, the unempowered one. Anne Mickelson claims that Jude and Sue reverse traditional gender roles in their relationship and adds, "Desperate to be loved and choosing submissiveness to gain this love (as many women do), [Jude] is the picture of the passive Victorian 'wife'—humble, effacing, patient, loving" (140). Jude never exercises the one power that his society allows him as a poor man—that of power over poor women, power within the home.

Very much like the women protagonists in the earlier Hardy novels, Jude finds himself attempting to move between two opposing worlds; however, in his case the cultural world does not bear down relentlessly upon him, but rather he desperately seeks to enter that world, even though it continually rejects him and refuses to acknowledge his existence. Predictably, Jude begins his life in a world aligned with nature. He lives in a little village, which he considers a "small sleepy place" (30) and from which he wishes to escape, in an old house with a great-aunt but no great-uncle—in other words, Jude's immediate familial situation is matriarchal. Jude finds his home, both the small town of Marygreen and the land around it, ugly and barren, although Hardy writes that "to every clod and stone there really attached associations enough and to spare—echoes of songs from ancient harvest-days, of spoken words, and of sturdy deeds" (33-34). Jude, however, is oblivious to such associations. As Kramer points out, he rejects the life of the land that surrounds him just as he rejects the friendships of the folk and the traditions they keep (158-59). His interests lie in books; even as a child, his great dream is to become a Christminster scholar—to enter the realm of the cultural.

Significantly, Jude's first setback on his path to scholarship comes from nature—in the form of sexuality. As Jude speculates on how he might possibly become a bishop one day (and thereby achieve distinction in the realm of culture), he is distracted by Arabella's throwing a pig's penis at him. The bipolar conflict that characterizes Jude immediately comes into play: he simultaneously sees Arabella through natural eyes, which reveal a sexually charged, beautiful woman, and through cultural eyes, which see a lower-class woman who, in spite of his own poverty, is socially inferior to him. Initially, Jude's assumption is that he and Arabella's interactions will be casual, and he winces at the idea that he is "coorting": "Courting in such a business-like aspect as it evidently wore to the speaker was the last thing he was thinking of. He was going to walk with her, perhaps kiss her; but 'courting' was too coolly purposeful to be anything but repugnant to his ideas" (64). Given the Victorian assumption that courting was a precursor to marriage, Jude's reluctance to involve himself with Arabella is understandable given his lack of means. But Hardy's word "repugnant" suggests another level to Jude's objection, one that has less to do with finances and more to do with a cultural sense of his social superiority to the women he intends to walk with and kiss but not marry. However, Jude's views quickly change; nature takes command of him, causing him to claim that "[i]t was better to love a woman than to be a graduate, or a parson; ay, or a pope!" (68). Nevertheless, such natural impulses hold sway only temporarily in him, having faded even before his marriage to Arabella occurs, after which he continues his reading and adheres to his dream of success in the "other" world. In addition, Jude shares Angel Clare's misconceptions about women in nature as well as his earlier precursor's cultural understanding of "innocence." He is disturbed to learn that Arabella's hair and her dimple are artificial, claiming that "in the country it is supposed to be different" (79). Although only on the boundaries of culture, he has assimilated its division of women into good women/fallen women. Peggy McCormack discusses that dualism at length, claiming, "From the outset, Jude conceptualizes the world as composed of binary opposition, with no successful mediation between extremes" (43). Seeing the world so polarized is, as feminist theorists frequently maintain, one of the aspects of patriarchal thought.

What marriage to Arabella cannot accomplish, the Victorian class system can. Once at Christminster, economic necessity requires Jude to work as a stonemason rather than study, as he had hoped. In a mystical moment, his intuitions, his bond with nature, allow him a glimpse of truth: "For a moment there fell on Jude a true illumination; that here in the stone yard was a centre of effort as worthy as that dignified by the name of scholarly study within the noblest of the colleges" (104). Jude's epiphany is temporary, however; he "lost it under stress of his old idea" (104). His desire to claim the cultural world as his own leads him to suppress the wisdom that would allow for happiness. He remains, from that point on, attached to the cultural, in spite of occasional book-burning. In his "irregular" life with Sue, the natural breaks through occasionally, but with the onset of her madness, Jude once again turns to the cultural. As he is very ill, the ghosts of Christminster scholars appear to him, and he tells Arabella, "[W]hen I am dead, you'll see my spirit flitting up and down here among these!" (413), indicating not merely his desire to attain the cultural realm but his awareness that he embodies it.

If Jude shares, to some degree, the tension between nature and culture that characterizes Hardy's women characters, he looks like them as well. He is very handsome—even in death, after a lingering illness, his corpse remains very attractive—and he possesses the dark hair and the powerful sexual nature that we associate with Bathsheba, Eustacia, and Tess. When he initially encounters Arabella, his desire for her manifests itself so fiercely that he is "held . . . to the spot against his intention, almost against his will" (60). The fire that occurs on the day of Jude and Arabella's first outing together is an excellent metaphor for the level of their passion—it blazes out of control. Jude is usually aware of and realistic about his sexuality. After Sue's photograph has begun to fascinate him, he recognizes his attraction for what it is; Hardy writes that the young man was "not altogether . . . blind to the real nature of the magnetism" (112). Similarly, he realizes that "he was a man of too many passions to make a good clergyman" (213), and responds to Sue's query about why people marry by saying, "they can't resist natural forces" (279). That "natural forces" affect his relationships with both Sue and Arabella is immediately clear. Even after he feels no love for Arabella, he is willing to spend the night with her in Aldbrickham, spurred on by his passionate nature.[11] Similarly, his love for Sue is very passionate as well as spiritual. Their clasped hands, the kiss at the train, as well as his honest admission of his feelings for her all indicate a powerful level of sexual response to her. However, Jude has lived in his culture long enough to have "learned" that his sexual desires are shameful. While at times he can straightforwardly articulate his desire and accept it as natural, at other times he reveals his cultural indoctrination by attempting to deny his sexual nature. For example, when Jude visits Sue at a schoolmate's house after she has run away from the teacher training school, Hardy writes, "*By every law of nature and sex* a kiss was the only rejoinder that fitted the mood and the moment. . . . Some men would have cast scruples to the winds and ventured it. . . . Jude did not" (178; emphasis mine). Hardy's rhetoric recalls his comment about Angel Clare: "with more animalism he would have been the nobler man" (216). When Jude begins to think in culture's terms, oblivious of and in opposition to natural law, he becomes destructive of self and others, as do all characters who behavior similarly in Hardy's canon. That destructiveness reveals itself most in Jude's dualistic thought after his night with Arabella in Aldbrickham. He refers to Sue as his "good angel" (206), which obviously indicates that the woman with whom he has been sexually intimate, by his own choice, is his "bad angel" for suggesting their liaison. Jude's thinking reflects the societal assumption that a sexual woman is a fallen woman, while a chaste woman is pure—in other words, that a woman's morality is solely dependent on her sexual behavior. Jude is not the only character in the novel who accepts society's co-optation of female sexuality; as I have already discussed, Sue readily assents to her own co-optation. Jude therefore reinforces her ambiguous, but ultimately negative, feelings about her own sexuality by putting her on a pedestal for denying him—and herself—sexually, oblivious of the appropriateness—and naturalness—of sexual desire between a man and a woman who love each other so deeply.[12] When, then, Jude rationalizes his relocation to Sue and Phillotson's vicinity by claiming he is proving his ability to resist temptation, Hardy almost smugly points out what Jude overlooks by citing Gibbons' line about how "insulted Nature sometimes vindicated her rights" (213). Jude learns that "the human was more powerful in him than the Divine" (227), which grieves him at times but which, ironically, associates him with the nature goddess figures of earlier novels, since "the human" in this context is associated with the sexual and the natural. In the power of his sexuality, Jude is the equal of Tess, Bathsheba, and Eustacia.

But Jude does not share the strength of his earlier counterparts. If anything, Jude's physical delicacy enables a reading of him as a feminine character. Although he is a stonemason, a profession that demands some degree of physical strength, his labor becomes his undoing. Jude is clearly not a Gabriel Oak or a Diggory Venn, either in terms of physical or emotional strength, as the pig-killing scene clearly reveals. Jude's extreme sensitivity, which prohibits him from acting directly, differentiates him specifically from Gabriel Oak, a man adept at his work with the animals, a work that obviously includes butchering even though the text does not focus on scenes of animal slaughter. Similarly, Jude lacks the kind of psychological strength that characterizes Tess and Eustacia. He frequently is dishonest with himself, rationalizing his behavior or lying about his motives. In his relationships with the two women, he never assumes any sort of power, unlike, for example, the way Eustacia interacts with Wildeve and Clym. The scene in which Jude rediscovers Arabella after her return from Australia is telling; catching sight of his estranged wife "destroyed at a stroke [Jude's] momentary taste for strong liquor as completely as if it had whisked him back to his milk-fed infancy" (200). Essentially, the two women turn Jude into a child, unmanning him. While Hardy's women characters are often dominant in their love relationships, usually the power is somewhat more equally distributed. However, Jude has no power, even to relinquish.

Jude's relationship with nature further distinguishes him from Hardy's nature goddess figures. One might claim that Jude experiences no true relationship with nature—he lacks an understanding of the natural, the result, not surprisingly, of the little time he spend in natural surroundings.[13] His childhood in Marygreen, during which he is oblivious to nature's nuances and her subtle beauty, begins what will become the pattern of his adult life. Significantly, as a boy, he is also afraid of the dark, another point of contrast to the major women characters, who, Hardy repeatedly stresses, experience no fears in the dark and often wander at will regardless of the time of day. The motif serves to emphasize Jude's removal from, and discomfort with, nature, as does his interaction with the birds he is supposed to be scaring away from the wheat field. While initially his sympathy for the birds may appear to indicate his unity with the natural, a closer analysis reveals an ignorance of nature on Jude's part. Kramer points out how the purposes of agriculture demand that birds be frightened away and emphasizes how Hardy consistently supports that which enables agriculture in his works (151). Jude's response is sentimental, growing out of his consciousness of himself as a victim. Identifying the birds as sharing in his own oppression, Jude represses the knowledge that is obvious were he able to view the scene from a non-neurotic perspective: his clackering is neither starving nor frightening the birds. Hardy writes, "At each clack the rooks left off pecking, and rose and went away *on leisurely wings*, burnished like tassets of mail, afterward wheeling back and regarding him warily, and *descending to feed* at a more respectful distance" (34; emphasis mine). Jude's sympathy for the birds is disguised self-pity and becomes the means whereby the boy can defer an unpleasant task; his response ultimately has less to do with concern for nature than with his own discomfort:

> He sounded the clacker *till his arm ached*, and at length his heart grew sympathetic with the birds' thwarted desires. They seemed, *like himself, to be living in a world which did not want them.* Why should he frighten them away? They took upon them more and more the aspect of gentle friends and pensioners—*the only friends he could claim as being in the least degree interested in him,* for his aunt had often told him that she was not. (34; emphasis mine)

When Farmer Troutham catches and punishes him for his "sympathy," Jude decides that "Nature's logic was too horrid for him to care for" (37), leading William Goetz to justly accuse the boy of "nostalgic self-deception" (208). Jude's perception of nature is one shared by the modern civilized world, which sentimentally chooses to avert its eyes from the recurring death and destruction that characterize the natural world. Having never lived close to nature, Jude can conceptualize neither the inevitability and appropriateness of death nor the constant resurgence of life that typifies all life on the planet. The sacredness of the unity of nature, including the sacredness of death, is obscured by culture. The scenes Hardy routinely depicts in his earlier works—scenes of a character wandering about at night, under the stars, or sleeping in the open—are all but absent here. In only one instance does Jude sleep outside, and the narrative treats the scene summarily to deemphasize it. Similarly, the sympathetic identification Hardy typically develops between nature and his main characters occurs only once in Jude's case. As Jude sets out to visit Sue, unaware that she and Phillotson have become involved with each other, "The trees overhead deepened the gloom of the hour, and they dripped sadly upon him, impressing him with forebodings—illogical forebodings" (129). However, usually nature is depicted as distant in the novel, not claiming the agency it wields in Hardy's other works. Even Jude's suicide attempts, both of which involve using nature to achieve his ends—once when he attempts to fall through the ice and drown, the other when he deliberately allows the rain to drench him—fail because nature does not accept Jude in death in the way she accepts Eustacia, or for that matter, Jude's mother. The absence of a bond with nature denies Jude a peaceful death; rather, he dies embittered, mumbling scripture to himself.

But Jude is not merely separated from nature but from community as well. Michael Millgate calls attention to the "rootlessness of the nomadic life" (333) Jude lives. Rootlessness in Hardy is often symptomatic of a removal from the natural and repeatedly is associated with the characters that are dangerous and disruptive, for example, Alec D'Urberville and Edred Fitzpiers. Mickelson also notes Jude's excessive movement and elaborates upon that flux: "There is no community sympathy and understanding . . . for Jude, as we see in *Tess* when she suckles her illegitimate child and the rustics express concern for what has happened to her" (127). Jude's alienation identifies him as modern man, removed from community, from tradition, from the ritual that imparts meaning to life.

Jude does, however, remain bonded with Christianity, which distinguishes him from the earlier Hardy characters, who are set in opposition to it. As a boy, Jude is already firmly located within the Christian tradition; one of his first acts in the novel is praying to see Christminster, a prayer that is answered within minutes, revealing his harmony with the Christian God. As he moves into adulthood, Jude remains both emotionally and physically close to the Christian church, praying frequently, studying to become a clergyman, and even working as a church restorer. Sometimes his attachment to his faith might even be labeled obsessive. His interest in the Jerusalem model is such that he "could examine it for hours" (127), and he goes so far as to recite the Creed in Latin in a Christminster pub. He views Arabella's presence in his life as divine punishment for his sins, an indication of how deeply he has imbibed Christian thought, compared to Tess, for example, who remains skeptical of Christianity throughout her ordeal. He even occasionally compares himself to Christ, aware that he falls short of his role model, but nonetheless conscious of his attempt to structure his life on Christ's.

Hardy's contemporaries did not, of course, see Jude as Christlike, specifically because Jude "lives in sin" with Sue for a significant portion of his adult life. Nevertheless, from the standpoint of the late twentieth-century, Jude's views do not position him in opposition to Christianity. His belief that his sexual instinct "had nothing in it of the nature of vice, and could be only at the most called weakness" (82) is one to which much of the Christian church could currently assent, and the acceptance of divorce within most branches of the church affirms Jude's sense of the ridiculousness of basing "a permanent contract on a temporary feeling which [has] no necessary connection with affinities that alone render a life-long comradeship tolerable" (90). Jude's only other lapse from the faith, at least as a young man, is his Pagan psalm to Diana, the source of much guilt for this otherwise devout young man. However, Jude's momentary lapse into goddess-worship has less to do with Paganism, with the adoration of the natural, than it does with his obsession with learning. Jude's praise is directed at Classical Greek scholarship, not at the ancient goddess of the moon. Furthermore, the end result of the event is Jude's moving even closer to Christianity, since the incident leads him to abandon secular writers for patristic ones.

Jude's temporary break with his faith results from Sue's influence. Following her intellectual approach to Christianity, Jude begins reading the "uncanonical books of the New Testament" (224) and shortly afterward claims, "[M]y doctrines and I begin to part company" (235), adding that if he has Sue's love, he'll "never care about [his] doctrines or [his] religion any more!" (235). It is true that Jude regards Christianity differently from this point on. He grows almost contemptuous of theology, most especially when he hears two clergymen debating the "eastward position" shortly after the deaths of his children. Along the same lines, he becomes more tolerant, more philosophical, viewing the horror of Little Father Time's destruction of the children from a sociological and psychological perspective rather than considering the act divine retribution, as Sue does. When he confronts Sue debasing herself out of an obsession with sin, he lashes out most directly at Christianity, claiming, "I am glad I had nothing to do with Divinity—damn glad—if it's going to ruin you this way!" (370). At this point Jude and Sue have seemingly switched places: she has accepted belief in a completely nonintellectual way, while his faith is largely intellectual. However, Jude is far too passionate a man to ever be as spiritually empty as Sue has been. While he may have intellectually moved away from the doctrines of his childhood, emotionally he is still as tied to Christianity as he ever was. Frank Giordano, in discussing Jude's death, claims, "In terms of a pagan ethos, Jude's act of self-destruction may be seen as a heroic affirmation of his personal being" (*I'd Have*, 180). I disagree, seeing no affirmation at all, but simply despair. On his deathbed, in a delirium, Jude recites the words of the biblical Job, venting his fury and despair at his creator. Jude's act reveals his unconscious acceptance of the Christian God, since his anger at God implies complete belief in God's existence and omnipotence. Hardy emphasizes Jude's ties with Christianity by specifically mentioning Jude's age as being "near thirty years" (425), the age at which he had earlier intended to begin his ministry, in emulation of Christ's life. Circumstances, most specifically an unjust, classist society, prevent Jude from fulfilling his dream, but unto death Jude's heart is where it has always been—firmly within the Christian tradition.

His ties to Christianity also serve to bind him to the culture that has grown out of the religion, the same culture that rejects him for his poverty and his sexuality, ultimately destroying him. Jude's enculturation is evident in his acceptance of culturally mandated definitions of gender and status. His dismay at Arabella's dimple-making is one such example. He is intellectually aware that "there is no harm in it" (81), but he nevertheless tells his wife, "I don't think they improve a woman—particularly a married woman" (81). In dividing women according to their marital status and in prescribing separate modes of behavior for unmarried and married women—not to mention in presuming the right to dictate a woman's behavior at all—Jude is acting on a cultural "truth," that a woman, once married, is her husband's possession, and that unmarried, she should follow the higher wisdom of the males around her. Along similar lines, when Sue reveals the details of her first relationship to Jude, he again assumes his right to pass judgment on women, declaring, "However you have lived, Sue, I believe you are as innocent as you are unconventional!" (169), never considering that his ruling on Sue's guilt or innocence is entirely irrelevant and inappropriate. His conventionality also reveals itself in his anxiety over sexual matters. As he gradually falls more and more in love, first with Sue's picture, and then with the woman herself, he is wracked by the "immorality" of his emotion. Similarly, he is appalled at Arabella's bigamy, not questioning (as he will later do, admittedly) the law's right to intervene in private matters of the heart. After he and Arabella spend the night in Aldbrickham, he "felt heartily ashamed of his earthiness" (207), again accepting societal dicta regarding sexual behavior rather than considering the problem to inhere in a system that condemns his very natural and healthy response to an attractive woman.

Jude's ties to culture reveal themselves in other ways as well, most obviously in his obsession with scholarship, a drive so strong that it results in his having visions, indicating how desperately he wants to participate in the cultural, that is, patriarchal, world that denies his being. In this respect, Jude again functions as a female character. As a male, even a poor male, Jude is always already a part of the patriarchy, but within the novel Jude is forever on the outside looking in. Although he struggles to achieve the patriarchal ideal, in both the sacred and secular spheres, he is never admitted to either. He, like Hardy's women characters and women in general within the patriarchy, remains forever "other." Jacobus writes, "The sturdy Wessex world of Hardy's earlier novels has been ousted by 'the ache of modernism'" ("Sue," 320). That modernism is characterized by a feeling of alienation, of a detachment from place and tradition, of a purposelessness and an uncertainty about self-identity. The mythic world that informed the other novels is completely absent here; Jude's world is located exclusively within the fallen, historical world, which accounts for the novel's tone of gloom and despair. Giordano claims that in this work, "Hardy explored the situation of man in the modern world—an alienated, isolated consciousness confronting the void created by the absence of God" (*I'd Have*, 133). However, God is present in this work, in the sense that characters believe in him and act either to please or consciously oppose him. The deity who is absent here is she who informed the earlier novels, the Great Goddess; the loss of a Pagan consciousness, with its understanding of the sanctity and the unity of all, is what dooms Jude.

For all Jude's movement—both intellectual and physical—within the novel, he actually does not travel far, ending up, as I have shown, still very near the faith of his childhood, although he has substituted a bitter cynicism for his earlier hope. Similarly, Phillotson makes a complete circle, ending up where he begins, behaving conventionally in spite of instincts that suggest other, more ethical, modes of action. Although not nearly so well developed a character as either Sue or Jude, Phillotson is nevertheless an intriguing and complex character, a testimony to Hardy's genius. Most readers would, I suspect, share the Widow Edlin's and Sue's assessment of him as hard to stomach, although it is difficult to say why—he is generally a kind man, certainly well-intentioned, and at times downright heroic. However, Hardy has constructed the text so as to encourage readers to dislike and distrust Phillotson. Consistently, the narrative voice champions the natural; as a schoolmaster and a minister, Phillotson signifies the patriarchy in both its realms and hence stands in opposition to the natural. He embodies the sterility of the modern world to which Hardy so often alludes and which he so clearly dreads.[14] From the very first paragraph of the novel, which speaks of the piano that Phillotson once bought but never learned to play, he can be read as an emblem of the limitations of the patriarchal world. While he possesses learning and religion, he does not possess an aesthetic sense; as the piano illustrates, lacking the feminine within him, he is incapable of creating beauty. He is not whole, his instinctive, creative side having been repressed by the patriarchal world he embraces. By comparison, one need only look to Gabriel Oak with his flute; the earlier Hardy character had denied neither his instincts nor his creativity, achieving as a result a kind of integration of self unknown to Phillotson.

Given both Phillotson's attachment to patriarchal forms and his alienation from nature (needless to say, Hardy never associates this character with any form of nature), it should come as no surprise that he appears at his most dysfunctional in his interactions with women, specifically women in loving/sexual relationships with him. From the beginning of Phillotson's relationship with Sue, his response to her is completely appropriate by Victorian standards, and hence completely misguided according to Hardy's sense of what love entails. He never seriously considers the age difference between him and Sue, since his society condoned generational-gap marriages when the man was the older partner. More significantly, he never heeds the signs that indicate Sue's psychological distance from him. When, for example, Sue writes to thank him for not visiting her at the training school, he puzzles over her feelings but ignores the obvious—that she simply does not love him. Even as he marries her, he has no indications of her feelings for him, because Victorian culture did not enable a discourse for couples to speak their feelings other than in conventional forms. Given his society's prohibition of premarital sex, Phillotson does not even consider the possibility of engaging passionately with Sue. However, the fact that he and Sue have had no sexual exchanges—not even subtle ones—indicates both his distance from the natural and also his enculturation, as well as his culture's alienation from the natural. Phillotson is playing by the rules; the problem is that the rules are senseless. Having no access to his instinctual side, as I have already shown, Phillotson does not perceive Sue's revulsion at their lovemaking and is astounded when she quite literally flees their bed. Under no circumstances can one imagine Sue forcing any enthusiasm for the sexual act prior to her actual removal from the bedroom, but her husband, accepting his culture's beliefs about women and their sexuality, cannot read her hesitations as anything other than proper modesty. Once he is confronted with the depth of Sue's disgust with him, he naively assumes that his kindness to her will be enough to guarantee a successful marriage, oblivious to the importance of sexuality in human fulfillment. In response, he accuses Sue of being "monstrous" for what she feels, his ignorance of even human nature revealed in his assumption that feelings can be governed by will. He even goes so far as to label her dislike of him a sin, a view to which Victorian society would give assent, but which is psychologically ridiculous. In creating Phillotson as he does, Hardy allows for a thorough critique of his society's sense of marriage.

For the most part, Phillotson is routinely conventional, a quality Hardy emphasizes in the scene involving his and Sue's first wedding day, when he asks Sue to wear her bonnet, emblematic of matronly respectability, under the tulle veil Jude purchases for her. Similarly, once he learns of Sue's unhappiness with their marriage, he is most concerned that someone else learn of her unusual behavior, claiming, "I hate such eccentricities" (242); he would prefer to live a celibate life with a wife who abhors him rather than be the subject of gossip that would tarnish his respectability. It is to Phillotson's great credit, however, that he reconsiders and frees Sue. Significantly, this action, the moment of Phillotson's greatest heroism, results from *instinctual* behavior, the site of Hardy's consistent attribution of moral action. Phillotson tells his friend: "I know I *can't logically, or religiously,* defend my concession to such a wish of hers; *or harmonize it with the doctrines I was brought up in.* Only I know one thing: *something within me tells me I am doing wrong in refusing her*" (251; emphasis mine). He explains that until his encounter with Sue, he would have assumed that a husband was obligated to restrain his wife by any means possible should she desire to flee. However, he reconsiders: "But *is that essentially right*, and proper, and honourable, or is it contemptibly mean and selfish? I don't profess to decide. *I simply am going to act by instinct, and let principles take care of themselves*" (251; emphasis mine). Phillotson at his most moral responds humanely to the plight of another, yet his response can also be called natural, since one must question the psychological health of a man who would choose to live with a woman whom he knows finds him repulsive; however, Phillotson's culture dictates that his humane, natural response is the wrong one, that the proper response is the one that would assume the woman is the man's possession to control. Throughout the entire scene with Gillingham, Phillotson's words are wise and just, precisely because they are in complete opposition to the cultural norm. He defends Sue and Jude's love, saying, "an extraordinary affinity, or sympathy, entered into their attachment, which somehow took away all flavour of grossness," adding, "The more I reflect, the more *entirely* I am on *their* side!" (252). Free of his culture's blind spots, Phillotson can make the leap from the specific case of Jude and Sue to the general principle; he defends the concept of matriarchy, arguing, in answer to his friend's conventional query about the situation of the family should the husband lose supreme authority, "I don't see why the woman and the children should not be the unit without the man" (252-53). However, such subversive views cannot be tolerated within the patriarchy; hence Phillotson becomes the victim of Victorian propriety. He does not waver, however, claiming, "I am more and more convinced every day that in the sight of Heaven and by all *natural*, straightforward humanity, I have acted rightly" (267-68; emphasis mine). His decision based on nature leads him into battle with the forces of culture, literally so when a brawl begins at the public meeting held to discuss the matter. Predictably, "the respectable inhabitants" (268) oppose the schoolmaster, but the folk, in this case itinerant fair workers, come to his defense. The fracas encapsulates the action within the Hardy novels as a whole; the folk, representing nature, momentarily gain some ground, but their victory is short-lived. Culture wins, as Hardy understands it has won, resulting in Phillotson's loss of status and economic security for daring to oppose cultural norms. The narrative voice is noticeably ironic, but also bitter, as it comments on the societal injustice that results in Phillotson's losing his position and experiencing virtual poverty: "No man had ever suffered more inconvenience from his own charity, Christian or heathen, than Phillotson had done in letting Sue go" (377).

It is only when Phillotson acts in opposition to his instincts that he once again becomes a despicable character. After Sue's tragedy, when she begs him to take her back, he agrees, although he is aware that "he was not quite following out the humane instinct which had induced him to let her go" (388). Acting according to cultural and especially religious expectations costs Phillotson his moral status. The lines are very clearly drawn here: the cultural precludes the possibility of moral action. To ease his guilt at behavior he knows to be base, Phillotson agrees to a sexless marriage—his immoral action has led to his further removal from the natural. Instead of being a celebration of love and sexuality, Sue and Phillotson's marriage, if it may be called that, is purely a social contract wherein they are bound to each other for the purpose of social propriety. Jude accurately assesses this union as a "fanatic prostitution" (380). Finally, however, Sue's madness/masochism leads her to force herself to Phillotson's bed, a scene that allows Hardy to depict the appalling depths to which humans may fall. Phillotson takes Sue to his bed even as she shrinks and clenches her teeth to avoid crying out in disgust. The scene is sickening—no dignity is left the schoolmaster for approaching a woman whose response to him is so clearly one of terror and revulsion. However, this scene is also to some degree "typical" of a lovemaking scene in a culture that views the act of sex as gross and obscene. Sue, in her disgust, fulfills the Victorian woman's role, clenching her teeth and tolerating—just barely—the touches she considers it her duty to abide. Phillotson is exercising his right as husband. The fact that neither partner is in any way enjoying this encounter is irrelevant. Given Hardy's continual opposition to the mores and values of Victorian culture, specifically because they deny what is natural to the species, he could have crafted no more fitting scene with which to end his career as novelist.

Throughout *Jude the Obscure*, the problems faced by Victorian society are frequently discussed, sometimes directly by the narrative voice, at other times through one of the characters. The most obvious of these problems is the institution of marriage as it existed then. The narrative voice frequently employs sarcasm in its discussion of marriage, but beneath the sarcasm lies a deep bitterness. At Jude and Arabella's first wedding, the narrative voice snidely remarks that "the two swore that at every other time of their lives till death took them, they would assuredly believe, feel, and desire precisely as they had believed, felt, and desired during the few preceding weeks" (78). The caustic narrative voice reappears in a passage that calls attention to itself for its seeming gratuitousness, its deliberately self-consciousness. After Jude's second marriage to Arabella, their landlord, having observed the two affectionately embracing one evening, decides they must not be actually married and is arranging to evict them. He changes his mind after they quarrel fiercely, reading the quarrel as the semiotic indicator of their legal status as husband and wife. But it is through the character of Sue that the text most frequently calls attention to the problematic nature of the Victorian concept of marriage. Sue tells Phillotson that she married him because she "thought [she] could do nothing else" (242). Hardy reveals here an understanding of the political and economic situation of women in a society that denied status to unmarried women. Furthermore, Sue's claim that "Domestic laws should be made according to temperaments, which should be classified" (243) restates Hardy's great theme: that social law should evolve from natural law. As Goetz points out, the novel demonstrates that "civil marriage sanctioned by society may find itself at variance with a more natural form of marriage, one that does not depend on social conventions to validate it" (190). Marriage in Hardy's time had little to do with natural law, since it did not spring out of a natural attraction allowed to grow and flourish through a couple's sharing of both their pleasures and their labors; therefore, Hardy could not endorse its existence.

Marriage is not the only cultural institution that Hardy opposes in the novel; Christianity as it was practiced in his time also comes under attack. Using slightly barbed humor, the narrative voice comments that when the youthful Jude sees Christminster as the new Jerusalem, "there was perhaps more of the painter's imagination and less of the diamond merchant's in his dream thereof than in those of the Apocalyptic writer" (41–42), calling attention to the tie between Christianity and classism, a tie that has throughout history led to the attitude that those who are poor deserve to be so, a result of their being out of favor with God. The humor surfaces again in the schoolroom brawl, when "a church-warden was dealt such a topper with the map of Palestine that his head went right through Samaria" (269); Hardy's delight at the scene is apparent from his language. Whereas in the earlier novels Hardy's strategy was repeatedly to align many of the unlikable characters to Christianity in some way, here he is more direct in his approach, acting out physical violence, admittedly not severe, against a churchman. But the narrative is also serious in its critique of Christianity. When Phillotson prepares to marry Sue for the second time, he claims he will use "a little judicious severity" (386) to control her, adding that his vicar had encouraged him to restrain her "with a wise and strong hand" (386). Biblical rhetoric notwithstanding, Hardy makes very clear the position of women within the Christian patriarchy: they are on a level with animals that can be owned and that are beaten when they become headstrong. For Hardy, "a religion in which sexual love was regarded as at its best a frailty, and at its worst damnation" (236) can only lead to destruction because it so ignores all that is natural to the species. Enstice, citing the scene in which the huge, horrific cross gleams luridly over the pathetic figure of Sue crumpled on the floor, claims it is "the nearest approach to a sense of real evil ever to be found in Hardy's work" (*Landscapes*,

177), and adds, "It is the supreme symbol—of the system Man has created for himself in the world" (170). While he no doubt intends his "Man" to be read generically, a gendered reading of the word makes the point even clearer. Within the system of Christianity that men have created, women are denied voice and agency and are deprived of their sexuality and power. But not only women suffer under the doctrines of a religion that sets itself in opposition to nature. As Gregor points out, much of Jude's true hardship begins at the time that he paints the ten commandments on the wall of the church ("A Series," 241), inscribing the very letters that will kill him as they have destroyed the Pagan world of Hardy's imagination.

Finally, Hardy uses his novel to attack Victorian prudery and intolerance. The narrative sympathies lie with Jude, who is a victim not of fate, as some have tried to claim, but of a sexist, classist society. Hardy speaks with Sue when she tells Jude that "[w]hen people of a later age look back upon the barbarous customs and superstitions of the time that we have the unhappiness to live in, what *will* they say!" (236). Jude's problem, after all, is not, contrary to some critical claims, that nature led him to father more children than he could afford; those children would not have been financial burdens had their parents not been denied work at Aldbrickham for choosing a living arrangement that met their needs, even if it did not conform to societal expectations. As Sue tells Jude, with the narrative voice assenting: "I can't *bear* that [the folk of Aldbrickham], and everybody, should think people wicked because they may have chosen to live their own way! It is really these opinions that make the best intentioned people reckless, and actually become immoral!" (322). The problem, as Hardy mentions several times, is that "the letter killeth," and Victorian society was obsessed with the letter, and the Word. As Goetz so aptly states, "*Jude* is depicting a new world, one in which the opposition between the letter and the spirit no longer operates; it is the world of the letter alone" (213).

What occurs in *Jude the Obscure,* then, is not so much Hardy's renunciation of nature as his bitter realization that society has renounced nature. The letter, the word, culture, in essence, precludes the possibility of the edenic world's existence, hence no glimpses of that world appear here. Hardy presents a desacralized world; when the sacred is gone, all that is left to fall back on is the form, the letter—and the letter killeth.

NOTES

1. The house-as-self idea comes into play here, as it so often does in Hardy's works. The pulling down of the old houses can be seen as signifying the destruction of the old consciousness.

2. In Hardy, makeup and false hair are always associated with characters against whom there is a narrative bias (e.g., Felice Charmond in *The Woodlanders*) and who are characterized as bearers of culture.

3. Hardwick discusses Arabella in similar terms, seeing her as exploitative and unable to love.

4. Arabella is one of the least nurturing women in all of Hardy's fiction. Penny Boumelha calls attention to the fact that, for all Arabella's sexual activity, she bears only one child (whom she does not even raise), and suggests the possibility that Vilbert and his "female pills" allow her a means of dealing with unwanted pregnancies (152). Sue, whom many critics see as emotionally frigid, mothers not only her own several children but Little Father Time as well and does so effectively.

5. Springer regards Sue similarly, claiming Sue's sexual dysfunction "[stems] not from physical frigidity, nor from lesbianism, but from a socially conditioned association of eroticism with sin" (161).

6. Blake points out that Sue in her wide reading likely acquired some of her distaste of sex from Victorian feminism, which was fairly separatist. It tended to view the ideal state for women as removed from men, and as a result opposed the ready availability of contraceptives because it would render women subject to greater pressure to engage in sexual activity.

7. Mary Jacobus comes close to a similar reading, claiming the ending makes psychological sense, given Sue's "self-punishing impulse hinted at earlier" (321).

8. Anne Mickelson comments appropriately, "Sue's constant references to the harsh religion she thought she had exchanged for happy paganism is proof that the early paganism she flaunts is but a thin covering over old beliefs and is easily punctured" (145).

9. Interestingly, the place in contemporary society where Sue's attitude appears is in sadomasochistic pornography, particularly in the more well written material, where a recurring motif is that of the victim's coming to a deep love of the torturer through being completely emptied of his/her own will. Given Sue's sexual dynamics, the parallel is perhaps not accidental.

10. Hardy treats this attitude in several of his other works, most obviously in *Tess of the D'Urbervilles*, where an underlying assumption, shared by Tess herself, is that Alec in some way can control Tess' actions because they have engaged in sex. In *The Woodlanders*, a similar attitude is found when Felice tells Grace that she can no longer order Fitzpiers out of her presence because he has "had" her.

11. Jude is apparently quite an expert lover as well. Arabella abandons her Evangelicalism and experiences profound desire for Jude after merely reencountering him casually. She marries him again apparently to enjoy him physically, since he is in no position to provide for her and so is not, in colloquial terms, a "good catch."

12. Marjorie Garson makes this point as well, claiming that Sue is constituted by Jude's desire: "[Sue] is what she has to be in order to arouse Jude and to thwart him. Jude creates her as a spiritual being before he ever sees her, and then expects her to satisfy him physically as well" (162).

13. Mickelson also raises this point, calling attention to the fact that Jude and Sue usually meet indoors (129), compared with Tess, Eustacia, and Bathsheba, who are rarely portrayed in interior space.

14. Geoffrey Thurley speaks of Phillotson's "negation of the life of the body" (195), which is essentially saying the same thing. Negating the life of the body is a way of negating the natural.

Works Cited

Bailey, J. O. "Hardy's 'Mephistophelian Visitants.'" *PMLA* 61 (1946): 1146–84.

Beegal, Susan. "Bathsheba's Lovers: Male Sexuality in *Far From the Madding Crowd.*" In *Sexuality and Victorian Literature*, ed. Don Richard Cox. Tennessee Studies in Literature 27. Knoxville: University of Tennessee Press, 1984, 108–27.

Beer, Gillian. *Darwin's Plots: Evolutionary Narrative in Darwin, George Eliot and Nineteenth-Century Fiction.* London: Routledge and Kegan Paul, 1983.

Björk, Lennert A., ed. *The Literary Notebooks of Thomas Hardy. Vol. I.* New York: New York University Press, 1985.

Blake, Kathleen. "Sue Bridehead, 'The Woman of the Feminist Movement.'" *Studies in English Literature, 1500–1900* 18 (Autumn 1978): 703–26.

Bonica, Charlotte. "Nature and Paganism in Hardy's *Tess of the D'Urbervilles. English Literary History* 49 (Winter 1982): 849–62.

Boumelha, Penny. *Thomas Hardy and Women: Sexual Ideology and Narrative Form.* Sussex: The Harvester Press, 1982.

Brick, Allen. "Paradise and Consciousness in Hardy's *Tess.*" *Nineteenth Century Fiction* 17 (September 1962): 115–34.

Brooks, Jean R. *Thomas Hardy: The Poetic Structure.* Ithaca, N.Y.: Cornell University Press, 1971.

Caless, Bryn. "Hardy's Characters and the Significance of Their Names." *Thomas Hardy Yearbook* 4 (1973–74): 10–16.

Carpenter, Richard. "The Mirror and the Sword: Imagery in *Far From the Madding Crowd.*" *Nineteenth Century Fiction* 18 (March 1964): 331–45.

Casagrande, Peter J. "A New View of Bathsheba Everdene." In *Critical Approaches to the Fiction of Thomas Hardy*, ed. Dale Kramer. London: Macmillan, 1979, 50–73.

Cixous, Hélène. "The Laugh of the Medusa." *Signs* (Summer 1976): 875–93.

Cixous, Hélène, and Catherine Clément. *The Newly Born Woman.* Minneapolis: University of Minnesota Press, 1986.

Clark, Anna. "The Politics of Seduction in English Popular Culture, 1748–1848." In *The Progress of Romance*, ed. Jean Radford. New York: Routledge and Kegan Paul, 1986, 47–70.

Coxon, Peter W. "Hardy's Use of the Hair Motif." In *Thomas Hardy Annual No. 1*, ed. Norman Page. Atlantic Highlands, N.J.: Humanities Press, 1982, 95–114.

Davidoff, Leonore. "Class and Gender in Victorian England." In *Sex and Class in Women's History,* ed. Judith L. Newton, Mary P. Ryan, and Judith R. Walkowitz London: Routledge and Kegan Paul, 1983, 17–71.

Deen, Leonard W. "Heroism and Pathos in *The Return of the Native.*" *Nineteenth Century Fiction* 10 (1960–61); reprinted in *Hardy: The Tragic Novels,* ed. R. P. Draper. London: Macmillan, 1975, 119–32.

Ehrenreich, Barbara, and Deirdre English. *Witches, Midwives and Nurses: A History of Women Healers.* New York: The Feminist Press, 1973.

Eliade, Mircea. "Cosmic Religiosity." *Myths, Rites, Symbols: A Mircea Eliade Reader,* ed. Wendell C. Beane and William G. Doty. New York: Harper & Row, 1975, 126–29.

Elsbree, Langdon. "Tess and the Local Cerealia." *Philological Quarterly* 40 (October 1961): 606–13.

Enstice, Andrew. "The Fruit of the Tree of Knowledge." In *The Novels of Thomas Hardy,* ed. Anne Smith. London: Vision Press, 1979, 9–22.

———. *Landscapes of the Mind.* New York: St. Martin's Press, 1979.

Firor, Ruth. *Folkways in Thomas Hardy.* Philadelphia: University of Pennsylvania Press, 1931.

Gallop, Jane. *Thinking Through the Body.* New York: Columbia University Press, 1988.

Garson, Marjorie. *Hardy's Fables of Integrity: Women, Body, Text.* Oxford: Clarendon Press, 1991.

Giordano, Frank R., Jr. "Eustacia Vye's Suicide." *Texas Studies in Literature and Language* 22 (Winter 1980): 504–21.

———. *"I'd Have My Life Unbe": Thomas Hardy's Self-destructive Characters.* University, Alabama: University of Alabama Press, 1984.

———. "The Martyrdom of Giles Winterborne." In *Thomas Hardy Annual No. 2,* ed. Norman Page. London: Macmillan, 1984, 61–78.

Goetz, William R. "The Felicity and Infelicity of Marriage in *Jude the Obscure.*" *Nineteenth Century Fiction* 38 (September 1983): 189–213.

Gregor, Ian. "A Series of Seemings." *Hardy: The Tragic Novels.* Ed. R. P. Draper. London: Macmillan, 1975, 227–47.

———. *The Great Web: The Form of Hardy's Major Fiction.* Totowa, N. J.: Rowman and Littlefield, 1974.

Guerard, Albert J. *Thomas Hardy: The Novels and Stories.* Cambridge, Mass.: Harvard University Press, 1949.

Hall, Nor. *The Moon and the Virgin: Reflections on the Archetypal Feminine.* New York: Harper and Row, 1980.

Hardwick, Elizabeth. "Sue and Arabella." In *The Genius of Thomas Hardy,* ed. Margaret Drabble. New York: Alfred A. Knopf, 1976, 67–73.

Hardy, Thomas. *Far From the Madding Crowd.* New York: St. Martin's Press, 1977.

———. *Jude the Obscure* . New York: St. Martin's Press, 1979.

———. *The Return of the Native.* New York: St. Martin's Press, 1979.

———. *Tess of the D'Urbervilles.* London: Macmillan, 1975.

———. *The Woodlanders.* New York: St. Martin's Press, 1977.

Harrison, Fraser. *The Dark Angel: Aspects of Victorian Sexuality.* London: Sheldon Press, 1977.

Hazen, James. "The Tragedy of Tess Durbeyfield." *Texas Studies in Language and Literature* 11 (1969): 779–94.

Heilman, Robert B. "Hardy's Sue Bridehead." In *Hardy: The Tragic Novels,* ed. R. P.

Draper. London: Macmillan, 1975, 209–26.

———. *"The Return*: Centennial Observations." In *The Novels of Thomas Hardy*, ed. Anne Smith. New York: Harper and Row, 1979, 58–90.

Horne, Lewis. "Passion and Flood in *Far From the Madding Crowd." Ariel: A Review of International English Literature* 13 (July 1982): 39–49.

Hyman, Virginia R. *Ethical Perspective in the Novels of Thomas Hardy.* Port Washington, N.Y.: Kennicat Press, 1975.

Jacobus, Mary. "Sue the Obscure." *Essays in Criticism* 25 (July 1975): 304–28.

———. "Tess: The Making of a Pure Woman." In *Tearing the Veil: Essays on Femininity*, ed. Susan Lipshitz. London: Routledge and Kegan Paul, 1978, 77–92.

———. "Tree and Machine: *The Woodlanders.*" In *Critical Approaches to the Fiction of Thomas Hardy*, ed. Dale Kramer. New York: Barnes and Noble, 1979, 116–34.

Jarrett, David. "Eustacia Vye and Eula Varner, Olympians: The World of Thomas Hardy and William Faulkner." *Novel* 6 (Winter 1973): 163–74.

Jordan, Mary Ellen. "Thomas Hardy's *Return of the Native*: Clym Yeobright and Melancholia." *American Imago* 39 (Summer 1982): 101–18.

Kozicki, Henry. "Myths of Redemption in Hardy's *Tess of the D'Urbervilles." Papers on Language and Literature* 10 (Spring, 1974): 150–58.

Kramer, Dale. *Thomas Hardy: The Forms of Tragedy.* Detroit: Wayne State University Press, 1975.

Lacan, Jacques. *Écrits: A Selection.* Trans. Alan Sheridan. New York: University Press, 1975.

Laird, J. T. *The Shaping of "Tess of the D'Urbervilles."* Oxford: Clarendon Press, 1975.

Marken, R. N. G. "'Sick for Home': The Theme of *Tess of the D'Urbervilles." English Studies in Canada* 4 (Fall 1978): 317–29.

McCormick, Peggy A. "The Syntax of Quest in *Jude the Obscure." New Orleans Review* 8 (Winter 1981): 42–48.

Meese, Elizabeth A. *Crossing the Double-Cross: The Practice of Feminist Criticism.* Chapel Hill: University of North Carolina Press, 1986.

Mickelson, Anne Z. *Thomas Hardy's Women and Men: The Defeat of Nature.* Metuchen, N.J.: The Scarecrow Press, 1976.

Miller, J. Hillis. *Thomas Hardy: Distance and Desire.* Cambridge: Belknap Press, 1970.

Millgate, Michael. *Thomas Hardy: His Career as a Novelist.* New York: Random House, 1971.

Morgan, Rosemarie. *Women and Sexuality in the Novels of Thomas Hardy.* London: Routledge, 1988.

Paterson, John. "The Continuing Miracle: Nature and Character in Thomas Hardy." In *Budmouth Essays on Thomas Hardy,* ed. F. B. Pinion. Dorchester, Dorset: The Thomas Hardy Society, Ltd., 1976, 140–53.

———. "Introduction." In *The Return of the Native* by Thomas Hardy. New York: Harper and Row, 1966; reprinted in *Hardy: The Tragic Novels*, ed. R. P. Draper. London: Macmillan, 1975, 109–18.

———. *The Making of "The Return of the Native."* Berkeley: University of California Press, 1960.

Rogers, Katharine. "Women in Thomas Hardy." *Centennial Review* 19 (1975): 249–58.

Schwarz, Daniel R. "Beginnings and Endings in Hardy's Major Fiction." In *Critical Approaches to the Fiction of Thomas Hardy*, ed. Dale Kramer. London: Macmillan, 1979, 17–35.

Springer, Marlene. *Hardy's Use of Allusion.* Lawrence, Kansas: University Press of

Kansas, 1983.

Sumner, Rosemary. *Thomas Hardy: Psychological Novelist*. New York: St. Martin's Press, 1981.

Tanner, Tony. "Colour and Movement in Hardy's *Tess of the D'Urbervilles*." *Critical Quarterly* 10 (1968): 219–39.

Thurley, Geoffrey. *The Psychology of Hardy's Novels: The Nervous and the Statuesque*. St. Lucia, Queensland: University of Queensland Press, 1975.

Van Ghent, Dorothy. "On *Tess of the D'Urbervilles*." In *Hardy: A Collection of Critical Essays*, ed. Albert J. Guerard. Englewood Cliffs, N.J.: Prentice-Hall, 1963, 77–90.

von Franz, Marie Louise. *The Feminine in Fairy Tales*. Dallas: Spring Publications, 1972.

Walker, Alice. *The Color Purple*. New York: Washington Square Press, 1983.

Weinstein, Philip M. *The Semantics of Desire: Changing Models of Identity from Dickens to Joyce*. Princeton, N.J.: Princeton University Press, 1984.

Wickens, G. Glen. "Hardy and the Aesthetic Mythographers: The Myth of Demeter and Persephone in *Tess of the D'Urbervilles*." *University of Toronto Quarterly* 53 (Fall 1983): 85–106.

Williams, Merryn. *Thomas Hardy and Rural England*. New York: Columbia University Press, 1972.

Wing, George. "Hardy and Regionalism." *Thomas Hardy: The Writer and His Background*. New York: St. Martin's Press, 1980, 76–101.

Wotton, George. *Thomas Hardy: Towards a Materialist Criticism*. Totowa, N.J.: Barnes & Noble Books, 1985.

Wyatt, Bryant N. "Poetic Justice in *The Return of the Native*." *Mark Twain Journal* 21 (Fall 1983): 56–57.

Index

About the Author

SHIRLEY A. STAVE is Assistant Professor of English at the University of Wisconsin Center-Waukesha County.

ISBN 0-313-29566-2

90000>

EAN

9 780313 295669

HARDCOVER BAR CODE